To Ezzy

May this never

happen to you

luv

Siri

The Story of
Jane Doe

The Story of Jane Doe

A book about rape

Jane Doe
Illustrations by Shary Boyle

Random
House
Canada

Copyright © 2003 Jane Doe

Illustrations copyright Shary Boyle

All rights reserved under International and Pan-American Copyright
Conventions. No part of this book may be reproduced in any form or by any
electronic or mechanical means, including information storage and retrieval systems, without permission in writing from the publisher, except by a reviewer,
who may quote brief passages in a review. Published in 2003 by Random House
Canada, a division of Random House of Canada Limited. Distributed in Canada
by Random House of Canada Limited, Toronto.

www.randomhouse.ca

Random House Canada and colophon are trademarks

National Library of Canada Cataloguing in Publication

Doe, Jane
        The story of Jane Doe : a book about rape / Jane Doe ; illustrated by
Shary Boyle.

ISBN 0-679-31153-X

        1. Trials (Rape)—Ontario—Toronto. 2. Trials (Police misconduct)—
Ontario—Toronto. I. Title.

HV6569.C32O583 2003   362.883'092
C2003-900140-7

Design by Carmen Dunjko

Printed in United States of America

10 9 8 7 6 5 4 3 2 1

for all the Jane Does

"Satire and the laughter of 'free' [women] is a potent weapon against

tyranny and oppression, whether domestic or political or both."

—George Orwell, *Essays*

VICTIM: POLICE USED ME AS RAPE BAIT

Memos show cops disbelieved attacked women: Pages 4-5

12 m...
root...
Sha...

Pat Burns on Leafs: 'it's sad to see'

Contents

Force must pay Jane Doe $22...

From Page B1

"In this case, they failed miserably in their duty to uphold women's Charter equality rights and women's right to the security of person," Ms. Peterson said at a press conference called by the lawyers yesterday. "It establishes a very important precedent, not only for women, but for other communities as well, whether it be people of colour or lesbian and gay community or any other community that might be subject to discrimination by police or to unfair police officers."

In fact, the president of the National Action Committee said the ruling could benefit other minority rights or communities that feel police have discriminated against them.

"I would say it could complicate things for the police service," he said yesterday. "It might open up the door for other people who are minorities if they weren't satisfied with what had taken place then we might be liable to be sued.

Mr. Gertner said he had a tough job.

> 'We have had situations where people have claimed to have been sexually assaulted, where no sexual assault took place.'

making the claim... making a false acc...

And when it was Gertner that his kind of attitude ha... had toward the... time, Mr. Gertner cases, there is that in other cases, the evidence."

In her judgment... suggests evidence... Doe was that po... into reports of rap... victims very serio...

It remains to be... lice will do with... ing indictment...

The background

ON an August night in 1986, Jane Doe became the fifth reported woman raped by a sexual serial predator dubbed the Balcony Rapist. The rapist stalked single women who lived alone in second- and third-floor apartments in a downtown Toronto neighbourhood. He scaled the outside walls of high-rises located within a six-block radius and entered the apartments through locked balcony doors.

Despite the fact that the police had full knowledge of his modus operandi, they made a conscious decision not to issue a warning about the rapist to women in the neighbourhood. Their rationale was that women, hearing the news, would become hysterical, and the rapist would flee the area. Informed of their decision a few days after her rape, the woman who became known as Jane Doe quickly realized that she, in particular, and women, generally, were being used by the police as bait to catch the rapist.

The woman who became Jane Doe was actively involved in the then thriving women's movement. She worked for a high-profile film festival and was experienced in public relations and marketing. She took it upon herself to organize a series of press conferences, postered her neighbourhood with warnings and delivered a deputation to the Police Services Board, demanding that the police be accountable. The rapist was captured as a result of a tip received after Jane and other women distributed two thousand posters—including one to the home of the man who raped her—alerting the community to the danger women faced.

During the criminal prosecution that followed, Jane Doe became the first raped woman in Ontario to secure her own legal representation.

This strategy allowed her to sit inside the courtroom while the hearings involving her rapist proceeded, instead of out in the hall where victim-witnesses were usually cloistered from the ongoing testimony. As a result she heard details of the police investigation that were normally withheld from women in her position. When the rapist was convicted and sentenced to twenty years in prison, the comfort Jane experienced was cold. A shocking degree of police negligence and manipulation had been revealed during the hearings, and Jane realized that the same type of crime that had been committed against her could easily take place again.

By 1986 a number of external elements combined to provide a small window of redress for women who experienced crimes of violence. The Canadian Charter of Rights and Freedoms was a new constitutional document with a section designed to prevent gender discrimination. Feminism had established awareness of sexual assault as a prevalent social crime, as opposed to an ugly fact of life. Since criminal law did not serve raped women, the women's movement looked to civil prosecutions as an alternative. Jane Doe became a test case: the right woman in the wrong place at the right time. Political, educated, presentable and a risk-taker, she was in her early thirties and there was no doubt as to her "good girl" status. In 1987 Jane Doe sued the Metropolitan Toronto Police Force for negligence and Charter violations in the investigation of her rape. The rest became legal history.

Of course history is a long time in the making. Over the next eleven years, Jane engaged a legal system and its players as no other woman in her position had previously done. Unwilling to play the traditional victim role, she battled with a series of her own lawyers to ensure that she, the person most involved, directed her case. In 1991 the Ontario Supreme Court ruled that Jane Doe had a cause of action and that she could proceed to trial. Until that ruling, it had not been possible to hold police officers responsible in a court of law for their actions in the investigation of a crime.

Jane plowed on. She developed strategies, secured witnesses and challenged her lawyers to push the boundaries of the law. They often were not amused. When the civil case finally came to trial in 1997, Jane was dismayed to learn that, as she had predicted, her sexual, medical, employment and family history was used against her to support the police defence that any damages she had suffered had existed before her rape and that her lawsuit reflected the delusional posturing of a bitter, man-hating feminist.

The ensuing nine-week trial was a media bonanza as retired police chiefs, celebrated psychiatrists, police officers of every stripe and station, forensic profilers and an FBI agent from Quantico, Virginia, testified to the "non-violent" nature of Jane's rape and her police-bashing agenda. After the trial was over, the judge deliberated on the evidence for six months. She ruled in Jane's favour, and a common-law legal precedent was set. A citizen could sue the police. She could even win.

But it didn't end there. It hasn't ended yet.

The Story of
Jane Doe

A preliminary note from Jane

RAPE stories are not new stories. They are as old as war, as old as man. Many bookstores have sections devoted to them, and I read them. I read them "before," too.

I have found most rape stories to be either chronicles of fear and horror, victim tales that make me want to run screaming from the page (although I do not), or dry academic, feminist or legal treatises on why rape is bad, written in language I must work to understand. All are valid. But all somehow limit me from reaching a broader understanding of the crime: why men do it; the myriad ways women experience it; and how rape is used to maintain the status quo socially, politically, legally. No book has ever reflected my experience of the crime.

I learned early in my political life to pose the question "Who benefits?" when attempting to understand social inequities and injustice. It is clear that rape is bad; that it has dire effects on the entire social fabric. We read the alarming statistics—sexual assault is the only violent crime currently on the rise—and try to teach our daughters well. Everyone, even some rapists, would like rape to stop. In the seventies and eighties some viable solutions were crafted to address the crimes of rape and violence against women. But in the last decade, those services have been cut and law and order agendas are now trumpeted as the single remedy for the crime.

In this book I explore who benefits from, and who controls, this state of affairs. I hope to help any reader who comes along for the ride to ask questions, develop answers, and experience what I experienced: the horror of it all, the honour and the humour, the theatre of the absurd known as the contemporary courtroom, and a cast of real-life characters that could have come from Dickens or Rohinton Mistry.

I want to challenge and respond to "popular" ideas about rape that still inform the way police and society behave around raped women. Popular, social, psychiatric and legal mythologies about rape tell us that women lie about our rapes; file false reports to seek attention, revenge or money; or, ludicrously, that we enjoy rape. The myths hold that rape can be non-violent. That a woman can be predisposed to being raped. That women will become hysterical if told a rapist is preying on their neighbourhood. They tell us that a woman can be a good or bad rape victim. Some myths insist that women cannot be raped at all, and that men cannot physically control the biological urge to rape.

I wanted to write a book about rape that is not about being a "victim." I want to startle you with art and humour. I'm not referring to comedy but to the comic theatre of life, which is sometimes too outrageous, too wild to be believable. I often regret that I was a central player during the civil trial, as it prevented me from fully appreciating what was going on all around me. I laugh now about a lot of it, a sweet, tragic fantastical laugh. The kind that keeps you from losing your faith. Or your mind.

I'VE taken a few liberties in the telling of my story. Everyone else has. I have changed some people's names where to do otherwise would cause pain or harm. I have fictionalized the voices of Bill Cameron, Kim Derry and Margo Pulford, the three police officers most involved in the Balcony Rapist investigation. I wanted to tell some of their stories in a manner that would humanize them and allow some insight into why historical and current relations between police and the citizens they serve are so fractious. I was mindful of the tradition in policing and in the law that *requires* officers of those institutions to speak on behalf of, and define the experiences of, raped women. To be their voices. I reclaimed that voice, made it mine again. While I have invented some details of their personal lives and thoughts, especially what they may have thought about me and about each other, all information about the direction of the police investigation into the crimes of the Balcony Rapist, and the decisions they made in pursuing it, is lifted verbatim from courtroom transcripts of their testimony, or the interactions I had with them. Bill Cameron's and Margo Pulford's kindnesses toward me are likewise factual.

I WANTED to write a book that would be a revolution. A book that would place rape on the table, in the mainstream, where it belongs. A book that would subvert stereotypical notions of the crime of rape and the women who experience it. But revolutions require more than the power of words, and to effect one, we must fight in different ways, with different voices. The art and images of Shary Boyle help illuminate places where words fail. Her visual narrative is another way to read rape, to look sideways at pain and victory. I want to surprise readers with angles and images that can be read from the inside out, or from the bottom up to better understand the cryptic puzzle of rape, in order to untangle and solve it. I wanted to describe and translate feminism and its impact on me. But my feminist analysis is also influenced by art, anarchy, labour, romance and lapsed Catholicism and it is developing still—as is its nature. The feminist movement is much more than what you will find in these pages. There are many more readings of it still forming, still waiting to be written. This book is meant to be a reflection of rage that is focused and smart, an expression of subversion and joy; it is supposed to shake us up, to help us think in new ways. The old ones aren't working.

MOST of all, I wanted to celebrate what is most common in human nature: our ability to overcome. To shuffle the deck and play the next hand, and sometimes to win.

I'll open with the first entry of the journal I kept during the civil trial, just to give you a flavour of what's to come. And then I'll step back and begin at the beginning—which is a place I still don't like to think about.

❖

alcony rapist" victim Jane Doe hold a den
civil suit against Metro police started yes

ictim sues

... hold a demonstration outside the courtho...
... tarted yesterday.

Civil trial journal
Jane Doe v. the Metropolitan Toronto Police Force

September 8, 1997

10:00 a.m.: Must take notes, document, everyone says so . . .
So many people showed up that the judge had to find a
larger courtroom. Women who came to picket helped my
lawyers carry their hundreds of briefs and cases across
University Avenue. Like a parade of crows and smaller
birds, robes and placards flying in the wind. Demo was huge
success. Arrived early and hid behind an office building to
watch demonstrators and media, all of them there for me, all
of them waiting for me. Huge feelings of excitement and sadness. Exhausted and thrilled. I did it. My trusty camera
crew catching it all. How brilliant to have pulled that one
off. My sister is here, holding my hand, touching my sleeve.
Lots of entering of documents and legal posturing.
Postering outside. Motions but little movement.

1:10 p.m.: The cops have amended their claim to say that I
was warned from newspaper reports, friends, most emphatically by my brother. Which brother? Do they know that any
of my brothers would come down here and rip their faces off?
If they knew. Do they get to change their defence like this?

2:00 p.m.: My lawyer Sean's opening statement. Telling the
story of my rape, all of a sudden his story, not mine. So

private to be so publicly stated. Pain in heart. Must blank out for a while. Blanket over. Hmmm, Sean's quite the performer, seems to enjoy it. What's he on about, though? Wonder if he'll say systemic. Sean, say systemic. I know you can say it. This is where you should say it, you bastard. He didn't say it.

Bryan Finlay, Q.C., is representing the police. Sounds like he's saying, "The whore of the rape of Jane Doe," instead of the horror. Hard to breathe. Anxiety attack? What in hell am I doing here? Oh gawd, now he's saying that the police were working with us to effect change! That's it, they were working with us, what were we thinking? I feel ill. But then it's fabulous because he keeps saying "systemic gender-based discrimination."

Other Finlayisms: "We're going to call the chief of police who was then the chief of police." "The best experts we could get."

I feel claustrophobic, surrounded. Don't know who's at my back. They say I'm sitting at a good vantage point for the judge to see me. I say fuck the judge. Sean should have me beside him at the plaintiff's table, and why hasn't he shown me the defendants' list of witnesses? Damn, am I going to have this fight all over again?

(To be continued on page 198)

Safe at home in bed

1:

August 24, 1986. Sleeping on a hot summer city night. In the white noise of a box fan and all-night traffic, I am drinking sleep. Restoring. Cells mending, creams moisturizing, dreams in the background like a drive-in movie, floating, sorting, safe.

Deep in dreams, I am jerked out. Pulled up by arms around me, a body spooned into mine, a voice in my ear, something sharp at my neck. The room is black and I smell sweat and chemicals. "Don't move. I have a knife. Do as I say and I won't hurt you." I am captured. A prisoner, a bug. Terror rises unbidden from my bowels. I inhale it up and breathe it out, and on the way it explodes my heart and shrapnel strews, imbeds, explodes again and I believe I will die now. I want to die now to stop it, to return to sleep, and he says it again, "I have a knife, do what I tell you," and somehow in those seconds that last forever, leave me never, I make a decision. I decide to live. Just in time to replace the fuse, reattach the wire that kick-starts my heart, and I take another breath. I will live. I will memorize you, every sound, smell, touch, word, as I do what you say, whatever you say, anything you say, because I have decided to live. And if I do, I will get you. I will tell.

EVERYONE knows something about rape. From our own experiences, the Sunday night TV version or Hollywood movies. There are a few things about my rape you should also know.

The man who raped me was a stranger. It was nighttime. I was asleep in my bed with the doors locked. He had a knife. He wore a mask. He covered my face. When he was done he escaped back into the night. I called the police. I was freaked out—you can imagine. They call it shock. A particular kind of shock where I got real quiet. No tears, no apparent fears, just a controlled alertness. When the police got to my apartment, I answered their questions calmly, with little emotion and a steely gaze. Kind of like Clint Eastwood.

I always refer to that quietness, remember it, as a state of "self-protect." No one was going to get close to me, especially not one of those huge police officers, none of whom I knew, all of whom were fully dressed while I wore a robe and dripped rape semen. I was placed in the situation where I was expected to trust these strangers to protect me, to fix what the bad man had done to me. As if my rape had rendered me senseless and useless.

The 911 operator stayed on the line with me until the police got there, told me not to touch or move anything, asked if I needed medical attention, told me I would be okay. When the police rang my buzzer, it startled me so badly I screamed with fright into the phone and she thought the rapist was back. So did I.

I opened the door and was surrounded by a half-dozen cops. A few uniforms, plainclothes, at least one in a suit. Questions flew from all sides as they scanned my living room with their camera eyes. A few fanned off into the bedroom and kitchen, careful not to touch or disturb, skating into the investigation, dusting, circling, handling the situation like players on fresh but familiar ice. I sat on the couch, stiff and upright, as they fired questions at me. Did you see him? Did you know him? What colour was he? What did he do? What did he say? Did he have a tattoo? Visible scars? Where was the knife? Did you see it? Did you see him? Penetration? Ejaculation? Age? Accent? How long? How many times? Did you see him? What colour was he?

I wanted to vomit. I needed to pee. I needed to be quiet. I needed to put some clothes on, clean up, call home. To walk. I needed these huge men to stop looking at me and my things. I needed to be in control. But you can forget about any of that. Especially the control stuff.

When I got up to use the washroom, one of the officers stopped me and said I shouldn't, it would be better if I could wait. Wait for what? was the unasked question as I moved purposefully toward the bathroom door,

NOTE: Patient should *postpone voiding,* if possi

AG #1 — CLOTHING (Removed by Nurse at di

1-A Have the patient stand on the two layers of
separately. Place articles of clothing in separ
ld the TOP sheet of paper to enclose an
lothing, paper and large green garbage bag to

BAG #2 — BODY EVIDENCE (Done by Nurse at

-A Place any FOREIGN MATERIAL (dirt, fibre
fold carefully and replace in envelope.

2-B Remove swab from envelope 2-B. Moisten in
any SEMINAL-LIKE STAINS on the skin. Air

-C Unfold paper 2-C containing comb. Have pa
combing hair. If at least 50 hairs are not she
back and sides of the head. Fold paper 2-C

-D Take ORAL SWAB using swab 2-D. Smear s
swab in tube 2-D.

2-E To collect a SALIVA sample, first ensure tha
oral sex has occurred or if patient has take
thoroughly and discard rinse). Have patient
tissue. Allow to air dry. Place in envelope 2-E
sure that sample is completely dry before seali

BLOOD: A TOTAL OF 25 ML. IS REQUIRED.
CONTAINING ALCOHOL FOR CLEAN

2-F Take 10 ml. of BLOOD for grouping. Place in

2-G Take 10 ml. of BLOOD for alcohol and drug a
For hospital analysis for Reagin (V.D.R.L.)
sample is not included in the kit).

Proceed with general examination. (See opposite pa

AG #3 — GENITAL/ANAL AREAS AND CAVI

Guidelines: *Respect need for privacy and appropria*
aginal Specula: (For procedures 3D-3G) wai
nts.

a) *Prepubertal: (If no evidence of genital*
speculum exam).
Specula: Walton-Pederson (4" x 5/8" blade
infant vaginoscope (6.5 x 0.9 cm.).

b) *Postpubertal:*
i) Previously Virginal — Walton-Pederson S
ii) Non-Virginal or Parous — medium sized

c) *FEMALE COMPLAINANT — COLLECT 3*
MALE COMPLAINANT — OMIT 3D-3G I

3-A Cut out any apparent SEMINAL-LIKE DEPOS
in envelope 3-A. Fold carefully and replace in e

B Comb the PUBIC HAIR for loose hair, fibres, e
ings on paper provided in envelope 3-B, fold
envelope 3-B.

C Pluck 12 PUBIC HAIRS and place in plastic
discretion of physician. This will not affect the

3-D Place any FOREIGN MATERIAL (hair, fibres
velope 3-D, fold and replace in envelope.

E Take 2 swabs of the VAGINAL FORNIX. (Plac
DO CERVICAL SWAB AND SMEAR FOR G
NOT INCLUDED IN THE KIT.)

Use syringe and tubing provided to introduce
posterior VAGINAL FORNIX. Aspirate and pla

3-G MOTILITY EXAMINATION — Prepare a wet
(40x lens on standard microscope) for the prese
in slideholder 3-G.

ake ANAL SWAB, smear slide 3-H and place i
ake RECTAL SWAB. Smear slide 3-I and pla
tube 3-I.

Collect URINE and place approximately 10 ml.
COLLECT 10 ML. URINE — FOR HOSPITA
TEST. (CONTAINER FOR THIS IS NOT INCL

Rape kit checklist

walking through him. "Okay then," he mumbled, ". . . leave the door open though and uhm . . . don't wipe yourself or wash up." I watched them watch me through the crack in the door. I felt nothing but was aware, attentive, almost as if I found it all interesting.

They said that if I wanted to file charges, I would have to go to the hospital and take some tests for what they called a sexual assault kit. They told me to sign a form saying I agreed to the tests even though I didn't know what they were or what the officers were talking about. They kept saying I had to sign before they could proceed, and when I did, they called an ambulance. They asked if I wanted to phone someone and that was the best idea I'd heard all night. I called my friend Susan, who is calm, and asked her to meet me at the hospital. The ambulance arrived and I was told to lie on a stretcher. They wanted to wheel me from my home like something broken or sick. A crowd had gathered in the hallway because the police had awoken everyone in my building. I insisted on walking out but they wouldn't allow it, and my first standoff with the police occurred. After a few rounds of argument, a woman medic approached me. "Listen honey," she said, "*sit* on the stretcher and put this blanket over your head." I agreed, simply because she had heard me and spoken kindly to me. I was wheeled out of my home disguised as Casper the Friendly Ghost.

At the hospital I sat some more on the stretcher in a hallway, waiting for the medical team to see me. Apparently two other women had reported their rapes that night and there was a lineup. While I waited, the cops were all over me again with their chorus of questions. Did you see him? Tattoos? Weight? Ejaculation? How many times? Was your door locked? What colour was he? Where is your boyfriend? Did you see him?

The officers all looked alike but some had new faces. I wondered where Susan was.

Then my number was called and I'm wheeled into a medium-sized room where three women in white lab coats are waiting. They speak softly, tell me their nurse and doctor names, what they will do. They ask more questions, record the answers. Like an annual physical, they light my eyes, touch me, bend, tap, prod and weigh me. They ask if I take medication, have attempted suicide, been admitted to a psychiatric hospital. If I have had children, abortions, recent consensual sex. What is my alcohol or drug consumption? Regular periods? Then they ask me to tell my rape. They write everything down, record the data on forms with numbers and codes that have been waiting for me to be raped. All of it is standard procedure. The women who treat me explain everything to me in apologetic tones, whisper commands in powdered voices—things better not spoken too loud. They are efficient and distant as they spread a circular plastic sheet on the floor and ask me to stand on it and remove my robe. They brush the hair on my head and count out fifty hairs and then they brush between my legs and pluck fifteen pubic hairs by the root and it should hurt but I don't feel it. I don't feel anything. One bends before me and scrapes skin from my shin. Another holds a tissue and I spit delicately into it. My mouth is swabbed. They take some blood and then take more and more and then—*and then*—they do an internal pelvic examination, stirrups, gloves, stainless steel inside me, entering, expanding. From a nearby microscope a woman's voice says, "We've got sperm here, one's still alive." I tell her to kill it and she looks at me and smiles. Everything is collected in vials and plastic or under glass, labelled with my name. All these pieces of me are placed in a kit to be touched and examined, probed and considered some more, somewhere, by someone, for something. More needles—these ones filled with antibiotics. And pills that gag me, coat my throat and mouth, to prevent fertilization by errant rape sperm. They give me Gravol for the upset the medication is sure to cause. And does.

Before leaving home, I had gathered some clothes, mindful to choose my highest heels, my blackest blacks and my leather jacket. After I had dressed, the nurse moved to fold my robe for me, but I wouldn't take it, even though it was velvet and blue and my favourite. A gift from my mother. I told her that I didn't want it anymore, and I could tell that she wanted to cry.

After that another police officer, a woman this time, began an in-depth interrogation of me in a hospital waiting room. She was on duty when the call went out, at my request, for a female officer to attend. She was young and kind and asked me to tell her everything I had done starting twenty-four hours before the rape, what I ate, who I was with. She wrote it all down. She was interrupted twice by older, busier detectives who asked if she was finished yet, how much longer? They parted the curtained walls with ham fists to ask me again what the rapist had said, what I had seen. I could see she was annoyed. I couldn't understand why Susan hadn't shown up. When I was done, I telephoned her and she answered in a panic, "Where are you? The police called me back and said I shouldn't come to the hospital. Are you okay? What happened?"

The female officer offered to drive me to Susan's house. It was morning now. The city was waking up and everything seemed normal and nothing was ever normal again. In Susan's kitchen I ate a little and vomited and fell into something like sleep. I hadn't shed a tear. I wouldn't for years.

WHEN I woke up, more friends were there with clothes, love, tears, Valium, rage. I got dressed and sat with them for a while but didn't say much. Then I went to work.

I had a management position with an international film festival and was responsible for a staff of twelve employees. Having a place to go and something to focus on helped me to feel myself a little, to think and to recognize the fury that was building inside of me. The thought that surfaced first, and surfaced the most, was quite simply: This is not to be borne. None of it. Not by me. I had gone to bed with my doors locked, my lights on, in the city I love, in my bed, my space, the safest place I could ever be, minding my own business, and some piece of shit I don't even know gets to crawl in and rape me at knifepoint? I don't think so.

Certainly there were other feelings. Like fear. Fear like I had never known, wouldn't know if only . . . what? If only I had or hadn't what? Gone to bed? Lived alone? Been female?

The thing about me and fear is that when I am frightened, I get angry and then I will fight. I don't care who wins. I will fight. It's not always the best reaction. Sometimes it would be better to run, or shut up and realize that the adrenalin rush will fade, or that what has scared you is not so scary after all. (If they have you pinned with a knife at your throat, you should consider the wisdom of fighting at that moment.) But I felt that this time there was something worth fighting, something I could almost see, grasp. If only I could sleep. Weep. Understand.

IN two days the police made contact again. One of the investigating officers called me at work and asked to meet with me back at my apartment. I hadn't been home yet and asked my friend Maurice to come with me. My instinct was to arrange that kind of support, or witness, whenever I spoke with the cops. I got to my apartment first, but before I could really register the disorder, the sadness of the place, my buzzer screeched and Maurice and I screamed and then someone started banging on the door really hard and yelling for us to open up! Police!

The detective's name was Bill Cameron and he was a really big man. Bigger than any of them yet. His head was massive (and I have a large head myself). I was most struck, though, by the fact that he looked like one of my brothers. He spoke softly and had sad eyes, which offset the requisite cop moustache and unhealthy pallor. He took hours to ask me the same questions I had already answered at the hospital, which I had already answered at home. When I asked him why I had to go through this again he responded that as the officer in charge, he preferred to get the information directly from me. Straight from the rape victim's mouth. He ended his first interrogation by informing me that he was convinced that the man who raped me was responsible for a series of rapes that had taken place in my neighbourhood in the last few months. The attacks were cyclical—on the full moon, in fact. The rapist stalked the women he chose, and we all shared certain characteristics. We lived in second- and third-floor balcony apartments and were physically alike. I had been raped by a serial rapist.

I asked him why I hadn't been warned.

"What?" he said.

"Why didn't you tell me that my life was in danger?" *You bastards! I knew there was something! You used me! As bait! To catch the guy! You let me sleep while he broke into my home! YOU DIDN'T WARN ME!*

"What do you mean?" he said.

"The papers, the TV—I look at them every day, and there was nothing. You should have warned me if you knew all those things. You could have put out an alert, posters, something!"

"We have a policy for these things, ma'am, and we followed it," he countered. "If we warned the public like you say, a lot of the ladies would get hysterical and the perp would probably stop and move to another precinct, and our whole investigation would be out the window."

I was beginning to understand. This was about police procedure, not about crime prevention. Not about protecting or serving.

⁘

"First interrogation"
(in the voice of Bill Cameron)

2:

SHE was so little. The occurrence report said she was twenty-one, but she was thirty-one and no bigger than my Sarah, who'd just turned twelve. Sarah was big for her age, mind you. She gets that from me. I hate these rape cases, the way they tear up the victim's lives. I'd kill any perp who hurt my girls like that. But twelve years on the job and you learn to treat it like other crimes. This vic was different though, even her place was different, a big apartment where she lived alone, with furniture from the fifties that reminded me of my mom, and lots of art. She had this fish bowl with furniture and plastic fish in it—one of them was lying on a little bed. The forensic guys had dusted and I could see the circle on her table from where she'd moved it. Anyway, I interviewed her there and she had brought this friend. Some guy, looked kinda fruity and kept gunning me off like I was gonna hurt her or something. So I explained the procedure and of course it was a little different from other investigations 'cause of sensitivity issues and such, and I could see right away that she was gonna be a handful. Not that I didn't like her. She spoke real soft and was polite, and the first time I saw her smile it made me smile even though I didn't know I felt like it.

The hardest thing about a rape investigation, well one of the hardest things, is interviewing the victims. We take a two-day course on it, but really, you learn on the job. The ladies are very traumatized by what has happened to them and have a few standard reactions. They're real quiet or afraid. The worst are the ones who can't stop crying, especially when they're really young or really old or can't remember. Some are mad at you and some act like nothing happened. It's a whole other ball game if it's a sex three. That's a level-three sexual assault, where the perp has hurt the victim physically and she needs medical care. No cop wants to catch those, but we do and we gotta do our job and so we have to sort of get hardened. If you show your emotion it takes away from doing your job, but man it's hard. Anyway, this one was a sex two, where the guy has a weapon and threatens her but doesn't use it, and that's not easy either—to investigate, I mean. I can almost tell you what the vics will say and how they are gonna act once I get a line on their trauma type. But damned if she wasn't hard to read, and she kept looking at me as if she was trying to read me too. Which she was.

This case was already driving me crazy. The perp was moving back and forth across the line, the street, that divided two downtown precincts, and when that happens it's easier to drop the ball, what with the chain of command and paperwork and all, and we did. Well they did. When I was assigned, first thing I did was check with the desk at 51, and fucked if they're not sitting on a couple unfounds,* and doublefucked if it's not the same identical MO as our two, and now we got a big problem because he's moving faster and these guys don't stop. So now it's a major occurrence and the boys upstairs are screaming and they put me in charge of a special force with Kim Derry, this Young Turk I was working the Two Toes case with. Then we have to start from the beginning and interview all the victims. So we do.

The first incident was six months ago and she's mad as hell at us because the cop who caught the call at 51 didn't believe her, didn't find cause to file a charge and even then suspected it was her boyfriend who did it and arrested him! According to the report, she had sex aids, handcuffs and ropes all over her bedroom. Jesus. The second vic's apartment superintendent said she was a troublemaker and her boyfriend says she's nuts and there's something about potato chips on the bed that sinks us, but that happens much later. The third girl lives in the same apartment building as the second, and 51 files that one but doesn't connect the two. That bothered me right from the get-go. But there's something you gotta understand about cops, about us: it ain't easy. Oh, there was a time when it was better,

---

* Police "found" (pursue) or "unfound" (do not pursue) sexual-assault charges based on the evidence they collect in their investigation, which includes their estimation of the credibility of the woman involved.

when people were glad to see us show up, when we were the good guys. I had some of that back at the beginning of my career, but honestly I'm glad to be out now in my own business and with the pension coming in. I earned every penny. So I'm not laying any blame on the cops who are still in and especially if it's a sex assault or domestic violence situation, because nobody wants to catch them.

The fourth girl he raped was on my side of the line, and I made that call and the pieces fell into place.

Young Kim and I set up special stakeouts based on the fact that the crimes appear to be cyclical, just before the full moon, and that the guy breaks in from the balcony of second- and third-floor apartments in a six-block radius. The immediate consensus was that our offender lived in the area and there were many reasons for thinking that, like the fact that he wore a mask and no one ever heard a car drive away. The only way he could have got out so fast was if he lived nearby. In a comfort zone. They usually do. And the other thing is that all the victims look alike and are single and they all recall the exact same details of the attacks and the guy is a real perv. He even cut one of them a little.

So we pull some more men out of robbery and we wait. Not that it was that simple, I mean, we were in full investigative mode. According to his pattern he was gonna strike again on August 25, 1986, and the thing is this was pretty reliable because these guys don't stop and all of the data points to escalation. This is proven by the FBI and Scotland Yard.

Detective work is shift work and I was off-duty the weekend of the twenty-fifth, after an eight-day log.* Kim was off, too. On the night of August 24 that little lady was raped by the Balcony Rapist.

I got the call at home. I drove my oldest to her swimming competition in Buffalo the next day with my mind on rape in Toronto. My girl did good and I don't think she noticed that her old dad wasn't focused on her for every single moment the way I had planned. Funny I should remember that. It was so long ago.

When I got back, I called the vic and arranged to meet her at her apartment. So she's sitting there and I explain that we believe she was raped by a serial rapist and she stays calm but gets real pale. She didn't miss a day's

---

* A shift.

work and has been staying with a friend but is about to move back in. By herself. I ask her to walk me through her life, back a few months and then up to the attack, if she has enemies and such. It takes a long time and she is very composed and a good witness. She works for some film place and has a bum for a boyfriend. He's in jail right now. When I'm done, she asks if she can ask me some questions and I say sure. She wants to know why I didn't tape the stuff I just asked her and why I didn't get it all from the uniform who took her first statement, 'cause she thought that was a good one and took even longer and why did she have to do it all over again? I explained that as one of the investigating officers I needed to speak directly with her and hear about the incident from her. Then she wants to know why, if we had all of this information about the perp being a serial and the specificity—that's the word she used—of the attacks, we didn't issue a statement to warn her about the rapist. Now of course we had considered this, but the truth is warnings can backfire on you. They scare the females, even make them hysterical. Also the perps are more likely to flee if they know we are on to them, and then our investigation is compromised.

Her face got pink when I said that and her friend looked real uncomfortable, but all in all I thought everything was going well. She was stuck on the warning thing, though, and kept asking me about it. And then she says right out of the blue and real quiet, "Well, Bill,"—I had asked her to call me Bill—"if you're not going to issue a warning, what if I put one out?"

And then I knew that she was acting out a control-type response to her trauma and that explained a lot of how she was behaving. I told her it wouldn't be a good thing for her to put out a warning and that we were gonna take care of things and we needed her co-operation. We would be in touch and she was to phone me if anything came up, like if she found something that could be evidence even if she didn't think it was, or got any phone calls or noticed anyone suspicious around her. And she thanked me and shook my hand, and her hand was so little.

❖

Ruined blue party dress

3:

JUST before I was raped I had found a new doctor. She was a general practitioner named Carolyn Dean who practised a holistic approach to medicine. The massive amount of drugs that doctors administer during the gathering of the sexual-assault evidence kit, combined with the trauma of rape, can cause you to miss your period or otherwise mess with your menstrual cycle and make you feel unwell. After I was raped I kept vomiting regularly, and of course I assumed I was pregnant. So I went to my new doctor and explained my situation to her. I also wanted to be tested for HIV. After the blood tests and the internal—back in the stirrups again—Carolyn asked me if there was anything else I needed, and I said yes, I needed something to ward off evil. She didn't bat an eyelash. I told her that I could still smell the man who raped me, that my home held the memory of him, a sense of him. She took out her prescription pad and wrote a series of chants for me to repeat as I burned sage and walked with it through my apartment. She suggested that I open all of the windows, sweep the floors and visualize a white light around everything. She wrote it all down for me on her pad, ripped off the prescription and handed it to me, telling me to call her any time.

A group of friends helped me burn the sage and chant and imagine the white light, and afterwards my home started to feel like it was mine again. I had never done anything like that before. But I believed.

While we were cleaning and sweeping rape from my place, I found a white shawl in the corner of my hall closet. Two holes had been cut out of it. My blue party dress was hacked in half. Bill Cameron had told me to call him if I found anything unusual or out of place and so I did. He

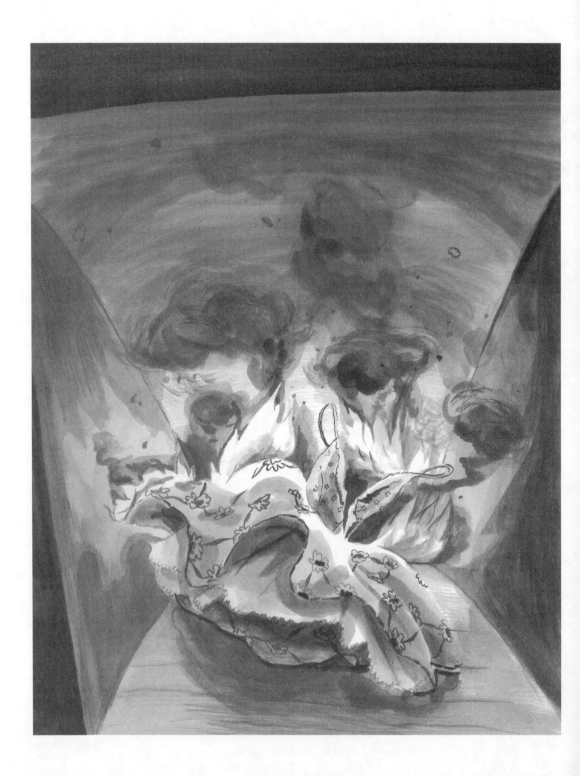

showed up with his partner, Kim Derry, who was all business and seemed a little bored. Bill identified the shawl as the mask the rapist had fashioned in order to cover his face and took it away for tests. He said the blue dress was a failed attempt at mask-making and they didn't need to take it. When they left, I threw it down the building's incinerator. Maurice and Penny, another of my friends, cried. It was a beautiful dress.

THE festival I worked for was hosting a retrospective of Russian films, and one of my responsibilities was to make touring and shopping arrangements for the visiting artists. I was arranging bus trips to Niagara Falls and excursions to Honest Ed's, the famous bargain emporium (Ed's prices and variety are renowned, even in Russia). The festival had also produced a series of T-shirts and posters in the style of Soviet art, which were selling like Russian hotcakes. Thousands of people converged to buy them, along with tickets, passes and program books, and off-duty cops were hired for crowd control. I was really busy and that was good. When I was working I didn't have time to remember that the man who raped me was still out there, that he could be watching, waiting, planning to return.

One day Bill and Kim showed up at work to ask me some questions. They attempted to be discreet but they couldn't hide their discomfort in the presence of so much communist propaganda and the insolent stares of the kids who worked with me, who knew a cop when they saw one. Bill wanted me to go through another kind of interview with different officers who were working on creating a profile of the rapist. I balked a little. How many times did I have to tell them the same things? Was it a test? If I tell it the same way three times I win? Or were they just not paying that much attention as I relived my rape for them?

I again asked if they had considered issuing a warning. Kim countered that this was a police investigation and I shouldn't interfere. That I could be charged with obstruction if I did. They left and I got back to work. Back to not dwelling on the fact that the man who raped me was still at large. He knew everything about me and I had never seen his face. I figured he must be close by. The only reason he could disappear so completely into the night and elude the cops after five rapes had to

be because he lived in my neighbourhood and could move quickly back into his home. I'd seen it all on *L.A. Law* and *Hill Street Blues*. I loved to watch lawyer and police TV dramas and had learned from them that sex offenders usually mask themselves when they live in the area in which they rape. I was very frightened and extremely pissed off. How does rape happen to four of my neighbours and no one tells me? I needed to do something about it.

People always ask me how I managed to do what I did. Take on the cops. The answer is that I did what I could. What I was capable of, what came naturally to me. It would have been much more difficult to have done nothing. Remember the two little girls in the news recently who were playing tent or picnic or something with their mother's sheets when they looked up and saw a baby about to tumble four storeys to his certain death? They didn't stop to make a decision about what they would do or what they could do. They remembered what their hero Pippi Longstocking had done. They held a sheet out and caught the boy in their net because they could, because they knew how and it was the right thing for them to do. It was like that for me. I caught myself in my own net because I knew how. I was not a girl at the time of my rape. I was a woman in my thirties. I had a life history and experience to call on to help me cope with what had happened to me. I was already a political person who had organized a union in my workplace, demonstrated for women's issues and against racism. I had been in therapy for a few years. I had rallied against sexual assault, war and homophobia. I understood the power of the media. By the summer of 1986 I had owned my own business, lived abroad and had my heart broken. I had plans and at least a little insight into life. It was not difficult for me to get organized around my rape and to understand the broader systemic issues as they presented themselves. It's what saved my life.

"She's not such a tough nut"
(in the voice of Bill Cameron)

4:

THE Sexual Assault Coordinator's Office—SACO, for short—wanted to bring the victims in to build one of those personality profile things the FBI developed in Quantico, called Viglass or Sunglass or something. Okay, I'll get it right: VICLAS, the Violent Crime Linkage and Analysis System. Bobby Qualtrough and Margo Pulford were working SACO, and they both had a hard-on about using all this technology to solve serial sex crimes. I dunno, I mean, did profiling help them catch Wayne Williams in Atlanta? I'll tell you what caught that friggin' scumbag: old-fashioned police work, methodical footwork, interviews, tips. In Jane's case, because she was kicking up such a fuss, there was talk about contacting the building superintendents in the targeted apartments and that they would then advise tenants—especially single women—about the occurrences under investigation, and they would then tell the police about any suspicious types. But I didn't like the idea. It was messing with procedure.

My experience was to do it by the book. Experience is what allows you as an investigator to do all the right things, which will result in creating an atmosphere within your investigation that will generate the luck required to solve the case. Not too many crimes are solved like Hercule Poirot, you know, where a light bulb goes off and all the pieces fall into place. My experience says it's about luck. And following procedure. You do the right things and you generate the good luck that's required. And you hope you're in the right place at the right time.

SACO wasn't procedure either, but they've spent the money on it and the old man wants it justified. So I talk it up to the vics and bring them in. Jane first.

I like Margo Pulford. She's a good cop, a looker too. I never know what Bob Qualtrough's talkin' about exactly. Statistics, projectors—it all seems to be after the fact. But we gotta do something. We think the perp did another B&E in a girl's apartment right across the street from Jane's. According to his MO he'll be back for her. She's an actress, Lori Martin, and she's co-operating fully. Number six on his list. She looks so much like Jane I had one of those déjà vues. Case is gettin' fucking creepier.

Anyway, as per usual, Jane says she wants to bring a friend with her to the interview and what can I say? It's her right. I pick them up and we go over to the old fire hall on New Street, where the SACO is. When we get there she asks where's the can—she doesn't feel good. The ladies' room is two flights up, and I ask her does she want the men's because she's awful white and it's right there. She says yeah, and I stand outside the door and I can hear her dry heaving and then she comes out and says, "Okay, let's do it." I don't know if she knows that's what Gary Gilmore said right before they executed him, but she smiles back at me.

So Bobby and Margo meet with her for about two hours, and Margo sends me a report a couple of days later and it's from the "Zink Cookbook"—Oliver Zink, an FBI agent who developed this recipe for categorizing serial rapists. The profile they've decided that fits our perp is "Gentleman Rapist, power reassurance." Why don't they tell me something I don't know? There's a bunch of other stuff, charts and percentiles, and Margo wants to meet, but I have to get over to number six's. Maybe tonight I can figure out who's the model citizen keeps replacing the light bulbs that we removed from the back of Jane's building. How're you gonna stake out a location under a hundred-watt light? Anyway, Kim is more interested in this profile business than I am, so let him take the meeting.

Just like I figured, the guy replacing the bulb was a neighbour. He says he was looking out for his girlfriend, who works nights. He didn't want her coming out of the parking lot in the dark. He was about to call us, because every night he'd replace the light bulb, and the next day it would be missing. They live right under Jane, and we'd interviewed him earlier. Richard Element. Get it? Light bulb element? He thought we were skels at first.* Didn't figure that cops were removing the bulbs. Kim going off on him

---

*Police slang for "criminal."

JANE DOE

didn't help much—the guy was just doing the right thing. But everyone is tensed up, waiting, driving around, sitting in a car, no leg room, no a/c. And now there's that Alison Parrott murder. Her face is in all the news boxes. A sweet little girl like that. Mother of Christ, what's this city comin' to?*

Anyway we straighten Element out, enlighten him you could say, and I relieve McCoy who's on surveillance at Lori Martin's apartment. There's not much going on, but that's the way of it. It's been three weeks now. That hump is gonna hit again, soon, we're heading for another full moon, and the pressure is on from upstairs on this one.

We're pretty sure our guy's an Indian—Canadian Indian I mean, not from India. One of the vics saw him silhouetted in her doorway, and she described him as holding the knife in the air just like you see in the movies when the Indians raid the settlers' homes. Later we showed her a *Maclean's* magazine with a photo spread of some Natives who had been drinking antifreeze and she pointed to one of them, saying the rapist looked something like that. Plus all the vics report that he had no body hair and that the hair on his head was shoulder length. Then there's his ability to climb.

We're also canvassing the neighbourhood, knocking on doors, telling people they should be watching out for prowlers. We probably knocked on his door and talked to him personally or certainly a close relative of his. We don't want to let him know what we are doing, so our method is to conduct the canvassing by saying there are a lot of burglaries taking place in the area, break and enters through balconies, and to prevent them, the public should take precautions. As a matter of fact, there were an inordinate number of B&Es in the area. So our plan had a twofold purpose. We were trying to protect the females in the immediate area, but the officers doing the canvass were advised not to bring up the subject of sexual assault, to warn them instead about possible thefts.

So to make sure we get all the right buildings, we generate a list of single

* The brutal murder of eleven-year-old Alison Parrott, a promising young athlete, marked what many felt was a loss of innocence for "Toronto the Good." In his testimony during my civil trial, Jack Marks, the police chief at the time, stated that community demands to address the Balcony Rapist investigation detracted from the investigation of Parrott's murder. Her killer was convicted in 1999.

women living in second- and third-floor balcony apartments and make sure we canvass those addresses. Goddamned if Jane's name and address isn't on the list—this is *after* her incident—and some rookie cadet knocks on her door. So then I get calls from the both of them. The cadet is practically shitting himself since it seems Jane got him to *show* her the list and spill his guts after she side-swipes him with who she is. Jane calls and starts again with the stuff about warnings and adequate information so that women can make informed decisions—I know it off by heart, she's said it so many times. And then she says, "What's with this B&E effing bullshit?" which kind of surprised me because I never heard her curse before. Why were we sending cops to women's houses late at night and don't we think that might be kind of scary itself? For a little dame she can make a lot of noise. Frankly, I don't necessarily disagree with some of her ideas but unfortunately they aren't in the law. And we have to comply with the law.

By now Jane and a bunch of other ladies are rattling cages with this feminism stuff. She doesn't look like a feminist, but she admitted to me that she was. Asked me about my girls, how old they were, and did I ever think about introducing feminism into my understanding of their lives. What the fuck? As if I don't have enough to think about right now.

❖

"Our own worst nightmares"
(in the voice of Margo Pulford)

5:

THERE'S this notion that female cops *want* to work on sexual assaults. That we choose it. There's this big deal that we're the ones who should take the statements and conduct the interviews, in order to be more sensitive to the victims who, let's face it, are all women and would probably rather talk to women. But does anybody ask us what we want? Vice and sex assault—that's where we're sent, how we're ghettoized, and it's not as if we're in charge of the investigations. Oh no, we're the decoys or the sensitive ones. They bring us in to flash some skin or to listen to our own worst nightmares and then let the boys do the police work. Well screw that. I'm a cop. A good one. But if this is where I'm stuck right now I'll do the best bloody job possible and get promoted out.

SACO is my baby. There's a budget line dedicated to the development of technology in police work and I'm cashing it in. Toronto needs a squad devoted to sexual assault, and SACO is the first step. The idea is that all serial or stranger assaults are coordinated through our office using FBI model-profiling, forensic and tracking technology. We translate and share that information with the investigating officers who are from the Major Crime units. This summer alone there are three serial rapists operating in the downtown core. That's not unusual, but the public is paying attention. Women's groups are organizing around the crime, telling us the way we're treating it is not good enough. They're right.

When the Balcony Rapist starts making headlines—after Jane Doe became his fifth victim—I meet with the old man and convince him that this is the time for SACO to become more centrally involved in investigations. I prepare a cost analysis for the chief, an overview of his own operational policies, get the data from Quantico and copies of newspaper stories criticizing current investigative procedures. He's a leg man, so I wear my new Italian slingbacks.

Bill Cameron and Kim Derry are the lead investigating officers. They're sergeants from Old Clothes,* alley rats who have investigated all manner of crimes. Bill is senior, thank God, Kim is so flat. I think there's someone in there, but it's hard to tell. He'll probably go far. Bob Qualtrough and I were given carriage of the interviews. Bob is okay to work with and I like his wife. I think his real calling is science, though.

The idea of creating a personality profile is to work with the conscious and unconscious impressions and memories of victims. No information or response is discarded. Victims are encouraged to relate any notions, triggers or associations that surface, as well as give us a detailed retelling of the incident. The procedure for developing a criminal profile consists of a series of questions—personal, general and specific—that we ask sequentially. The responses are correlated and shipped to Atlanta where forensic and psychology experts analyze the data through VICAP to create a portrait or behavioural composite of the predator and his prey.** We send a tape recording of the interview, and photographs of the crime scene and the victim.

It's important to create an ambient setting and to establish a supportive relationship with the subject. Our building was remodelled to house police administrative staff. It has high ceilings and windows and beautiful floors, and it's located in an upscale residential part of town. SACO has a small office on the second floor, but we have access to a larger meeting area. Since Jane Doe is the most recent vic, she is our first interview, as per VICLAS profiling procedures.

Bill Cameron brought her in and she brought a friend. No one informed me that she would agree to co-operate only if she were accompanied by someone she knew. Before I meet her, Bill tells me to go easy, she's not feeling well. What does he think, I'm going to attack her? She's in the room, already sitting down, when we come in. We do this on purpose: allow her

---

* A term for "plainclothes" used by Toronto police in the eighties.
** VICAP stands for the Violent Criminal Apprehension Program, the American serial-offender computer profiling system on which the Canadian system, VICLAS, is based.

to occupy the space first, assume more of a power position. She's wearing a white T-shirt and black skirt, and heels with no stockings. Her friend has spiky hair and looks ready for battle. Jane Doe is a tiny woman. Not so much skinny as small, in proportion, older than she looks, long nose, pretty, a killer smile—although I don't know that for quite a while.

We begin well, Bob and I playing off each other, but mostly me explaining things. Jane is attentive. When Bob asks permission to tape the session she says sure, as long as we don't mind her taping it too, and she pulls out a banged-up tape recorder. Bob freezes. He explains that this is not procedural. Jane says if she has to put hers away, we do too, and we sit there for a while, tape recorders loaded, staring each other down, until I blink and say it's fine, we'll all tape. We all relax, except now Jane can't get hers to work, so Bob helps her and we begin again. It's necessary to enter a physical description of the subject on the tape, and I do so in an anecdotal manner, saying I see you have blue eyes, are wearing whatever and have red hair. No stranger to the bottle myself, I inquire if this has always been her colour and Jane bristles. She tells me she dyed her hair red immediately after her rape, as she was aware that her natural hair colour was a factor in the perp's choice. Likewise, she says that pre-rape she had not worn the half dozen silver bracelets that threaten to snap her slender wrist at any moment, but does so now to better arm herself.

This is not going well. When Bob takes out the Polaroid to snap her picture, Jane and her friend Spike make as if to leave. Jane explains she thought this meeting was to provide an opportunity for her to assist in the investigation by contributing her own assessments and impressions, as opposed to being another lengthy interrogation including tape recordings, physical judgments and photo ops—all of which portray her as a helpless object.

This is one high-maintenance rape victim, I'm thinking, and then before I even finish the thought, something shifts. She sits back and smiles and says, "Look, this is the first time anyone has asked me what I think, so if you want to, let's finish this—only if I don't like the photo of me, you take more and *I* choose which one is submitted." I realize that she wants this guy caught and that's what we're here for. She's smart, I like her shoes, and she can be on top. For a while.

When we're finished and Jane has picked a photo she can live with, she asks us if she can ask a few questions. She wants to know about SACO, what we do and how I like being a cop. She said "police officer." I can tell when someone is trying to play me, and I'm not saying she wasn't, but she also seemed interested in my answers, said it must be hard to be a female cop. I told her that SACO was being modelled to become a separate crime unit dealing only with sexual assaults and that part of the preparation was increased training and awareness in interview and investigation techniques. Then she asked me about Bill and Kim, if I had worked with them before. And she wanted to know what I thought would happen next and why I thought a warning hadn't been issued. Before she left she said that I had done a good job and she was sorry it had started badly. As if I were the one being interviewed. Then she asked if she could call me if she had questions, and I said, "Of course, that's my job. I was just going to suggest it."

BY the end of the week we had interviewed the four other victims involved, and I FedExed the results to the VICAP headquarters in Atlanta. The material is sorted by computer and then analyzed to create a profile. Within forty-eight hours we had their results. I met with Kim to discuss them. The perp fit perfectly into the Power Reassurance/Gentleman Rapist category, which is the majority of all stranger rapes. I was excited about the finding, but Kim was less enthused.

A few days after our meeting, I got a call from Jane. She had been awakened the night before by shouting and glass breaking in the park just outside her building. She was frightened and had called the police, and the on-duty who answered told her that they could hardly send out cars every time someone got drunk in the city. Even after she told him she'd just been raped and the perp was still at large and she was supposed to call if she saw anything unusual, he told her to call back in the morning and hung up on her. She had his name, and I told her I would take care of it. When I spoke with him, the officer still didn't get it. It's not like he was technically wrong, but what does it cost to exercise a little sensitivity?

❖

What's a Gentleman Rapist?

6:

ONE morning after my rape I was sort of listening to Peter Gzowski on the CBC. That's how I did things. Sort of ate, drew breath, went to work. Sort of. Suddenly I realized that the woman being interviewed on the radio was telling my story. The balcony, the mask, the knife, the rapist's party banter—they were mine! A second guest identified herself as a counsellor in the hospital sexual-assault care centre where the police had brought me. The first woman's story of police treatment was outrageous. They had not believed her until several other women had reported identical crimes. Although he was sympathetic, Gzowski questioned her claims and also quibbled about the prevalence of the crime. I knew that this woman and I had been raped by the same man.*

Within twenty-four hours I had contacted the hospital counsellor, who passed on my name and number to the woman, along with an invitation for her to call me if she wanted to. The counsellor's name was Patti McGillicuddy, and with that call we began a political relationship and personal friendship that continues to this day. The other woman returned my call. Her name was Alice. (Well, actually it wasn't. I've changed it to respect her privacy.) We agreed immediately that it wasn't wise to discuss our rapes, but we consoled each other for about ten minutes. We talked about our fear that the guy was still out there, that he carried bits of us around, could follow us still or come into our homes. We talked about the hospital care centre, the counselling it offered, and

---

*I wrote to Peter Gzowski following this interview and challenged him about his resistance to a raped woman's story and experience. He sent me a letter of apology and requested that I call him if he could ever help.

a bit about Patti, whom Alice seemed to adore. She told me that she had spoken with another of our co-raped and that she, too, was doing okay. When you are freshly raped and doing okay, it means that you aren't dead. Before I hung up we agreed that we should tell Bill Cameron the content of our conversation. We didn't speak again until after the trial, but that night I felt a little better and almost got some sleep.

When I told Kim and Bill about speaking to Alice, Bill looked at me with his sad face and Kim started yelling that I was interfering and could be arrested—witnesses to a crime can't talk to each other, it could taint our evidence, confuse us, and don't I watch TV?

SHORTLY afterwards, I woke up one morning and couldn't move. Well, I could move, but I couldn't turn my head, and my neck locked with pain when I tried. I had always enjoyed excellent health. When people like me, who have always been healthy, do develop something, we assume the worst, and I was certain that I had either stroked out or developed MS. I mean why not? At that point it would have been a relief, because at least I could define those conditions, they had names and there were treatments. Sort of. Maurice took me to the hospital and didn't leave my side for a minute.

I didn't have to wait too long for an ER doctor, who poked and prodded and asked me if I had been in an accident or had fallen recently. I said no. Then he asked if I had undergone any recent trauma. I hadn't put the two things together: the rape and my frozen neck. Sometimes you think your heart can't take any more and then it does and you survive but it's like when John Travolta plunges the hypodermic into Uma Thurman in *Pulp Fiction*. It's almost more than you can take. That's how I felt. Anyway, the doctor said that I should see my GP and get a referral to a chiropractor. So I went back to my new doctor and she said she knew just the guy, and although I never see male medical practitioners if I can help it, my witch doctor recommended him and I trusted her.

The chiropractor's name was Larry and his office was close to my home. I liked his receptionist and he had a decent manner. When he read "rape" in my referral he didn't flinch, and he said that he could help me. I was in pain and frightened and I needed to believe him and I did.

OLIVER ZINK RAPE COOKBOOK

ER REASSURANCE   THE GENTLEMAN RAPIST

OF ALL RAPES

RPOSE:
      1.   No intent of harm or to degrade th

      2.   He is resolving doubts about his o

US OPERANDI

Assaults between 12 midnight and 5 am

Assaults occur in victim's residence or in a
area

Victim is alone or in the company of small ch

Will select his victim through peeping-tom ac

Will probably bring weapon or threaten the us

Will only use the force which is necessary to
the victim's resistance

If confronted with resistance he will: negoti
                                  desis
                                  flee
                                  resor

Uses little or no profanity.

Will demand verbal activity of a personal nat
the victim, ie, tell me that you love me, etc

He explained that my injury was brought on by the physical force of my rape. I saw Larry a lot over the next year, and miraculously my neck got better. Although he advised me that I needed long-term maintenance work, I couldn't afford it. My neck still attacks me when I work out too hard or get too tired or sad or when I have the dream that my rapist is in the next room and I can hear him shredding my clothes but I cannot move because I am paralyzed, and I struggle against the weight of my body to lift myself up, to scream, to run, and I cannot.

WHEN I lay awake at night and went over things, I became firmer in the conviction that I had to do something. That I *could* do something. Armed with that understanding, with anger and with forethought, I informed the investigating officers again that if they were not prepared to do so, I would issue the warning to the women of my neighbourhood myself. Kim Derry got really riled up again. He went off too fast and too often and always struck me as heart-attack material. I think he and Bill believed I wouldn't dare. They could not fathom the concept that I might involve myself in my own rape case.

I decided first to approach the media for assistance. I wrote to well-known activist June Callwood and asked for her help. She directed my letter to a *Globe and Mail* reporter who met with me and translated my claims to print. She quoted me as saying that I was raped by a gentleman. It was a mistake that spoke loudly, since it was, of course, the investigating officers who had used the term "gentleman rapist," and I had only repeated it to her as an example of the direction and nature of the investigation. When I called her about it, she insisted that her article and the notes that informed it were accurate and that I had called my rapist a gentleman. There was no retraction, and nothing much happened as a result, except that Johnny showed up at my office the day the story appeared.

Johnny, my boyfriend, my ex-boyfriend, my forever boyfriend— never partner. He had recently been released from jail and was living in a halfway house. We'd been in and out of a relationship for eight years. Mostly out. Definitely out at the time of my rape. But he remained the love of my life (more about that later).* He'd read

* Or go to page 100 now.

the article and said he knew it was me. He just knew, and he walked out of the halfway house to come and find me. He put his arms around me and I leaned into him for a while and felt a little better. He said he would get a pass and come see about me, but he had to get back before they missed him.

I WAS taking a night class at the University of Toronto. From a notice on one of the bulletin boards there, I learned of a feminist coalition that was inviting new members to its weekly meetings. "Direct action to confront violence against women" was the stated agenda. I went to the meeting and sat quietly at the back of the room, the newspaper article about my rape in my pocket, listening to a small group of academics and counsellors.

The group had recently produced a cable TV show about sexual assault, and they were talking about the telecast and child-care issues. One woman was knitting. I had been raped and was looking for radical, screw-the-system action as promised on their poster. I wondered if I was in the right place. An hour into the meeting, the door opened and two women walked in. They were expensively dressed. Fresh air and energy swirled about them. I breathed a sigh of relief. They introduced themselves as Lori Haskell and Melanie Randall.

Finally the group's chair asked about any new business and I raised my hand. I asked if they would help me to poster in my neighbourhood. Some of the women resisted the notion but Lori and Melanie didn't simply say yes, they enveloped me in their glamour and charm. I did not have to explain my situation or my thinking to them—they understood immediately. Within a week we decided to rename the group WAVAW, or Women Against Violence Against Women, seek new members and raise some feminist hell.

The concept of postering neighbourhoods or workplaces where a rapist is known to be operating was not invented by me. The Toronto Rape Crisis Centre (TRCC) had been promoting and engaging in postering for years. Feminist writers and anti-violence activists supported it as a way of addressing a crime that was swathed in silence and denial. It was radical but not that radical. With Lori and Melanie's support, I drew up a plan of action designed to use my rape as a flashpoint to organize locally and to address the sexist nature of the police investigation of sexual assault and their failure to warn women. Because of my work with numerous arts organizations, I was familiar with the media and with ways of getting their attention, which wasn't really that difficult, because let's face it: Rape Sells.

I wrote the press release and made sure it was also delivered to local and provincial politicians and union organizers, and I designed the warning poster. I drew up a map of the neighbourhood that highlighted apartment buildings in the area (there were about twenty) and alerted women about the danger they faced. The poster also invited them to a community meeting in a hall we had booked. The posters were red and stark and handmade. By my hand. The TRCC let me run off copies on their new colour Xerox machine. A week before the meeting date, about fifteen women recruited through local women's agencies, most of whom I had never met, worked in groups of twos and threes to put a poster in every mailbox or under the doors of every apartment in my neighbourhood. We also plastered telephone poles, hoardings, bulletin boards and bus shelters.

At the time, the Royal Ontario Museum was exhibiting art on loan from the Vatican. Its media campaign included posters with the slogan "The Pope Sends His Best" in huge letters that were displayed in bus

shelters all over the city. Our poster proclaimed in large letters, "Rapist in this Area," and we delighted at opportunities to combine our message with the Vatican's. The Pope Sends his Best *Rapist in this Area*.

Within twenty-four hours of our postering, headlines blasted the news that the rapist had been caught.

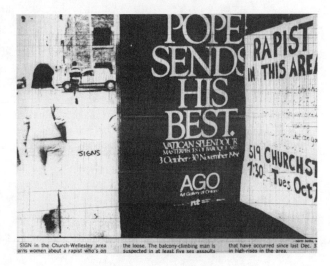

SIGN in the Church-Wellesley area arns women about a rapist who's on the loose. The balcony-climbing man is suspected in at least five sex assaults that have occurred since last Dec. 3 in high-rises in the area.

BILL Cameron called me early that morning so I would hear it from him first. I went to my corner market and the papers were full of the news, including the rapist's address, an apartment one block south of mine where he lived with his wife and child. His building was on our map. We had delivered a poster to his home. I wanted to see, to speak with, the man who had raped me. Remember, he'd worn a mask and then covered my head. I needed to know what he looked like, what made him do it, why he chose me and how. Who was he?

A friend and I walked down to his building and rang the super's buzzer. I told him I was a newspaper reporter looking for personal information about the serial rapist who lived in his building. What was he like? The super was clearly distressed about it all and assured me that buddy was a nice, quiet man who minded his own business.* The last person he would have suspected. I thanked him and went out and drank too much.

Other women might not have felt the same urgency, the curiosity or desire to see the man who raped me. But for me it was as if by seeing him I could undo some of my rape. Until now he had held the power of anonymity, he was the man in a hood and could be any man. He maintained complete control of that night.

IN a voice that would be soft if it belonged to anyone else, with breath soaked in rum (from a bottle my mother brought home from a cruise, which he chugalugged in my kitchen before coming to get me), the rapist whispers in my ear as if we are old friends, ex-lovers, reunited and

---

* In this book, I do not give the man who raped me a name, but I have to call him something. In Newfoundland, "buddy" is a common—sometimes dismissive—term for an unnamed man. Buddy it is.

RAPIST
IN THIS AREA

He, is medium build, black ha
white, enters thru 2 & 3rd fl
galeony apts, armed with a kn
he police are not warning
women. Why? What can you
o? Attend a public meeting at

519 CHURCH S
7:30 pm TueS Oct

catching up. "Do you have a boyfriend? What does he do? I'm going to get up now and stand by the window. I have the knife. Wait until I tell you to and then turn and look at me." He does and I do. He is wearing something white over his head with holes gaping for eyes and a butcher knife brandished above his head with the moon behind him. Even in my terror I read that he likes this part a lot. It's his beginning.

"How old are you?" My answers are brief. How old do you want me to be, I think, because that's exactly how old I will be, and I plead, "Please don't hurt me," and I promise myself that I will get out of this, it will end. Do as he says, answer, listen, don't breathe too much. And then more things I don't want to write, and he takes my pillowcase and wraps it around my eyes, and I can hear him removing his clothes. He has left the knife balanced against my cheek. I know from the sound of his pants hitting the floor, the clink of a belt buckle, that he is wearing jeans. I have already memorized the feel of his long-sleeved shirt as he held me. He climbs on top of me and kisses my mouth. "You have a beautiful body," he says. I am sure he is insane, will sink the knife inside me.

There is more, not really anyone's business. But I never saw his face, and the power that gave him was now mine to take back when I finally put a face to him.

THERE was no peace after the rapist was arrested. The police questions continued, often over the telephone, often at night around ten or eleven o'clock or later—whenever the shift changed. I was a routine task to be gotten off their plates.

Sleep has never been my friend. Imagine my sleep now. Every time I lay down or even thought of sleep, I thought of rape. The violent acts that plunged me into shock that night had left a hole in me that was leaking into my system, my brain, my concept of what was safe and civil. It was making an awful mess that did not show up in medical examinations. If I thought about it too long, stayed in those thoughts, I would shatter.

A few rape weeks after I was attacked, I was walking down a lovely street—my street, my city, my home—when I saw a man approach. The way he walked, his face, his eyes, his suit, convinced me that he intended to stab me in the back when he walked past me. I could feel the knife going in, cool blade, hot pain, not too much blood at first, and I looked around for help. "Scream," I thought. He was so close. "Shut your eyes. Don't faint. Breathe." Then I thought, "Do it if you're going to do it! Stab me! No, he won't, stop yourself, *snap-out-of-it*!" And then he passed me by, intent on his own business, enjoying the day. It happened again in the grocery store and on the subway platform. And again.

And then, with all of this going on, sometimes in the background, sometimes in the foreground, but going on and on always, *then* I would get phone calls from the cops when I was sleeping or trying to get there. "Do you want your sheets back?" they'd ask. The police always take your sheets—and your underwear—in the hopes of matching blood or semen. To this day I think of that. How many pairs of women's under-wear do they have and what do they do with them?

"Which hand was he holding the knife in?" I mean, can you imagine? They're asking this at my bedtime! And I had been blindfolded!

I had already answered these questions in official statements. I'll never understand why cops don't tape-record their interrogations of women who've been raped. How many times do they have to hear all of this stuff? At the time, when I suggested taping, they said it wasn't part of police procedure. (Six months later, during his testimony at the crim-inal trial, one of the investigating officers wasn't able to read his own notes about statements I'd made to him. I swear to God.)*

When I questioned the need for these late-night intrusions or the inconsistency of their information gathering, they treated me at first with gentle patronization. I became more demanding: "So what have

* In 1986 I felt strongly that the police should have tape-recorded their initial interviews with me rather than have me constantly repeat the story of my rape. While I believe that would have been the most efficient way to proceed *in my case*, the underlying reason for not tape-recording was that police officers (consciously or not) do not believe women's accounts of rape or believe that they are not reliable witnesses. In 2003 the situation has changed. Women who file sexual-assault and wife-assault charges are videotaped. The videotape becomes the property of the police, and a permanent record of her experience that follows her throughout the legal process. If she strays from that taped version—if, for example, she remembers something important a few days or weeks later or if she chooses not to proceed with a criminal investigation—the taped interview can then be used against her. If she appears intoxicated or stoned or too emotional or not emotional enough, if her wounds are not visible or she is too angry or not angry at all, the tape can be used against her. Women in these circumstances can be charged with mischief, obstruction or filing a false complaint. Or they can simply be discredited.

The police blew it

Metro police just blew a chance to reassure the women of the community that they're as interested in preventing crime as in catching criminals. No police officer showed up Tuesday night at the Church St. Community Centre, where 100 residents met to discuss a series of sexual assaults that have occurred recently in the Church-Wellesley area.

Some assault victims are particularly angry because police didn't warn them a rapist was on the loose in the neighborhood so that they could take the necessary precautions. Police have said such information would have made it harder to catch the suspect, who is now in custody.

If the police really believe this, why not go to the meeting and make the case? A police spokesman said yesterday the letter asking a police representative to attend didn't arrive in time and that one of the two officers specifically invited wasn't authorized to talk about rape and the other was unavailable.

These excuses won't wash. How much notice does the police department need? The letter arrived on Oct. 2 and was preceded by telephone invitations. What's more, the letter said that if the two named officers couldn't come, another officer experienced in investigating rape cases would be welcome.

Although 5,000 of Metro's 5,400 police officers have had some training in dealing with sexual assault, the failure to attend Tuesday's meeting is evidence that there remains considerable insensitivity to the crime and its victims among members of the force.

torstar Oct 9, 75 A22

you done today? Don't you have a computer you can feed this information into? Didn't you read the rapist's profile?" Then I got angry: "No, I
won't hold. No, I can't come to the station at two o'clock tomorrow, I'll
lose my job!" As the articles began to appear in the paper and we postered
and I led deputations in front of their bosses at the police commission*—
their attitude shifted. I became the troublemaker, the big mouth, the
feminist.

The cops' manner toward me became more aggressive and offensive
as I continued to attempt to make them accountable to me. They would
holler and threaten, hang up the phone, lie, equivocate or just plain try
to avoid me. Their behaviour was and still is considered acceptable, a
tolerable component of romanticized perceptions of police officers as
surly but heart-of-gold heroes who always get their man. I was to put up
with the transgressions: half-naked pin-up girls on calendars over their
desks, inappropriate endearments (dear, sweetie, little one) that morphed
naturally into infantilizing and paternalistic attitudes; sexist and
misogynist beliefs blatantly displayed. But what do you expect? They're
police officers and they don't really mean it, and didn't they catch the
guy and don't you have a political axe to grind, fish to fry, a point to make?
Get off that high horse and get off their case.

From the moment the cops entered my apartment after my rape, I was
aware that they perceived me in a way that worked in my favour. I had
all of the elements necessary to make them believe that I had been raped.
To make them accept me as a real rape. A good rape. A real good rape.

My home and work and dress are acceptable. I am white-skinned and
perceived as heterosexual. My rapist was a stranger to me, as opposed
to the majority of rapes, which are committed by fathers and husbands
and doctors and dates. I played on my preferred status and attempted to
parlay it into my larger political agenda. Now that I had their attention,
I reasoned, they would be more likely to listen, to understand the com-
plexity of the crime. That it is not isolated or random and that there are
reasons women do not report it. In my dealings with the police, I never

---

* A group of politicians, lawyers and business leaders, appointed by politicians on municipal and
provincial levels, to provide civilian oversight of police operations. It has since been renamed
the Toronto Police Services Board.

raised my voice or expressed my anger in a way that could be used against me. I dressed in my best and borrowed my friends' best clothes to wear when meeting police. I did not expect help or justice from them. At least not the kind I needed. And although I woke at night screaming and soaked in sweat, which I thought was blood falling from the mouth of the monster above me, I was not afraid to fight the force by day—the system that presumed to define justice for me. A community of women with a history of activism and resistance supported me. Feminism and a belief in social justice sustained me.

But what if any of this good-girl presentation and support were missing? Would I have been so fearless, so confident? Would I still have picked up my phone and dialled 911?

"Goddamn, if she didn't poster"
(in the voice of Bill Cameron)

7:

SO JANE goes to the media. And right there, on the front page, she says we're using women like her as bait, and I catch heat from upstairs, and the media is up my ass and then she says she's gonna warn women herself. I never thought she would. Kim did. He said we needed to rein her in.

Anyway, goddamn if she doesn't put up posters too, and the very next day—this is the part that drives me crazy—the day after she puts up the posters, we get a tip to look at this guy up on wife assault with rape priors, and damned if it isn't him. It was his parole officer who called in the tip, and she says this is the second time she's called about him but now she really thinks it's relevant as Jane's poster has ID information on him and such. So Kim and me tail the guy and he's on the move all right, with his face all banged up, and he stops to meet some other skels at this greasy spoon in the neighbourhood known by some as the Bugger Burger, and he's carryin' a sawed-off baseball bat, which is in direct violation of his parole stipulations. I put my hands on him as he comes out the door. "Police, you're under arrest," and he looks right at me and says, "You got me, I'm the one."

We bring him downtown and he spills everything. Details only he would know. He says his face was beaten by some drug dealers he owed money to. And I'm thinking, That saves me from beatin' ya then. We book him and he lawyers up.

But it's him and we got him and all I want to do is call those ladies he hurt, especially Jane, and before they see the papers. I called Jane first and she answered all sleepy, and when I told her, she didn't say nothing at first and then she said, "Thank you, Bill. Thank you for getting him." I told her

I was gonna call the other ladies, I mean women, and she could call me back if she had more questions. That she could call me any time.

Once you've arrested your suspect, cleared the occurrence, especially when you are confident that he is the guy, which in this case there was no doubt, you might think it's over—but it's not. There are a couple hundred things to do to prepare a case for trial.

When we checked balcony boy's latents, the computer screen started going off like a slot machine. He'd done a double deuce* in Abbotsford, B.C., for a series of rapes out West—same MO—and had a sheet full of other priors.** Bastard lived a block south of Jane's place with his wife, a social worker he'd met in the pen and then married. They had a little girl. He'd been beatin' on her—the wife—and was living with a girlfriend. Who are these women that would shack up with a guy like that? We searched the girlfriend's and seized jewellery and such that belonged to the victims. Combine that with the trace evidence and similar fact evidence and buddy boy was going down. Even though his mouthpiece, a slicker named Mel Green, had convinced him to clam up and filed notice of a not-guilty plea, which meant a trial. So now, even though we know he's guilty and he's confessed, we have to prepare for a full preliminary hearing and then a criminal trial.

The biggest problem we had was making a good ID. None of the vics ever saw his face. Even so, we do it by the book, arrange for a lineup and call the ladies in to see if they can pick him out. There was a snag in that the perp is Indian (he says half Indian) and we couldn't locate enough volunteers, civilian or otherwise, who looked enough like him to fill the lineup. So we switched to a photo ID although that was screwed too, because the perp's face is all smashed up, so we have to use an old black and white photo of him that's on file, and it's about ten years old and kinda grainy. So we go ahead, but no one picks him out.

Jane was pissed off the day she saw the photos. Afterwards, I showed her a current one of the guy. She didn't seem to want to let go of it—Kim had to sort of pry it out of her hand. She asked what happened to his face and she got this real sarcastic look when Kim said he'd been beaten by his

* A double deuce is four years.
**As in Toronto, he had used the balcony to access the apartments of the women he raped in British Columbia.

dope-dealer buddies. And then, get this, she asks if she can see him, if she can talk to him, and Kim starts raising his voice at her, and she snaps back for him to be quiet and never speak to her that way again, in fact never to speak to her again period. Wasn't she a citizen, co-operating fully, and hadn't she spent the entire afternoon at the station? Whether he liked it or not she was involved. It was her rape, not his.

The thing you have to understand about Kim's attitude is that by now, Jane has gotten together with some other ladies calling themselves Waves or something like that, and they've gone to the chief himself to say that the cops used women as bait and that they don't like the way we investigated the whole crime spree of the Balcony Rapist. And they did that in front of the media, too. There's about a hundred of them, and Jane herself is the boss (I saw a news release with her name right on it). Then the media calls the chief, and he makes a big deal out of responding that in hindsight, the police were the ones who should have issued a warning, and he figures that should settle it. But a few hacks won't let go and there are editorials, and Jane and her friends keep showing up at every police commission meeting demanding more, and then some politicians start chiming in. So naturally there is more pressure on us to make the case, which is under the full scrutiny of the media. Gathering all the evidence for a good prosecution in a rape case means you work with the rape victim. The other four ladies were fine, but Jane had her own ideas and she was driving Kim nuts.

Margo comes up with this notion of a voice ID, the first time it's been used around here. Seems all of the victims talked about his voice and the things he'd said, and they said they'd know his voice again, what with the heightened awareness of their eyes being covered, I guess. We go ahead and set it up. The ladies all agree. The whole thing required trained personnel and technology that was only available in one station in the suburbs. I was on hand but was told to lay low as it was felt I knew the vics too well and could unduly influence them. When I got out to the station, they let me talk to Jane for a few minutes and she looked bad. Like she was going to cry, which I had never seen her do. I told her to do the best she could and then watched her on the video monitor that had been set up so we could observe the process. His voice was the third one. The second he started talking she got even whiter, if that was possible, and she sort of stiffened and I knew she was gonna nail him, and then she asked to hear his and another voice again and then she picked him.

There was no washroom on that floor so I took one of those metal wastebaskets, it was clean, and waited for her to come out. When I told her she got him, I held it ready in case she was gonna heave, but she didn't, just asked if the other women had picked the third voice too. I told her two of the others did. And she said she felt real bad for the ones who didn't ID his voice and did they have anyone to talk to? You never knew what Jane was going to be thinking about.

"She's not the enemy"
(in the voice of Margo Pulford)

8:

I CALLED her after the accused was arrested and again after her
voice ID session, to congratulate her and ask how she felt. She asked why
I didn't attend the voice ID since it was my project, and she also told me
that except for Bill, who hardly said anything at first, the officers were cold
and distant. Seems they'd driven way out to Scarborough in a prowl car
with her in the back like a prisoner, and it smelled of sweat and cigarettes
and she was all closed in, couldn't breathe or speak to the officers in front.
They brought her in past the holding cells, then they sat her at a desk with
pictures of half-naked women on the wall over it, and when the officer
explained the procedure to her, she felt like she was under arrest. He kept
stressing that she could not ask questions during the process and if she
had any, she should ask them now. She's thinking, "How can I ask questions
when I don't know what they are and you won't tell me what's going on?"

She said she was so nerved up she thought she would be ill, but that
didn't stop her from recognizing his voice, and she was so glad to see Bill
sitting there when she came out. He drove her home.

Then she tells me about the lineup, how they'd kept her in a room for
two hours and told the friend who came to meet her that she wasn't there.
After all that, they cancelled the lineup and showed her photos that were
so worn they could have been anyone, and then Kim starts yelling at her
for what she says is the third time.

None of this is particularly remarkable except for two factors. One, she
is rational and intelligent—even funny—when recounting her experiences, and two, I agree with her. It's 1986 for God's sake, and this force is still
run like a rural wartime army camp. Every concept of modern criminology

and crime prevention technology dictates that community involvement and sensitivity training to race, gender and other social realities are critical to better policing and to reduce the occurrence of crime, especially sexual assault. Shit, it's 1986 and there are more horses in the police force than there are female officers. Doesn't that say something? I've had the training to conduct a voice lineup that would maximize success by working with female victims to explain the process clearly in a non-threatening manner that benefits from the victim's input and questions. Instead they leave me out and run it like she's the enemy.

So I have to admit I'm happy that Jane has organized, gone public and put up posters and then led deputations at the police commission. The whole issue of rape investigations and police sexism is getting a good stirring, and the old man has got to start liking the strategy of SACO as a separate unit investigating sexual assaults. And I'm the one most likely to head it.

9:

PRELIMINARY hearings are designed to assess whether the nature of the evidence provides grounds for the accused to be held over for trial. In the high-stakes poker game that is the law, preliminary hearings are definitely a face card. A jack, I'd say. Powerful, tricky, able to decide the direction of the game but also easily trumped. It all depends on the dealer, who and how many are playing, their skill and luck. Of course you must play by the rules. Bill Cameron and Kim Derry were my contacts in the game. I was not a player. I had no currency without them. They would explain everything to me, answer all of my questions— except for the questionable ones. It looked like this case was going to be fast-tracked. It was October and they promised a late January to early February prelim.

Meanwhile, WAVAW held its community meeting (as advertised on our poster). Every media outlet attended. Local and provincial politicians and women from my neighbourhood and across the city packed a meeting room in the 519 Church Street Community Centre. As the emcee, I announced WAVAW's intention to continue to address the police investigation of the Balcony Rapist and sexual assault in general. On behalf of several front-line women's agencies, WAVAW publicly demanded changes in police protocol, investigation procedures and training regarding sexual assault. The media carried our message. The following week Lori, Melanie and I appeared before the police commission and presented our proposal in person. We were outstanding. It helped that we had the support of Jane Pepino, the only woman on the commission and the obvious, if not appointed, leader of the group of

aging lawyers, politicians and retired businessmen who governed policing in the city. It didn't hurt that they believed WAVAW had an active
membership numbering in the hundreds.

As a result of WAVAW's work and because the women's movement
had been educating, marching and lobbying on sexual assault for several
years, immense pressure existed for accountability and reform. Just a
year earlier in Toronto, the force had withstood a maelstrom of public
scorn when an officer investigating a series of stranger rapes in a downtown park stated that women could prevent the attacks if they fell to the
ground and ate grass in order to induce vomiting. Vomiting, he reasoned, would be an immediate sexual turnoff. He had lifted the advice
from a police brochure printed in Florida.

By now the police force had been under pressure to change its ways
for a dozen years. In 1974, the Toronto Rape Crisis Centre was established in response to concerns regarding the manner in which raped
women were responded to by police, the legal system, hospitals and
society in general. One of the TRCC's objectives was to assist and
inform the police on how to respond to women. They produced a police
liaison handbook to that effect and formed a committee with police
bureaucrats to discuss problems and solutions from a feminist-
oriented perspective. They also called for the formation of a squad
dedicated to the investigation of rape.

But the police had a tough time listening. Disregarding the recommendations of the TRCC women, who insisted that the problems were
systemic, the force made cosmetic changes. For example, they began
referring to "sensitivity" and "safety programs" for women. They
sounded good and soothed the public into believing that real change
was taking place. Around then they introduced the popular myth of
community policing, instead of acting to address myths about rape
inherent in their own police training and investigation of the crime.
They undertook promotional, marketing and media campaigns to reinforce the impression that change was taking place. But the police did
not, would not, could not shift to looking at the crime of rape or sexual
assault from the woman's point of view. Frustrated and fed up, the
TRCC women had refused to work with the police again until the

TRCC joined the WAVAW deputation in 1986.

Chief Jack Marks must have thought, "Here these noisy women are again, only hundreds, maybe thousands strong, in the media, at my door, telling me what to do." Marks took a few meetings with his deputies and advisers, who, like him, completely misread the political situation, let alone the times in general, and issued a carefully worded apology for not warning us in this one instance. They just didn't see the failure to warn the women living in the Balcony Rapist's neighbourhood as part of a larger problem. The police thought that after the apology we would go away, that all they had to do was say, "Sorry girls," and they could get on with the business of the day. They were wrong.

"Apology Not Enough," screamed the *Globe and Mail*. "Women Decry Police Inaction," blared the *Toronto Star*. "Stick Your Apology up Your Ass," thought WAVAW (which at this time consisted of Lori, Melanie and myself). We insisted that instead of issuing lame apologies, senior police officers meet with, and take direction from, women working in the area of rape and wife assault, in order to reform their practices. Chief Marks agreed. He appointed Superintendent Jean Boyd, the highest-ranking woman in the force, as the police chair and assigned a dozen other officers to attend. The meetings were to start immediately.

Women from the Barbra Schlifer Commemorative Clinic, the Assaulted Women's Helpline, the Women's College Hospital Sexual Assault Care Centre (SACC), the Metropolitan Action Committee on Violence against Women and Children (METRAC) and the TRCC, as well as individual women working in the field, came together under the umbrella of WAVAW. Three committees were struck to examine police training, investigative protocol and public education on sexual assault. We met for almost a year.

The first few months went like this: We met at police headquarters. Minutes were kept by a police administrative worker. Community members made presentations to demonstrate problem areas identified by raped women who had reported their rapes or had decided not to report. The police told us why they couldn't do it differently, which seemed to hang on existing protocol—what they referred to as "standing orders." They also insisted that we provide them with the names, dates and badge numbers of the officers complained about so that they could check the stories themselves and, if necessary, discipline the individual officers involved. That was never our point. But this was where the back and forth between us began and where it always ended. Where it ends today. We explained that the problems were not only about the behaviour of individual officers but about how the police system gives individual officers permission to behave badly, how it sanctions their behaviour. The way the individual officers behaved was determined not only by pre-existing experiences and prejudices but also by the inherent sexism of police culture, which is built into the department's formal and informal rules, procedures and practices. I could never figure out which part of that message they didn't get, but it was sort of fascinating to watch them tag-team a response that always ended with a request for names and dates concerning an isolated incident. They ignored the systemic part—the sexist part—as if doing so would make us go away.

We shifted gears and requested copies of their standing orders and existing protocols regarding sexual assault in order to demonstrate how policy and operational change could increase the number of women who reported the crime. They said (a) there weren't any, (b) they were confidential, (c) no, and (d) okay, you can have them next week. We would spend at least the first thirty minutes of every meeting correcting the police minutes of the last meeting to reflect what had really been said. Our repeated offers to keep minutes were refused.

I sat on two of the three committees, which met weekly, on top of the main WAVAW meetings, which now included many more women. I was also preparing for the preliminary trial of the man who had raped me. Johnny was out and working, and he came around most nights all handsome and rehabilitated. He cooked for me and put me to bed and told me how wonderful I was, how he wished he was more like me. He slept in the living room, and when dreams and fear robbed me of sleep, I would go out there and crawl in beside him.

My friends had me over, telephoned, agonized about what they could do to make me feel better. "What do you need?" they would ask, wanting to do something, give me something, anything. "I really like those earrings, that bracelet," I would joke, and they would take them off right there and offer them up. I told my sister about the rape, but I didn't tell the rest of my large family. I didn't tell anyone that Johnny was back. Sort of back. One day I was sitting outside with my friend Susan and it was getting cool and we needed our jackets. "You get them," I said, "I've been raped."

"That was last week," she replied. We laughed and laughed, and then she got all quiet.

Weekends rolled round, Christmas approached, dinner parties, films, openings, music. Most people avoided my rape like the plague, changed the subject, changed the channel. They thought that talking about it would upset me when it was they who were upset, not wanting their own pain to surface and fearful that mine would. It was their sense of damage that bothered me most. I must be damaged in unspeakably tragic, intensely private ways, and once I came out of that, why then I would be fine. I had to put it behind me and then it would be over, a bad experience to be forgotten, devoid of social impact or message. I'd be only a little damaged then. Sometimes I believed it myself.

I functioned on the surface of that. The edges of life. Too tired and too sad to do more, except when working with WAVAW or in therapy or with a few close friends. I was fascinated and horrified by what had happened and what continued to play out. I read everything I could get my hands on about rape, discarding a lot,* repelled by people's notions of how I should be, sensing their discomfort, smelling their fear. Even as they loved me.

···

---

* Two books I found especially helpful were *Intimate Intrusions: Women's Experience of Male Violence* by Elizabeth A. Stanko and *The Issue is Power* by Melanie Kaye Kantrowitz. More recently I have read and appreciated Susan Ehrlich's linguistic exploration *Representing Rape: Language and Sexual Consent.*

"They tell me not to call her"
(in the voice of Margo Pulford)

10:

I HAD a few more conversations with Jane. Answered her questions, gave her information. It seemed that Bill and Kim were stonewalling her or avoiding her calls altogether. They told me that she was out of control and unmanageable. Interesting choice of words. Kim Derry actually walked into my office and ordered me (I'm sure he would say it was a suggestion) to have no more contact with her, said that I was jeopardizing the integrity of the investigation. More interesting words. Then I get a call from upstairs and it is further "suggested" that I devote maximum effort to drafting the mandate and structure of SACO to go into full operational mode. The chief's office has green-lighted it for next fiscal, and I've been assigned to oversee the implementation with a recommendation that I get the coordinator's job. Bob Qualtrough is back in Operations and Bill Blair has been seconded from Robbery to work with me. He's a close buddy of Kim Derry's. Nice guy. One of those blond, chiselled types who get flabby in middle age. Probably popular in school: football hero–knee injury–no money for university–police department kind of trajectory.

I'm also on one of the WAVAW committees Jeanie Boyd has command over. Patti McGillicuddy and Lori Haskell are members, too. I like both of them a lot. Too bad it's not going anywhere. Apparently WAVAW members suggested at one of the meetings the old man attended that the police members needed frontal lobotomies to eradicate their cowboy mentalities. He was really upset.

I think Jeanie gets it, though. She circulated a memo inside the force warning of the potential fallout if sex-assault investigation protocols aren't overhauled. But the other police members on the committee are dug in, and she retires in six months. While all of this is going on, Jane is getting ready for the preliminary hearing. I don't know what she expects from the committees or the prelim. I have a feeling it will be interesting. Sometimes I don't know what to think of her—she is half vulnerability and half steel, neither side able to blend with the other, preventing her from being either.

"Jane doesn't get it"
(in the voice of Bill Cameron)

11:

I ALWAYS figure a person has to do what they have to do. I've said as much to Jane, but how in hell can I do what I have to do as a senior detective investigating and prosecuting a major crime spree when she's out there shitting on everything we do? Oh, she's nice about it and all, and sometimes she has a point, but this is not TV. It's not one of those documentaries she works on that nobody ever sees. There are regulations, protocols, and they have to be followed. That's my job and I have to do it. I *like* doing it. She's in over her head, traumatized, thinks women are going to save her, going to solve rapes. She can't seem to understand that she is separate from the crime. Sure, it happened to her, but I need to look at the crime, not the person, and she keeps trying to be involved. Maybe Kim's right about her.

I hate these rape cases.

12:

THERE are a lot of things you should know about a rape trial, and you should probably understand them long before you are raped if you are going to cope at all well. After you are raped, you are too vulnerable, too objectified, too victimized by what has happened to attempt to navigate a system of waters so deep and currents so complicated they require a practised sailor to steer you through. Better you should chart those waters yourself before you have to jump in.

But it is not a learning we take to easily or like to believe is a necessary part of our education. We believe that rape is a matter between the perpetrator and his victim and that it does not affect us all socially, in our systems, in how we live. We don't want to think of the large cast of players that the crime sets into motion. I have sometimes pictured myself as a financial cash register for the legal system. Every report, investigation, stakeout, news story, interrogation, charge, motion, court appearance, jury selection, objection, witness, exhibit, conviction, appeal, sentence served or acquittal results in the creation or performance of a job, a salary paid and a host of additional economic spinoffs. You could almost say that rape pays.

You could certainly say that it has financial benefits. The police and the Crown attorney, lawyers, the victim-assistance people—they all present themselves as your guides, your captains. They describe the journey you are about to take as if it has been charted with you in mind, as if it is safe and won't cost you much. I have been there and have come back with an alternative view.

It's important to be aware of the physical layout of the courtroom before you walk into it. The courtroom is designed in a way that allows the judge, the lawyers and the rapist to hold centre stage. There is no designated seat or space for women who have been raped. Colours are muted, usually a version of beige. Lights are fluorescent. Chilled air maintains the comfort level of the heavily robed officers of the court. Space is limited. You are boxed in, overly lit and cold. The only thing on the walls in a courtroom is a coat of arms with lions and tigers and bears. Some rooms have windows, and some are larger than others. But it's not like in the movies.

Most of the officials of this room are still old white guys who wear long black priest-like robes. If they were priests, the judge would be pope. Everyone is required to stand when the judge leaves or enters the room. He can interrupt you at any time and tell you what to say. He can banish you from his sight. His word cannot be questioned. He does not have to explain. He answers to no one. Latecomers must bow their heads in supplication for disturbing his court. When you are a witness, he is the one you must impress (unless there is also a jury), for he is the one who will decide if you are lying or telling the truth. He will decide how serious your rape was and what penance or sentence the rapist will receive. If any. His decisions will be based, among other things, on his impressions of you. How you are dressed. How angry you are and if that anger is justifiable or in proportion. If he sees that your friends or family are with you, he usually considers that a good thing. If you speak English and speak it well, that is even better.

My case was high-profile and as a result, we were at the preliminary-hearing stage by February 1987, six months after the rapist had been arrested. For it to happen so fast is almost unheard of. Most women wait up to two years before their rapists get to trial. If there is a trial.*

I tend to think of the preliminary hearing as a trial. Technically it is not, but to call it a hearing (of all things) does not convey its true nature. It felt like a trial. That was how I experienced it. It lasted for five days.

---

* An overloaded justice system results in lengthy waits for trial for most crimes, not just sexual assault. But I suggest that there is a difference. The alleged rapist is rarely in custody waiting for trial and is almost always well-known to the woman involved. The wait for a rape trial is fraught with anxiety, suffering and danger for the woman involved, which isn't the case for "victims" of most other crimes.

There was a judge, lawyers, testimony, fear, grief and loathing. There was a verdict and a sentence, media headlines, pain and loss. It was one of the greatest trials of my life. The language of the law reduces this procedure to something kinder or softer than what it was. Something preliminary. But I can't.

About one week before the preliminary *hearing* began, the police took me to meet the Crown attorney assigned to my case. The purpose was to go over my statement of evidence with him, to ask any questions I might have had and mostly for him to get an impression of me and what kind of witness I was going to be.

One thing to understand very clearly is that the Crown attorney is not there to represent you. He represents the state or, more precisely in Canada, the queen of England—Regina. (It has been said that she is the only woman the Crown represents in a rape trial.) He operates under a specific set of guidelines defined by ancient rules of evidence and designed to serve the interests of a legal system established centuries ago by wealthy men to protect their property interests (which at that time included their daughters' chastity and access to their wives' sexuality and inheritance).

Todd Archibald, the man who worked as my Crown attorney, didn't articulate any of this for me. In fact he presented himself to me as if he were representing my interests. What he was really doing was sizing me up to see what value I might have in proving his case. He did not differentiate between me and the other four women involved. We arrived as a package, as if we were one.

Of course I questioned him about what he could do for me under the circumstances, and he gave me the whole Crowns are overworked and underpaid–the rights of the rapist must be upheld–the trial must be seen to be fair and impartial–long arduous process–I'll take care of you–the courts frown upon–let's get it over with and all behind you as soon as possible line of rhetoric.

Because he saw my (our) case and its high media profile as beneficial to his work, he did give me more than the usual fifteen-minute-interview-right-before-trial, which is what most women in my position are allotted. But he offered me very little information, as if he thought I could never understand the complexities of his job. As if my rape defined me, was all of me. It was as if he needed to separate me from the crime in order to proceed. I would never have chosen Todd Archibald as my conduit to justice if given the opportunity. I would never want anyone to represent me who spoke so quickly, who read some other document as he spoke, who barely made eye contact and who did not explain all of the small print. But I was not given a choice. The concept of choice did not exist in this circumstance. He was a Crown attorney, and my rape was assigned to him. My name, my thoughts, feelings, experiences were simply unimportant attachments to the crime.

THE Crown Attorney's Office has an agenda that is very different from yours. It is supposedly neutral and applies the same legal practices to rape as it does to a property crime, a B&E for instance. (Since rape is a crime in which women are sexualized, it would actually be a step up to be treated like a B&E.) The individual Crown attorney assigned to your case expects you to speak in his language, a legal language that is precise, exact, with times and dates attached. It seems to be the only language he understands. There will be no opportunity for you to explain your thoughts or actions, to equivocate or clarify. Any instinctive logic or knowledge you might have about what happened to you will be ignored. Any emotion you display in your speech or actions will be used against you. He will instruct you on what to wear, what to say and how to say it, with whom to speak, where to sit, how to sit and where to direct your gaze. He will manipulate you, define your experience for you, remove any vestige of control that you might still cling to. He will do it his way.

For example, oral sex was part of my rapist's MO. The Crown instructed me to use the Latin term "cunnilingus" when describing this on the stand.

"I can't say that," I objected. "It's not what I say, I can't even spell it. It's an embarrassing word."

"No no, you have to say it," he ordered. "It's what the courts require. Trust me, just say it."

When I testified to the act of rape-cunnilingus, the rapist's lawyer interrupted to ask, "By that do you mean oral sex?"

As with the police department, the behaviour and agenda of individual Crown attorneys is dictated or determined both by our system of law itself and the culture, practices and procedures developed within the institution of the Crown's office. Individual Crown attorneys are under a lot of pressure to function within the agenda of their employer (the government). Even if Crown attorneys understand the problems inherent in the system they represent, even if they have maintained that understanding through years of gruelling legal training and apprenticeship, how does one person make change? After witnessing the horrors and heartbreak of crime and withstanding the pressures of keeping their jobs—Crowns who try to defend raped women or actually represent their interests in court risk professional censure—who are they going to call to complain?

Recently we have been seeing more and more women Crowns. And some of them practise law from a coherent, feminist position, risking their careers and reputations. We could, and perhaps should, interpret this as progress.

But in critical ways it is not progress. Women lawyers may take these jobs because the sexism and misogyny of the legal system still keeps them out of better-paying positions in private law firms. The law is still a boys' club. Few women are interested or have the tools to change the behaviour, culture or agenda of the legal system. Few will be feminist in spirit, let alone through training or because of something they studied on the law school curriculum. These women are more interested in keeping their jobs and getting into the club. And why not? It's what they signed on for, paid hundreds of thousands of dollars for, find themselves in debt for. It's the law.*

I HAD presumed that I would be inside the courtroom for the full duration of the five days allotted for the preliminary trial. That I would get to see how my legal system dealt with what had happened to me. But I was told that a woman who has been raped is expected to sit in the hall

* As a result of the work of feminist academics, several law schools in Canada have developed course content that is feminist in name and legal nature. These courses are not mandatory, however, and women who teach them must deal with disruptive and threatening classroom behaviour.

on the appointed day and wait to be called in to testify, after which she must leave the courtroom again and sit in the hall in case some authority requires clarification of something she said.

I was cautioned that while waiting outside the courtroom I should not speak with anyone. Especially any women. The fear is that your friends or family or supporters might say something to you that would get you all confused about what really happened and then you'd mix everything up in your pretty (traumatized) little head, and your account would be tainted. This could lead to a mistrial.

Let's say that your sister or a friend is sitting in that same hallway and you need to talk to them or just touch them because you feel so bad. Well you can't. Or let's say that a woman from the rape crisis centre who is supporting you is there and you really need to talk to her now because you're going to vomit or scream. Not allowed.

Sometimes the rapist's lawyer has a cop or a private detective placed in the hallway or in the washroom to watch you in the hope of overhearing something he can use to get the rapist off. I swear this is true. Ask women who do court support* and they will tell you. So what usually happens is that one of the investigating officers will come and sit with you. To guard you.

All of this took me completely by surprise, and I decided that there was no way I was leaving that courtroom. They could drag me out and I would scream all the way. What use was this trial to me if I couldn't participate in it? Screw participate—I only wanted to watch. A stranger had raped me, simply because he could, and I needed to find out what my justice system was going to do about it.

I expressed my intention to the Crown and the cops in a more subdued manner, and they rolled their eyes and said that it was against procedure. Not illegal mind you, just against procedure.**

I couldn't accept their logic. Are women stupid? Do we confuse what

---

* Court support is one of the advocacy functions that rape crisis centres and other women's groups offer to clients who are entering the legal system. I have performed that service for two agencies and have monitored students who select court support as part of their field practicum in social and community service diploma programs.

** The practice of excluding raped women from court proceedings is not unique but is also imposed on others who witness crime. In Canada the practice is, in fact, discretionary but is always applied to women who are "victim-witnesses" of sexual assault.

Witness at rape case hearing allowed to stay for testimony

BY ANN RAUHALA
The Globe and Mail

A provincial court judge has ordered that a witness at a preliminary hearing be allowed to stay in the courtroom to hear part of the proceedings.

Representatives for women's groups hailed the ruling as a sign that the courts will be more cognizant of the needs and interests of victims, particularly of women who have been victims of violence.

Last summer, a series of rapes in downtown Toronto attracted public attention when neighborhood women complained about the way police handled the investigation.

They said police knew the rapist's patterns — he attacked single women at knifepoint in low-rise apartment buildings — and could predict when he would strike again, but did little to warn the public.

Community complaints led to an internal review by Metro Toronto Police, who eventually conceded that they may have erred in the way they dealt with the investigation. A citizen-police committee has since been set up to help police respond better to violent crimes against women.

A 32-year-old man has been charged in five incidents of rape with 13 counts including sexual assault, confinement, breaking and entering, assault with a dangerous weapon and possession of a dangerous weapon.

The witness involved, a woman who was one of the rape victims who testified at the preliminary hearing, asked this week that she be allowed to hear testimony from police and others about the investigation.

(At preliminary hearings, in which a judge decides whether a case should be brought to trial, judges customarily order that witnesses be excluded from the proceedings.

(The exclusion is based on concerns that witnesses might be influenced by what they might learn in the preliminary hearing and that a fair trial could be jeopardized.)

The witness's lawyer, Rebecca Shamai, appeared before Judge John Kerr and asked that her client not be excluded from the entire hearing.

In an interview later, Miss Shamai said she argued that justice must not only be done but also must be seen to be done.

"She requires for her well-being to see that justice be done" she said, noting that her client felt she had been victimized in the attack, traumatized by the investigation and was about to be shut out of the legal process.

"Let us not forget that she has suffered an incredible indignity," Judge Kerr said on Thursday in explaining why he approved the woman's request. "Is it not obvious that she has an interest in observing the process?"

In making the ruling, Judge Kerr pointed out that the request to remain in the courtroom was made after the testimony of all five victims in the case had been given.

hear the accounts of other victims, he said, and she had already given her own. "She's merely asking to sit in court to hear the balance of the hearing."

Judge Kerr noted that her testimony is on record in the event that she should try to change it when and if there is a trial. "This court does not see that a fair trial may be in anyway prejudiced."

Judge Kerr also disagreed with defence lawyer Melvyn Green's argument that Miss Shamai should not have had standing to make the request, saying "any counsel should have status in this day and age" of increasing awareness of the treatment of victims of crime.

Pat Marshall of the Metro Toronto Action Committee on Violence against Women and Children commended the judge's decision, saying it will encourage other women to come forward in cases of violent crimes.

"For the first time, there is a willingness to understand the view of the complainant," Ms Marshall said. "I think it will be a welcome sign to women . . . who are wary of the criminal justice system."

However, Toronto lawyer Clayton Ruby called the ruling unusual and surprising.

He said the object of excluding witnesses, at trials and at preliminary inquiries, is to ensure that evidence is untainted and to avoid any chance that testimony is consciously or subconsciously altered by hearing other versions.

"It's better for the administration of justice if her testimony is untainted," Mr. Ruby said. "She shouldn't be listening to evidence . . . until she's finished testifying.

"The bottom line is that she's jeopardizing the strength of her evidence and jeopardizing the conviction."

Asked about considering victims' rights and roles, Mr. Ruby said: "She has a role. She's a witness.

"It's only because she's a witness, not because she's a victim" that she is expected to leave the preliminary hearing, Mr. Ruby added.

The witness, who did not wish to be identified, said she credits Judge Kerr with taking "an important step" toward changing attitudes about violent crimes against women.

"For the first time since August (the time of the assault), I feel the system has allowed me to take an active part," the woman said. "I'm happens to us with what happened to someone else? Or with some other interpretation of what happened? Was I simply a piece of evidence to be used by the courts? Did they remotely understand the nature of rape and its effects? Did I have any role other than passive victim– witness–piece of evidence in this system?

I decided to get my own lawyer.

My plan was to have her argue my right to stay in the courtroom. God forbid I should be allowed to address the court myself. According to the law, a professional must define my experience to the other professionals. So just a few days before the trial began I was on the phone, calling lawyers. I was committed to working only with women who had a feminist analysis. I couldn't believe some of the responses I got: "Who do you think you are?" "You don't have a chance in hell." "You don't have enough money to pay for me."

The trial was to begin on Monday. On the Friday before, I found a woman who understood what I wanted and what I was talking about. Rebecca Shamai agreed to represent me. On the first day of court (which was also my birthday), the rapist's lawyer argued that my lawyer should not receive what is called "standing." That is, he didn't even want her in the room asking if she could be in the room. He said that I had the Crown and that it was not my lawyer's business to be there—she was not wanted or needed. Meanwhile, the Crown, the guy who's supposed to be watching out for me, didn't say a word.

Judge John Kerr reserved his decision until after I had testifed—I was to be on the stand first—then ruled that my lawyer be allowed to present my case. Our argument went like this: everyone accepts the notion that justice must be done and must be seen to be done publicly in a court of law—which includes me, the woman wronged, raped, the victim, the complainant. It was only just.

The judge agreed. He said that his decision was based on the fact that I had already testified, on my behaviour on the stand, on my composure in his courtroom (and maybe on the fur coat I had borrowed and wore to court every day?), on public interest in my case and on the presence of reporters. The next day my actions and his decision made headlines as precedent-setting, and I got to sit inside the courtroom for the rest of the preliminary trial.*

I learned later that Rebecca Shamai was criticized by other defence lawyers who saw her actions in representing me as a betrayal of their "side." She currently sits as a judge in the Ontario Court of Justice.

I wish now that I had hired my own lawyer much earlier. I would advise any woman who finds herself in the same position to do so. But it ain't easy and it ain't cheap. Who can afford a lawyer's fees? Why should we have to pay anyway? If the rapist cannot afford legal counsel, a lawyer is appointed free of charge to represent him. I support that completely. But surely one person's rights and representation should not override another's. Who benefits (and how) when raped women are not fully represented by the legal system after they've done the so-called responsible thing by coming forward and filing charges?

AT trial I finally got to see the man who raped me. He was thirty years old. His blue-black hair was badly cut in a seventies shag. A too-tight suit from the same era stretched over his small muscular frame. He had plain, even features. My very first impression was that he looked frightened. After all I had imagined, he was just a little man, a man so blank-faced he wasn't really there. In a fair fight, I probably could have taken him. Women in the courtroom taunted him quietly as he climbed, manacled, from the pits of the holding cell into the prisoner's box. "Nice suit, buddy." "Watch you don't fall down there and break your neck." He did not seem to hear them.

He remained blank and expressionless throughout our five-day trial, finally revealed as a cheap vicious thug. I positioned myself where I could watch his face, his body, for a clue, a hint, a sign of remorse, guilt, self-pity—anything. There was none. He was closed. Except for one

---

* Except for the *Globe and Mail* article reprinted on page 68, no record exists of this ruling. It is not reflected in legal transcripts of the preliminary trial or elsewhere documented. It cannot be used by lawyers or read by law students. In Canada since 1987, more women have been successful in obtaining legal counsel when raped. However any standing granted to their lawyers is at the discretion of the presiding judge and is argued against by the Crown Attorney's Office and the lawyer representing the accused. Obtaining independent counsel is costly and not covered by legal aid. Women who have experienced wife or partner assault are similarly disadvantaged if they seek legal representation. It's not much of an issue, though, as the right of the woman to have her own legal counsel is not well-known in the first place. It's sort of a secret.

moment during my testimony. Using the puritanical anti-sex language of the law and in keeping with the requirement that every detail, every position, every entry and exit be described, I testified that at one point the rapist entered me from behind. His bowed head reared back and he shot how-dare-you, liar-liar glares at me from dark widened eyes. Apparently there were some things he would not do. His lawyer clarified that we were not talking about anal sex here, and the rapist settled back into his coma-like state.

Of course everything I said he did he denied through his lawyer. (I understand why women who have been raped think of defence attorneys as co-rapists.) Worst of all, the rapist got to watch me too, to listen to and relive what he had done to me—the fear he had filled me with, the ways my life had changed. He got to experience all over again the power hard-on that drove him. To vicariously rape me again.

When I was called to give my evidence, the Crown led me through our rehearsed version of the story. I was nervous, afraid, but the very last thing I was going to do was let buddy see me in fear again. To deal with that, I disconnected. It was safer. Easier. I pretended there was no one else in the courtroom. I focused on the immediate, what was being asked of me, and on making truthful responses. When I couldn't focus, felt panicky or ill or angry, I looked at my sister and the faces of other women I knew who had come to court. Patti, Susan, Penny, Lori and Melanie. There were others there, some I didn't know. All of them nodding, with quiet smiles and comforting eyes.

I got through the first part well enough—the telling of my pain, fear and grief through questions put to me by the Crown who only wanted me to tell part of it. Then it was the rapist's lawyer's turn. The rapist had pleaded not guilty, presumably on this man's advice, even though he had previously confessed. Now his lawyer's job was to try to make me look like I was lying, exaggerating, as if my rape really hadn't been that bad.

Just so you know, if you're ever in my position, the rapist's lawyer will begin softly, to make you feel that he is a nice guy, on your side. His real job is to set the rapist free or to reduce his guilt, mitigate the seriousness of his crime, and therefore his sentence, in any way he can. I was aware that I faced an enemy here. A man more dangerous perhaps than the man who had raped me, because the law sanctioned his actions—his actions are the law. His lawyer began by questioning my ability to correctly identify any voice, let alone the rapist's voice. He questioned my memory of what had happened. He questioned the violence of my rape. He suggested that my doors had not been locked. That there had been no knife. That the threatening, insane things the rapist had said while he raped me were friendly comments intended to lessen my fear. He felt it was important to establish that the rapist had not robbed me or broken anything in my apartment.

The rapist's lawyer can ask you just about anything. Most of the time, the Crown will sit there and allow it. He will not object or defend you. Nor will the judge. I remember the experience of the two lawyers questioning me as humiliating and infantilizing. I was never allowed to describe the crime in my own words but was required to respond to a template designed to protect the rights of the rapist. I will never forget the final question put to me in defence of the man who had raped me. I was asked, as were the other four women, whether my rape had been violent. Despite the knife, the threats against my life, the forced entry, the ghoul's mask and the binding of my eyes, he asked if my rape had been violent. Despite the police manhunt, the public outcry, the rapist's criminal history of violence, the packed courtroom, and the media scrutiny, the rapist's lawyer asked if my rape had been violent. Despite everything we know about the violent nature of rape, he asked if my rape had been violent. When I did not answer, could not answer, the judge instructed me that because I had not been cut or stabbed with the rapist's knife, because he hadn't beaten or mutilated or (most decisive of all) killed me, I must answer that my rape had not been violent.

And my testimony was over.

THE ONE condition of my presence in the courtroom was that I would leave while the other women testified. So I waited in the hallway for the other four women to give their evidence before I took my contested seat back inside. I watched them enter the courtroom nervous and frightened and then leave spent and weeping. They all looked away when they saw me. I was the troublemaker. The wife of the man who raped me passed through that hall, too, as pale and tense as any of us. I wanted to speak to her, to say something kind. What must her life be like now? But Kim Derry, who was sitting with me in the hall, forbade me to approach her and then she was gone. I caught glimpses of her in the next four days but she was always surrounded, ushered in and bustled out. Later, Patti introduced me to a sixth woman raped by the man on trial. The police had said that in her instance there wasn't sufficient evidence to lay charges. She came to court every day just the same, one of us. She and I connected for a moment, and then she was gone too.

After five days of testimony, it became clear that despite his lawyer's best and most legal efforts to trick and baffle the witnesses, buddy was going down. And the rapist switched his plea back to guilty. At trial the Crown had not spoken with me outside of examining me on the stand. He hadn't objected or interrupted as the rapist's lawyer confused and insulted me. He told me I couldn't get a lawyer of my own to argue my way into court. Now, when the rapist copped a guilty plea, the Crown made a sentencing deal without properly consulting me.

He met with each of the women under the guise of explaining our options and soliciting our direction. He saved me for last. This was the deal: The rapist and his lawyer had agreed that to save us the pain and trauma of testifying all over again at a criminal trial and to save the state the expense, he would agree to a twenty-year sentence. The alternative prospect was to apply to have him declared a dangerous sexual offender (DSO) after his conviction in a criminal trial, which would take time and of course require us to testify all over again. Furthermore, the Crown informed me, we might not get the DSO.* The other four women involved had agreed to the plea bargain. It was four against one. The rapist got his deal. So what the hell was the preliminary trial about? I knew it was about proving there was enough evidence to take him to

---

* Under the Dangerous Sexual Offender Act the offender is placed in a maximum security facility where he is held indefinitely or until it is determined by a panel of experts that he is not a risk to offend again. The application of the act requires that he be a repeat or serial offender and that thorough and extensive psychological profiling and psychiatric testing indicate that he cannot or will not control the impulses and behaviour that led to his conviction. As I understand it, DSOs receive services and counselling at a higher rate and more consistently than other inmates.

trial, or getting him to plead guilty, but it also felt like showtime. Theatre. Were they just practising, testing us, clocking up salaries and reputations? I still don't get it.

APPARENTLY I was the first woman in Ontario to verbally deliver a victim impact statement in court. They say the statement is designed to allow victims of crime to have input into the judicial process. It was and is hailed as a progressive step in the legal system. The statement itself came as a three-page form, divided into sections titled "property loss," "financial loss" and "emotional reaction." A week before the trial, the police had asked me to fill it out, and it seemed like a good idea. But by this time I didn't trust anything the police were doing or suggesting, and when I lay awake at night, I would try to figure out who benefited from this new process.

Finally I decided that this statement (aside from its label of "victim," which I despise) was the first opportunity I had been given to describe what had happened to me in my own words. So I filled out the form. Financial and property loss items are easy to list. Bed, bedding, moving expenses, prescription bills, time off work, taxis, parking, therapy. It goes on.

Emotional damage isn't quite so easy to describe. How do you describe the fear that suddenly strangles you as you shop or when you get in an elevator? Also, if you're too emotional about your emotional response, they'll think that you're losing it and that you won't present well in front of the judge. They also don't like it if you are too political in your response or your understanding of what has happened. When you complete the statement it's returned to the police, who read it and enter it on a computer. It then becomes their property as opposed to your personal thoughts and reactions. The statement they returned to me was significantly different from the one I had given them. I had written mine kind of like a poem. They sent back a version that was all blocked out like an essay, with spelling mistakes inserted, and in a different order. When I explained my difficulty with this, they said that it would be better if I stuck to the official version. Meaning their version. Fortunately I had kept my original draft.

It's an illusion to say that victims have this wonderful right to read their statements in front of the court and that by doing so they are included in the process. Presenting such a statement is actually a very disturbing and controlled experience designed primarily to benefit the families of homicide victims. It does not fit rape well. You read your statement in front of the rapist, after a conviction but before sentencing. Your words are supposed to influence the judge's decision about how long he will be jailed (if he's even going to jail). What if you know the rapist well and fear his retribution? What if you are too frightened to speak, or if English is not your first language? As you read your impact statement, defence lawyers may guffaw or sneer or smirk, silently mocking you, and they are not censured for such antics.

Another thing to be mindful of when you present your impact statement in person to the court is that the rapist's lawyer can cross-examine you again on what you've said. That means that he gets another crack at trying to make you look like a liar, this time on the subject of how you have emotionally experienced your own rape.

VICTIM IMPACT STATEMENT:

You ask in this portion to describe to you my feelings on how being raped has affected me personally.

The other areas wer not so difficult.

I can itemize property and financial loss; I can explain physical injuries and list specifics that apply to them, but to tell you my feelings..to describe the terror of that night, the horror I have lived with since then.

In fact, I don not wish you to fully understand my feelings because that would make you, too, a victim of rape and I do not wish that on anyone.

The Crown decided that my presentation of what I had written would be helpful and that I could deliver it in court. (The other women chose not to, and the judge read their impact statements in private.) I had planned to speak about how failure to issue a warning had contributed to my experience as a raped woman. It was all part of the package, the same thing for me. The morning I was to testify, the investigating officers and the Crown took me aside and pleaded with me to change my statement. They feared that such comments would be the focus of media coverage and that all of their excellent police and legal work would be diminished. It would make them look bad. Now, I had just been through a gruelling, week-long trial. I was tired and I didn't have a friend or adviser with me during that particular conversation. So I caved. It's something I regret to this day.

IN 1987, a sentence of twenty years in prison for rape was unheard of. Nor has it been heard much of since. That same summer in Toronto, a man known as the Annex Rapist received eight years for sexually assaulting and beating four women, some of whom he bit until they bled. (The Annex Rapist had no known priors and was the son of a prominent West Coast attorney.) Because of the expediency of the trial of the man who had raped me, and the unusually long sentence, I was expected to feel that justice had been served. I was expected to put everything behind me, to forget and get on with my life, as if the conviction and prison sentence were remedies for what had happened. As if it could not happen again. As if it had not happened.

I didn't feel that justice had been served. Not the justice I sought. What purpose is served when a man is put in a cage for twenty years? Certainly through his actions and choices, the rapist has denied himself the right to be among us. He has renounced freedom, refused responsibility, and he has been put away. But to imagine that the same thing that happened to me that summer night in 1986 cannot happen again, has not happened again to others because of one conviction and prison sentence, is to deny our own individual responsibility and freedom. Where we send men like the one who raped me and how we treat them are reflections of our own humanity and desire to properly address the problems of violence against women. Rape is a social crime. Solutions based on militaristic

Metro's balcony rapist given 20-year prison sentence

FEB 27 1987 STAR

By Wendy Darroch Toronto Star

A man who became known as the balcony rapist has been sentenced to 20 years in prison for

"The violence, the horror never stops. That's what makes rape so much more chilling," assistant

known as the balcony rapist, and had women in the area of the attacks terrorized.

... the father of a little girl,

... five victims gave Archibald written victim impact statements yesterday. And one told the court of the horror she has suffered.

anguish has been so overpowering that one woman cannot face returning to her church and another moved in with family members be...

Columbia and has three assault convictions and a sentence for rape, court...

pist jailed 20 years

FEB 27 1987 SU...

By ZEN RURYK
Staff Writer

A rapist was sentenced to 20 years in prison yesterday for five sex attacks in which he entered his victims' apartments from their

knifepoint in their downtown apartments on different dates during an eight-month period starting Dec. 31, 1985.

Each victim submitted statements to court explaining what they've gone through

morning hours and get into their apartments through an unsecure door or window.

In at least four cases, he armed himself with a knife in the kitchen, said Archi...

Man who raped five at knifepoint sentenced to 20 years

FEB 27 1987 G&M

THOMAS CLARIDGE
Globe and Mail

A 22-year-old man who admitted raping five women at knifepoint in their Toronto apartment bedrooms was sentenced yesterday to 20 years in penitentiary.

... sat impassively in the prisoner's box as Provincial Court Judge John ... accepted a joint submission on sentence proposed by the Crown and defence. Crown attorney Todd Archibald de...

stark, psychological horror" involving "obvious planning and premeditation."

The five rapes occurred over an eight-month period from Dec. 31, 1985, to Aug. 24, 1986. All involved second-floor and third-floor apartments in central Toronto near Wellesley and Sherbourne streets.

Mr. Archibald told the court that in each case Mr. ... had stalked his victims and determined that they lived alone in a specific apartment and that he could gain

He said the man spent some time in each apartment, getting a knife from the kitchen before subjecting his victims to 45 to 90 minutes "of psychological hell."

The judge was given statements on the impact of the assaults from the five victims, all of whom were in the courtroom.

One of the women read her statement from the witness box. She told the judge of recurrent nightmares and an inability "to look any man directly into his face."

sexual assault, she told the judge that there "is no sex in rape — there is only pain."

Mr. Archibald read excerpts from the other four statements, one of which told of the victim feeling she was, "a prisoner in my own apartment."

"I'm scared to death of the dark," the same victim said. "Sudden noises scare the hell out of me."

One of the others said: "This whole nightmare has changed my outlook on our society. . . . I shouldn't be the one who

Mr. ... came from the Vancouver area to Toronto after serving a four-year term for a rape that was described as all involving an apartment break-in. He has a criminal record dating back to 1973, when he was 16. The court was told his previous offences included theft, common assault and impaired driving.

In agreeing to the sentence, Judge K... said he would recommend to the Parole Board that they have "a look at the matter before consi...

---

strategies that call for increased police presence and control, bigger prisons and longer incarcerations, which occasionally punish or make examples of individual offenders, deny the social and economic roots of male sexual violence. To isolate one series of rapes, one sensational case and conviction, and claim justice when countless more go unreported, fortifies people's desperate need to believe that rape and sexual assault are episodic—when it is justice that is episodic.

FROM the beginning, I ached to speak with, be comforted by and console the four other women who had been through the preliminary trial with me. Women who have been raped are bound together by an experience that catapults us into another reality where pleasures are reduced, where what was once safe, civil or normal gets tossed. We are united in disaster, like air-crash survivors or veterans of battle. We understand. During the rapist's trial, Bill and Kim cautioned the other women not to speak with me and told them that I was making trouble, that my actions could cause us to lose the case.

They did not join me in my successful bid to observe the trial. When the preliminary trial was over and we all returned to the courtroom for the sentencing, they did not sit with me. After I read my impact statement, Alice alone joined me.

I understand that those women did what they had to do to take care of themselves. In almost all cases, police officers who investigate sexual assault become the woman's single conduit to information about progress and process. Those officers position themselves as crime solvers and caretakers, social workers and avengers. Unfortunately they are not adequately trained or informed to play any of those roles. Investigating officers are by and large distressed by a raped woman's anguish. They want to see rapists punished and women safe. This I truly believe. Women who have been raped naturally look to these men for comfort and guidance. They place themselves in police hands and hope for the best. They need to believe that the best will be done if they do everything they are told to do. I suppose sometimes it is.

A hypothetical outcome of this intense relationship, wherein a man is protecting a woman who sees him as a hero, is that the relationship becomes emotionally explosive. Several romantic fantasies and realities are at play. The woman could use a knight on horseback; the police ride horses and wear armour. A bad man has hurt her; the person who stops or captures him is necessarily a good man, isn't he? I know this sounds like the kind of Freudian stuff you would not expect from me, but listen: I've been the woman whom the police "protect and avenge." It's very complicated. We are not prepared for, or informed about, rape but we are socialized to expect the police to serve and protect us. The police are not trained to understand the crime outside of a limited emotional context. Literature, cinema and crime fiction celebrate heroes who are drawn to extremes of behaviour in their need to protect women.*

But in the end I believe that we all do whatever works and if the other women involved needed to believe that the cops would take care of them, I respect that choice. But oh, how I missed them. How I miss them still.

ON THE day the judge sentenced the rapist to twenty years in prison, Bill and Kim invited the five of us to lunch. They promised to give us

---

* The film *L.A. Confidential* is an example. Didn't you cheer for Russell Crowe as the violent renegade cop who beat wife beaters, then sought revenge for Kim Basinger's damaged woman character? I did.

information that had not been allowed in court and that would help us fill in some pieces. Some of it I already knew. This is what they said: The man who raped us had raped before. He had served four years federal time in British Columbia for an identical series of rapes and while imprisoned had sexually assaulted a female corrections worker, who opted not to file charges. While in jail he met and wed the social worker assigned to his case—the woman I'd seen in the hall. At the time of his arrest he was facing wife-assault charges. He had been in all of our apartments before the nights of our assaults to figure out from the clothing, toiletries and toothbrushes whether we lived alone, which he suspected because he'd observed each of us eating alone at a local greasy spoon that he also frequented. He had taken jewellery and other pawnable items where they were available. He had stalked us. This was before the term had been coined and before the present toothless anti-stalking legislation was passed.*

He was arrested because a parole officer read the warning I had distributed. The arrest took place as he left the greasy spoon. He was carrying a sawed-off baseball bat and confessed to twenty rapes the moment the police identified themselves. Twenty, not five—or six, if you counted the woman Patti had brought to court, who had reported her rape but had not seen charges laid. There were fourteen more women out there who hadn't called the police. Either that or buddy was bragging, or perhaps he was referring to his entire career.

We all had questions. We wanted to know why his prior convictions had not been admissible. His lawyer had successfully argued that his past crimes could not be used against him. (Sometimes real courtrooms are just like the ones on TV.) We wanted to know if he had expressed remorse, but our rapist's only response to his sentencing was to request that he serve his time in British Columbia where his mother lived. Bill assured us that he and Kim would do everything in their power to have him sent to the opposite end of the country. I remember thinking that I did not wish that on him. I asked why, if the guy was on parole and had priors, they had not accessed this information through their computer

---

* Anti-stalking legislation was passed in Ontario in 1993 despite considerable resistance from women's groups who claimed that its watered-down content and intent would not protect women fleeing abusive partners and would be difficult to prosecute.

system or through the exhausting FBI profiling they had subjected us to. Or why they hadn't made us secure in their knowledge that he was the guy before we sort of survived a five-day trial that reduced us to quivering lumps of exposed nerve endings and anxiety? They didn't answer. I was still missing some pieces. I was still attending WAVAW committee meetings at police headquarters. Nothing felt resolved. I still couldn't sleep, hadn't wept, and was madder than hell.

BECAUSE I had fought for the right to watch the trial of the man who raped me, I learned some inside details of my rape and the role the police played in it all, information that had been kept from me. I learned about the cross-divisional politics that prevented the police from connecting the first three rapes. Bill Cameron testified that the investigation identified over one hundred similarities between me and the other women. Any instincts or theories I held about the use of women—myself in particular—as bait to catch a man in the act of raping were proven true. I got a first-person experience of the mindless mythology, held and practised by police, lawyers and judges, that a rape can be non-violent. I learned that there is little dignity or safety for raped women who seek a conviction and sentencing as a remedy for the crimes committed against them. The clearest thought, the strongest feeling I had, was that there was more. Lots more, but it was buried in police notes, in what Bill and Kim did not say, the questions they were not asked, what they did not do. I just didn't know exactly what it was. The preliminary trial was about establishing the guilt or innocence of the man who raped us, and that was accomplished. It was not the venue to determine negligence or discrimination in the investigation of his crimes, although evidence clearly pointed to both. I still didn't know the whole story then, and I wouldn't find out until years later when police documents that hadn't been entered as evidence for the criminal prosecution were produced in the discovery portion of my civil trial. But I knew that I had been used, that I and other women needn't have been raped. It was like something in my mouth I could not swallow.

⁙

13:

ONE spring day following the preliminary trial, I walked into my local market to find a camera crew shooting some kind of news program. They asked if I minded being part of the background scene, then said to just continue on about my business as if they were not there. I had been on film sets before and said sure, why not. As I approached the cash register, I saw a woman I recognized. It was Alice. She was being interviewed about the Balcony Rapist and her subsequent work as a guest speaker at C. O. Bick, the local police training college, where she now lectured cadets on rape from a victim's point of view.

She looked well and I was thrilled to see her. We chatted and reassured each other that we were both okay, and she gave me the same news about the other women with whom she had some contact. She had read about the community meetings that WAVAW was holding with the police, and agreed to write a letter to the committee about her experience as long as the letter would not be made public.

Alice is a dignified, articulate woman who is a successful stockbroker. She was the first woman we know of who was attacked by the Balcony Rapist. She lived in a high-rise a few streets east of mine and was engaged to a man who lived in the same building. In the privacy of her home and her relationship, Alice and her partner used and enjoyed sex toys. Lots of them. On the late December night on which she was raped—after she did the responsible thing by calling 911—a couple of officers arrived at her home to investigate. The proliferation of sex toys, the untidiness of her apartment, her statement that the rapist's voice sounded a little like her fiancé's, all led the detectives to the illogical conclusion that it was her boyfriend who had raped her, and they arrested him. Alice protested that the masked man who climbed over the balcony of her second-storey apartment, covered her face with her bedding and raped her at knifepoint was not the man she loved. She could tell the difference. But despite her sworn statements, conscious and detailed retelling of the crime, her certainty that her fiancé was not the guilty party, they led him away in handcuffs. Only to release him the next day. Only to list Alice's rape as a false claim and recommend that she be charged with mischief. (She wasn't.)

On the police occurrence report concerning Alice's sexual assault, the investigating officer painstakingly described each sex aid complete with measurements and accompanying photos. He documented his suspicion and interrogation of her boyfriend and provided additional photos and commentary about her housekeeping. He noted the large number of gifts under her Christmas tree, some from male friends she had known for years. Under the heading "Reason for Crime," he typed "sexual gratification."

HOW ATTACKED (COMMITTED OR ENTRANCE GAINED)					MEANS OF ATTACK (WEAPONS - TOOLS USED)		
~~Believed through balcony window~~					hands		
OBJECT OF ATTACK (MOTIVE - TYPE OF PROPERTY STOLEN)					VICTIM'S ☐	VEHICLE INVOLVED (YEAR, MAKE, TYPE	
sexual gratification					SUSPECT'S ☐		
SAFE ATTACKED	ALARM SYSTEM INSTALLED	ALARM ACTIVATED	NAME OF ALARM COMPANY (IF MORE THAN ONE, NOTE ON MTP 209)				
YES ☐ NO ☒	YES ☐ NO ☒	YES ☐ NO ☒	N/A				
NO LOSS OF PROPERTY IN THIS OFFENCE ☒	PROPERTY RECOVERED ALL ☐ PART ☐ NONE ☐		WAS PROPERTY INSURED YES ☐ NO ☐		TOTAL VALUE OF STOLEN PROPERTY $ Nil	TOTAL VALUE OF PROPERTY DAMAGED $ Nil	
CAN SUSPECT(S) BE IDENTIFIED YES ☒ NO ☐	BY WHOM Victim	APPOINTMENT TO VIEW PHOTOS YES ☐ NO ☒	WHEN		RESULTS - LOOK-A-LIKES		
SUSPECT NO 1 (NAME - LAST FIRST MIDDLE - NICK)					SEX	AGE	HEIGHT	WEIGHT
					COLOUR YELLOW ☐ WHITE ☐ RED ☐ BLACK ☐ BROWN ☐	MTP NO OR D.O.B	
ADDRESS		MEANS - DESCRIPTION OF SUSPECT					
NAT SKIN OCC INJ REL							
IF YES BELOW INCLUDE RELEVANT INFORMATION ON MTP 209		WARRANT ISSUED FOR LIST LAST NAMES ONLY (FULL NAMES & DESCRIPTIONS MTP 209					

Fortunately for her, for us, Alice is no wilting flower. Although the man who raped her was still at large and although the police did not believe her and judged her as loose and lying, and even though her relationship with her boyfriend began to crumble, Alice kept it together. She talked about what had happened to her, approached the media, called the police again and again to offer new evidence of missing property and things the rapist had said to her in order to persuade them to reopen the investigation. They did not.

Once, the police returned a phone call when Alice was in the shower. She called the officer back and explained why she hadn't been able to pick up. He remarked that he regretted not being there to see her in person.

When, five months later, the police began to connect the dots—dots so large and similar they formed the unmistakable pattern of a serial rapist—they did not return to the scene of Alice's crime with apologies, service and protection. She remained in the dark, uninformed, not believed and terrorized until the day the Balcony Rapist was arrested.

Alice detailed this sorry history in her letter to the WAVAW/police committee. The police members' response? They would hold all copies of the letter, and the committee at large should not address it at all in order to honour a rape victim's right to privacy.

BY this time, the WAVAW committee meetings with the police were disintegrating. The fact that we were meeting at all was in itself a victory but without much resonance. The meetings took place within an altered sense of reality and a heightened sense of paranoia. On both sides. The police members, even those who knew better and who wanted better, retreated behind the blue wall that fortifies their culture and customs. No matter what we did, how many examples we gave them, even when women of courage talked in the first person about their experiences in filing sexual assault charges, the boys resisted. They took shelter behind their regulations, behind their guns.

Some did it with furrowed brows and gentle tones. They spoke of their own daughters and wives, squeezed out a tear here, a drop of blood there. It was eerie. They became victims even as we railed against that role. If only the public could understand what it was like for them, how hard they worked, how often they were in danger, how their own hearts broke. There were others who just sat there and hated us with the heat of an oven.

We developed a series of codes and visual cues to communicate among ourselves and around them. A tug of an earlobe or a flicked finger meant "you take this one" or "let's move on."

They had us on a loop:

> Us: May we see your protocol?
> Them: There is no protocol.
> Us: How do you inform your officers about sexual-assault investigations?
> Them: We use the standing order.
> Us: May we see it?
> Them: No.

Or we would suddenly find ourselves on the "serious versus non-serious sexual-assault" merry-go-round, where they got to decide which crimes were investigated based on their perceptions of a particular scale of sexual assault. And we would ask to see the protocol for that and on and on.

The police members did all of the things they had to do to wear us down: minimization, obfuscation, wilful obtuseness. They crossed their fingers behind their backs and wallpapered the room with cop energy. Once in a while they would throw us a bone. Like when they brought in a celebrated homicide detective just off a child-murder investigation to sit on a committee. He was presented as a gift to us. See how important we think this is? What a big deal!

But the man was torn up, broken by what he had seen. You could see it in his eyes. One night after a meeting, he confided to me that if his wife or daughter were raped he would never let her report. He said it in a supportive way, to comfort me. His breath was laced with mints and alcohol.

On our side, some of the women who sat on the committees undermined efforts to stay on track politically. They strayed into the minefields of pornography and prostitution as causes and effects of sexual assault. They pushed this even to the extent of screening graphic and violent examples of porn for committee members to view. As the images flickered, women, one by one, left the room in tears. Only Patti and I stayed, watching the detectives watch porno.

One large women's agency with representatives on the committees was compromised by the police personnel and legal beagles who held seats on its board of directors. "You can't say that," their executive director would chide us. "Don't upset them." Lori, Melanie and I could operate with an autonomy that women representing different agencies did not have. The preliminary trial was over. We had no worries that we might have to call these same cops the next day to assist in filing a complaint for a woman beaten or raped, as other women at the table might. We were not accountable to government funders or other institutions. Only to the larger community of women who watched and waited and fought with us and had fought before us. But even when we wanted to scream, to pick up the table and turn it over in reaction to police stonewalling and insult, we stayed and did our work.

Over and over the police had asked that "real" rape victims be paraded in front of the committee to verify the written, statistical and second-party information that women representatives were providing. They wanted someone who would speak to them, to their faces and without the protection of anonymity, about police treatment.

Finally we brought them the woman they had been demanding. She was supposed to be their victim. It was her decision to be involved; she viewed it as part of her work as a political woman, something she needed to do, something she thought she needed to do. Her name was Claire.* She was a psychologist who had been raped by the estranged husband of a client during a contested divorce case. Claire was, is, the kind of woman we all wish we could be, and hope our daughters will be. She has the mind of a wizard, the heart of a lion. When Claire speaks she doesn't just tell you something, she paints it for you. Tells you and shows you.

---

* I've changed her name and some identifying details.

She came one night to a WAVAW meeting in the old police head-quarters on Jarvis Street and sat with us and with some of the brass who had supervised the investigation of her rape. She gave the police their example of an investigation gone bad, and she pinned them once and for all. For all of us. She left no place for them to retreat, made them see her and the truth of her experience of them, which had all of the hallmarks of sexual-assault investigative procedure considered standard and accept-able by police but negligent and sexist by women in WAVAW. Claire's testimony, the clarity of her example, made it impossible for the police to maintain their game that night, and we left thinking we had really demonstrated our points. We thought we had used a "good" raped woman, a highly articulate and "respectable" person, to nail them. One who had, or thought she had, nothing further to lose by coming forward, as it had become clear to her and her supporters that the police had blown the investigation of her case and were not going to catch her rapist.

But we underestimated the price of being right and the fury of their response. We forgot what happens if you embarrass some men too much, declare that they are naked or cause them to feel caught out. And we failed to identify Claire's vulnerability. We failed because we did not, could not, imagine the depths to which the police would sink to vindi-cate themselves. After the meeting, the police reopened Claire's case and, without her knowledge or consent, began speaking to and inter-viewing her family members, workplace colleagues and neighbours. At the time, Claire was involved in a child custody dispute with her ex-husband, who happened to be a criminal lawyer. He volunteered to the police that Claire's mental health was questionable since she had been treated for postpartum depression. Faster than you can say, "Both her ex and the police benefited from attacking her," Claire was forced to end her custody battle and send her children to live with their father. The investigation of her rape was again abandoned by the police, with a notation that the complainant (Claire) was not mentally stable.

WAVAW's work came to a smouldering end as a result of the intran-sigence of police brass, who saw themselves and their positions as infallible, and raped women as helpless victims who were either lying or should be happy to be redeemed by police assistance and deliverance. Police culture, which maintains that anyone not with them is against them, allowed police committee members to believe that they had met with us in good faith. They could reason that because we were not part of their culture, we just couldn't understand the crime. Force members believed this with the ferocity of fundamentalism, the ideology of generals at war.

When WAVAW decided to withdraw, we knew it was critical to document our foiled efforts. We created a chart that listed the examples of sexist and negligent police behaviour that had been presented in committee, the systemic context for each in the bigger picture of policing, and viable solutions for change that would assist women as well as police officers to effect a higher rate of reporting and stronger legal cases. And there it was on the page: evidence that reflected the consistent pattern of police failure and denial. I seriously doubt they ever looked at it.

We convened a media conference to release our documentation and to announce that we had no other option but to withdraw from the process, as the police were not sincere or committed in their participation. And that's all there was.

Not that it wasn't interesting or worth it. To be true, to stay with the work and resist regardless of the outcome, which we had done for a year—that's as good as it gets sometimes.

It was also an incredible education, a behind-the-scenes tour through a gallery of Bosch landscapes. Fascinating and repellent. But finally we were only visitors, unwelcome and barely tolerated. "Let us get on with the work of solving crimes" was likely the cops' parting thought, along with "Don't let the doorknob hit you in the ass on the way out."

In fact, WAVAW accomplished much more than I could see at the time. We publicly exposed the nervous system of the police infrastructure. We caused the police to engage with community members in a model of accountability and change under close media scrutiny. We were so successful that they apologized, admitted wrongdoing. We delivered a feminist critique from their insides out. Feminist academics and legal practitioners were likewise forging progressive change in the

Specific Issues & Indicators	Systemic Context	Recommendations
5) (continued) • Interruption of hospital procedures for questioning • Reports of police insensitivity to complaints of exhaustion		• Protocol must recognize the demands of a multidisciplinary response to sexual assault and the need to respect the role of other services.
6) Differential treatment of victims of sexual assault according to: relationship to assailant, class, race, profession, status, sexual orientation, physical or mental disability or presence of alcohol or drugs. Indicators: • Numerous reports of differential treatment from victim/survivors and professionals working with them. • Sexual Assault Evidence kits not submitted to C.F.S.	• Lack of awareness that the problem exists. • Lack of clarity re: boundaries of discretionary power of officers. • Hiring/screening does not address biases and inappropriate belief systems. • Training does not address biases and/or inappropriate belief systems.	• Protocol must address boundary of discretionary power. • Development and implementation of screening procedures in hiring which challenge inappropriate beliefs and biases. • Development and implementation of training programmes which challenge inappropriate beliefs and biases.
7) Investigative procedures which place women at risk physically or psychologically. Indicators: • In-depth questioning at scene of crime. • Line-ups in unsafe locations. • Notifying other family members of the assault without permission.	• Lack of awareness that the problem exists. • Focus on the accused and the ensuing investigation is so strong that needs of women are neglected.	• Development and implementation of alternate approaches to current investigative procedures • Written consent must be obtained prior to notifying family members or other individuals of assault.

social and legal status quo, which defined crimes of violence against women. Civil lawsuits were being discussed as viable alternatives to the criminal system for raped women.

The work of WAVAW caused the force to finally remove the crime of rape from the jurisdiction of untrained officers who usually investigated robbery and homicide, and to establish a squad dedicated to sexual assault. Money was poured into the fledgling SACO, and additional officers were recruited to work there. It was the first of its kind in Canada. Without us that would not have happened.

<A page from the WAVAW
document, which described
the issues raised in committee
meetings with the police

How I became Jane Doe

14:

MEDIA bans drive the media crazy. They are potentially dangerous. Our right to know what's happening in our legal system should be maintained and monitored diligently. I support that. The withholding of information in any form is not a decision to be made lightly or in the absence of public scrutiny. But let us be clear about the history, use and intent of media bans such as the one granted to women who file sexual-assault charges. The statistics are that one out of four women experience sexual assault in their lives and that most of that number—90 per cent—choose not to report the crime to police.

There is immense pressure to report and most of us would prefer to, but this is what happens if we do:

We are not believed.

We are shamed, subjected to unnecessary and invasive medical and forensic examinations.

We are humiliated through public exposure of our past lives, lied to and insulted by court officials.

We are sometimes shunned by our friends, family and community, and forbidden to speak of our experience again unless it is in the context of our eternal pain, suffering and trauma.

We can be charged with mischief.

If our rape is sensational enough, or if it's a slow news day, the scariest bits are reported in the media.

While fear is an important factor in our decisions not to report, the larger reason is that we're not stupid. Why would anyone choose to subject themselves to such shitty behaviour? Especially when the conviction rate for sexual assault is under 5 per cent.

The legal system, in its wisdom and compassion, and because the police and the Crown really, really want you to report, provides a small safety net. If a court official applies on a raped woman's behalf, she is granted a media ban that prohibits, under criminal sanctions, the public use of her name, likeness or any other identifying information. If you don't stipulate otherwise, the name they assign you is Jane Doe.*

Becoming Jane Doe was the only thing I did not have to fight the courts for. It will be a cold day in hell before I relinquish the favour. It is simply not safe, not wise or dignified to be identified as a raped woman. My rape or fall from any "good woman" status I previously maintained is not reversible. If the media ban were lifted, my public identities as teacher and culture worker would be replaced by the label "rape victim" in the blink of an eye. The sensational aspects of my case, especially the psychiatric evidence that was used to discredit me during my civil trial, would be connected with my real name and reputation. My parents would know.

While I do not believe that individual police officers wish me harm, my actions as Jane Doe proved the entire institution of policing guilty of criminal negligence and sexist bias—offences they continue to deny. I prefer that the seven thousand people employed by the Toronto police force are not familiar with my face and real name. The man who raped me will be out of prison one day. He already knows my name and face, but I choose not to have my image linked with his publicly and, if the past sixteen years of media coverage are any indication, reported sensationally. Removing this scrap of safety, this single nod to a woman's right to privacy and dignity when, at huge personal sacrifice and for the public good, she reports her rape, would result in an escalation of unreported crime.

Recently, more women—especially younger women—are choosing to use their own names when they have been raped and are entering the legal system. Usually these women have been raped by a stranger, and their decision is their right as well as a sign of their courage and strength.

---

* While this practice has become automatic in criminal courts in North America, it is still necessary to officially request that a media ban be granted in a civil procedure.

RAPE STATS*

❖ One in four Canadian women will be sexually assaulted during her lifetime.

❖ One-half of all Canadian women have experienced at least one incident of sexual or physical violence.

❖ 83% of women with disabilities will be sexually assaulted in their lifetimes.

❖ Of the women who are sexually assaulted, 69% are assaulted by men known to them: dates, boyfriends, marital partners, friends, family members or neighbours.

❖ Four out of five female undergraduates recently surveyed said they had been victims of violence in a dating relationship.

❖ 60% of college-age males indicated that they would commit sexual assault if they were certain they would not get caught.

❖ Only 6% of all sexual assaults are reported to the police.

❖ Only 1% of women who have been sexually assaulted by an acquaintance report the incident to police.

❖ In one study, 50% of women who did not report their rapes believed that police would do nothing about it. 44% of them were concerned about the attitudes of both police and the courts toward sexual assault. 33% were afraid that if they reported they would be assaulted again by the accused. 64% did not report because of shame and fear.

❖ 60% of sexual assaults occur in private homes. 38% of them occur in the victim's own home.

❖ Women are physically injured in 11% of sexual assaults.

❖ Nine out of ten women experienced on-going anger, fear and loss of trust in others as a result of sexual assault. Of women who have been sexually assaulted as adults, 20% use sleeping pills and 20% use sedatives.

*adapted from "Dispelling the Myths," a pamphlet issued by the Ontario Women's Directorate of the Government of Ontario, March 1995.

But my right, my choice, is to remain a Jane Doe. Although I am deeply proud of my work and would prefer to have my real name connected to it, I would not have acted politically nor would I continue to act without that anonymity. I could not have won. View it as an ongoing testament to the world we live in.

In 1987 I already had the protection afforded under law to maintain my privacy as a Jane Doe. But it was only after the police sabotaged the community response that WAVAW had initiated that I became *that* Jane Doe. Became her for life, in order to have a life, to be alive. But the transition was not instant. There was not a single moment when the decision to launch a civil suit against the police landed fully formed in my head.

What did I know from civil law? What did I care? I was a worker, civic-minded, a stronger feminist than many women I knew but not as developed as others. I was minding my own business, living my life, when rape barged in. The difference for me was that feminism allowed me to understand the intrusion and to meet it a little more prepared. One of the police defences during my civil trial would be that I was a feminist political mastermind who plotted the lawsuit from the moment I was raped, probably *during* the rape. They would seek to prove this to the judge by presenting my lengthy work history with socially progressive agencies as evidence, along with a list of all the feminist books I had read prior to my rape. On the list I included the Nancy Drew and Trixie Belden series I had read as a girl. By the time we got to court, someone had noticed and removed the titles. (I was more partial to Trixie.) Both documents were to be read aloud in court.

But my transformation to Jane Doe was far more holistic and much less deliberate than they assumed. The police tried to separate my feminism from me just as they tried to separate me from my rape. As if both were skins to be shed. But that was not possible. Becoming Jane Doe propelled me into becoming the person I was probably going to be anyway, but at a much greater personal cost and in a very different manner.

HOW did I decide to take the cops to court? It was the first summer after my rape. The end of Year One of my new life as a raped woman. I had just been hired to coordinate a documentary film seminar to be held outside of Toronto. I was doing a relatively good impersonation of myself, keeping busy, getting involved in community work and organizing as if I were a normal person. That work and my role within WAVAW translated into new possibilities for me, new ways of understanding and experiencing my new life.

Johnny was gone again. I forget where but never far enough. Police officers once came to my home looking for him, saying he had last been seen driving east on Highway 401 in a stolen limousine. A white one. I hate white limos and I hated him for bringing the law so close to me when I was so close to the law, for putting me in danger, for not loving me enough. Still, I thought he was all I deserved and all I was going to get. Even though I was in therapy and had many good friends, I did not completely leave him. I bled into another stage of my life, of life after rape, where you only see yourself when you look in the mirror and even then you are suspicious. Is that really me? Is that an *R* on my forehead, my breast, my heart? Can others see it? It's a stage where you swallow but don't taste, function but don't feel. Only when resisting, when fighting back politically and with others, could I see a clear reflection of myself. A strong, steely me.

Since I was unable to engage the police in meaningful dialogue and change on a community level regarding how they investigated rape, I decided to look to the courts again for redress. Perhaps the most damning outcome for the police, and the most life-changing for me, was that *Jane Doe v. the Metropolitan Toronto Police Force* crystallized as the ultimate, the perfect example of the individual case we needed to illustrate the systemic problems we had been naming in WAVAW. Only this time it would be a civil action and I would have legal representation and a voice in the system. I would not be a victim and I would not be alone. It would be different this time.

When I was not Jane Doe

15:

I AM the eldest of five children, an adultified child who grew up with too much responsibility and Catholic guilt. I left my suburban home when I was eighteen, got a job, travelled and returned to university part-time without financial or other support. Although I loved every minute of my young adulthood, I lacked the guidance and nurturing that might have better directed my life at that critical time.

I was always a political animal, although I wouldn't have used that phrase when I was young. But I started young, at my parents' knees. They both grew up in too-large families and in grinding poverty. Like many of their generation, the Second World War brought them the promise of economic stability and new beginnings. But my parents were not fools. They remembered the gnaw of hunger, the back-breaking, lung-scarring labour of coal pits and steel mines, and they naturally mistrusted bosses and politicians, who in my father's words were "bastards and thieves." My parents were active in labour politics and preached the doctrine that we should stand up, fight back and speak out, even though they were devout Catholics, and such a stance sometimes put them at odds with their church. While they have prospered beyond the wildest dreams of their own mothers and fathers, they were and are confounded by their eldest child, who spoke out at an early age against their church and government and fought against a social system that, she screamed, relegated her to second-class status. "What in the name-ah-Gawd is she on about now?" my father would yell, wanting to understand me but preferring that I shut up about this women's rights stuff.

People wonder about my decision not to tell my parents about my rape and trials; some think that my discretion is a dark reflection on them, their parenting, that my hurts, mistakes, bad choices are judgments on them. And in small ways I suppose that is true, as we are all our parents' children. But I can tell you this: Everything I learned about faith and courage and boldness, I learned from them. Hard work was their real religion. They survived war and poverty. They laboured and loved and played with equal ferocity, scrimping to buy us the best on sale at Fairweather's or just as good at Towers, filling up on what we left on our plates, cleaning toilets at the strip mall during winter layoffs, walking to save the fare or where there were no bus lines in weather so cold their clothing froze. They censored *Perry Mason* as too adult for our viewing. "No, you can't go to a party if boys are there, you can't pierce your ears, you must carry that beautiful purse Aunt Bridget sent you and do not talk back, you saucy pup."

They couldn't afford to send us to camp, but we drove down home every summer, to the Maritimes, seven of us in the car, at first a black Mercury and then a newer blue model ("Just tell the policeman your stomach is sore and that's why Daddy was driving so fast"). There were Sunday picnics at Kew Beach, rosaries every night in the month of May, playing hard at outdoor games that lasted for days, copying my father's shop steward reports in perfect child's printing because he did not write well.

My parents dressed up for card parties, at which uncles pounded the table, "Trump that, b'y," with Aunt Alice and Mom laughing in black dresses and pearls and scolding: "Don't tell me how to play the damned card!" Toasted cheese sandwiches and Canadian Club whisky and ginger ale. Us rushing down the next morning to fish for nickels and dimes under cushions and down the back of the chesterfield. "Be quiet this morning, kids. The Leafs lost last night and Daddy's in a bad mood."

As I grew, my mother's picks pierced bristled rollers and my scalp. "Be still! A woman's hair is her crowning glory." There were hugs with kisses before bed, unless my parents were working. "Night-night, my heart." And I woke up every morning to the smell of bacon and eggs and porridge and murmured voices, and in the winter a dose of cod-liver oil, lined up with my brothers and sister at the fridge, Mom laughing as we puckered. Then I'd run across the tracks first to mass and then to school.

My parents are the stuff this country was built on but no longer values. They lived at a time, in a moment, during which, with hard work, it was possible to own your home and to live in health and safety. They snatched that chance from the wreckage of their own youth and never let go. They occupied it. That time, that promise, their like will never come again. In their old age, which my father rages against but my mother embraces with the same energy that has always driven her, they live a middle-class life. Their children have all survived, all do reasonably well, all come home for the holidays. They delight in their grandchildren but are increasingly appalled at their behaviour, their clothes and sauciness.

But as we grew older it became obvious that our parents could not, would not, let our relationship with them evolve into an adult one. That we would forever be the children to their grown-ups. Not for our lack of trying or for lack of love, but because they would never relinquish the identity they carved for themselves from blood and sweat and loss. The parental authority that formed them, held them up. So we disengaged, all of us, to protect them from the harsher realities of our lives, remembering how much they gave us, wishing they knew us better. My father wakes at night now—he is very old—remembering his mother who died when he was a child, and his father killed the year after. He recalls pulling onions from the field and eating them raw with a bit of bread and mustard. The suit he shared with his five brothers, carefully placing the pants under a straw mattress they all slept on or off. A war that brought him his first pair of new boots and in which he killed other hungry young men. He wakes with tears in his eyes and roams the house for hours remembering.

I will not bring him more tears. He could not bear that his first child, his oldest girl, the one he allows to comfort him sometimes, was fighting her own war and also wept at night. He could not bear that things had changed so much after all he had worked and fought for. He would not understand that the faith and joy I grew up with in my parents' home sustains me as an adult because he has no memories of safety,

97

hugs and laughter when he himself was a child.

So that's why I didn't tell my parents, and I have never failed nor wavered in that decision. Because finally they do not really want to know. They do not watch what they call the death news, or movies with cursing or too much violence in them. "We're seniors, dear, we don't need this," my mother explains as she asks for her money back after walking out of a film.

One day, right after I had done a radio interview, she called me. "Daddy and I just heard a woman on the radio who sounded just like you!"

"Really, Mom? What was she saying?"

"Oh, I don't know, dear, I wasn't paying that much attention."

"No, Mom, it wasn't me."

"Isn't that funny! Are you coming up on the weekend?"

I never spoke on that radio station again. But don't misunderstand me. My parents are warriors still, strong and brave. Everything I know, I first learned from them.

AS their child, I was exposed to a socialist strand of Catholicism rarely found in conservative Ontario. Two of my aunts, one from each side of the family, were nuns, and I was named for both. They entered orders in which they were educated, travelled broadly and taught. One worked extensively with maximum-security-prison inmates. She swore and played poker. The other was a teacher in the Caribbean and became the Mother Superior of her order.

My mother tells the story of the boy who loved her sister and who wept at the gates of the convent on the day she entered. Then he grew into the brother of the man who announced *Hockey Night in Canada* every Saturday of every winter weekend of my youth. Each time I heard him, my heart would break a little in romantic anguish. My aunts' letters and visits, lessons in joy, the romance of their lives, contrasted with the sometimes cruel, sometimes loving wimpled nuns who taught me, or the woman as housewife/mother/second earner, who was modelled by my mother as my destiny.

I adored school and did well, won scholarships, sat on student councils, smoked cigarettes, had intense relationships in my all-girl schools, some of which have lasted my entire life. I walked for Biafra, marched against Vietnam, and crossed a big line when I returned home, posters in hand, from a pro-FLQ, anti–War Measures Act *manifestation*. "'Pon me soul ta Gawd! What is she doing now?" my father roared as my brothers snickered in delight. "She's really going to get it this time, goddamned French bastards!" It was time to go. My best friend and I hitchhiked out West for the summer.

I entered college and then dropped out to work full-time in order to save enough to travel to Europe. A Toronto-Amsterdam return flight, open for a year, was $225. I was nineteen. I turned twenty in Bethlehem. I was enthralled by socialism at this point in my life, and I even attended a few meetings of the International Socialists, which, while sounder, reflected some of the dourness and fanaticism of the religious doctrine I had been raised in. I had it in my mind to do the kibbutz thing, which I had researched for a sociology paper, and experience socialism first-hand. And I did, back in the days when Israel was seen (by most) to be David in the battle with Goliath. I wouldn't like to trade that experience or dilute it with memories of Arab workers who laboured more than we foreigners in fields and factories but were fed less and treated less well. I remember instead film nights in the desert—Fellini's *Amarcord* with Hebrew and Arab subtitles—bus rides to Eilat with rock and roll on the radio and history just outside the window. I remember falling in love with handsome Israeli soldiers and firing off their Uzis, the force so strong it knocked me back into their arms. I remember working in the orange *pardes* or orchards, then the laundry and finally, after I had proven myself and stayed long enough, in the children's house or *ga'an*, which had been my goal, my secret plan. All along I had been fascinated by the kibbutz model of parenting and child rearing.*

These were some of the things that shaped me. Decades later, during my civil trial, my political affiliations and paid work (mostly with non-profit and community agencies), my reading habits and my family relations

---

* In addition to mealtimes, children spend five hours of each day at home with both parents in activities that are exclusively family-oriented. They eat, sleep and attend school communally in separate buildings according to their age group. Adults also prepare food and eat meals together in a collective kitchen and dining hall.

were used against me as evidence that I was predisposed to anti-author-itarianism and was manipulating the legal system to rabble-rouse and score political points.

NOW I suppose I have to write about Johnny. My relationship with him was another wepon of the police defence in the civil trial. What shall I say about him? That I loved him madly? Badly? That he made me cry, walked backwards in front of me in winter to keep the wind away, believed that I could do anything, broke my heart repeatedly, fretted that I did not eat enough, built me furniture from pictures in magazines and then smashed it up, never bored me, won any prize I wanted in the midway games at the CNE, and was the only person that I believe truly loved me, good parts and bad.

Or should I simply say that adult women should stay away from dan-ger boys with *y*'s on the end of their names? Johnny was, is, probably manic-depressive or a variation thereof. There have been nods in that direction from brief, court-ordered encounters he's had with shrinks just before being sentenced for petty crimes (B&Es) committed to bankroll a drug habit that planted itself when he was twelve years old. I met him when we were twenty-five. He was publishing an underground music zine and managed a band. Johnny was a carpenter and electrician by trade. He could fix just about anything with only a knife and fork, and during the first two years of our relationship, he taught model-making to architecture students in a downtown community college and made 8mm films.

We had a huge flat on Queen Street West and went out at night to lis-ten to Rough Trade, The Curse, The Viletones. Saturday matinees with Handsome Ned at the Cameron. I didn't know about the drug addiction he had pushed to the side, until he stopped going to work, stopped washing and started leaving fits in the top drawer. (I had never seen a syringe in this context before and needed to believe his explanation that it belonged to someone else or that he had found it somewhere.)

When he trashed our apartment, I knew the honeymoon was over. But did I leave, take the hint, do as Ann Landers most certainly would have advised? No way. Because the thing about me, my weakness and my strength, is that I never leave. I will stand and fight even when retreat is the wiser path. And like many women in such a situation, I believed that he loved me, and I knew that I loved him and I was going to make it work. Hadn't my mom done that with my dad? Rescued a handsome, lost boy-man from approaching alcoholism and loneliness and built a model life together?

So I stayed for fifteen more years. Well, not consecutively and not always. I travelled, loved others, ventured into filmmaking, championed causes, but every time I was truly out, he pulled me back in. And I was never really out. Johnny and I enabled each other. That most pathetic of relationship clichés defined ours, and I knew it and I stayed. We mirrored each other. I was his goodness, he was my badness. What can I say? That I wasted love? That I am ashamed? All right. But there were times with him when I was completely happy. They are overshadowed now, memories of memories, lost friends. Johnny did one B&E too many, paused to wreak additional havoc in the home of an influential man and was sent up to do federal time. Five years. A blue note in the big house. And since then he's never stayed out. For a while I followed him there with letters and sweet telephone talk. I was his prison wife. Sometimes I would visit him behind metal detectors and electronic doors, steel slamming against steel, until finally I realized that he had chosen that house instead of mine, ours.

With time he became institutionalized, unable to function at all outside of the cold discipline and structure of jail. Queerly, he finds his good self again when physically imprisoned, writing articles that take on the penal system, working so hard to introduce harm-reduction models from the inside that he is paroled early, thrown out because of his work to allow inmates access to condoms. But soon he is back. The monkeys are monsters now, on his back, in his face. He fills himself with bile and chemicals until he forgets his goodness, is afraid to live outside, and his drug mortgage is stamped paid and final.

But I remember him still, and sometimes I think I see him or that he is calling my name, and I forget for a moment that I don't love him any more.

SOME of these pieces of my life sabotaged me, and I looked for ways to better understand who I was and why I made the choices I did. Seeking out a therapist seemed natural to me: why not talk to a totally objective person who is paid in a professional relationship to devote listening skills and insights to you and who enjoys doing it? There is a consensus, even among those who should know better, that therapy implies that you are weak, damaged, crazy. This is an assumption that is often located in fear and certainly in ignorance. Which is not to say that there aren't a lot of shitty therapists out there, because there are. Dangerous even. Criminal yet. But therapy has always worked for me. Therapy is the best gift I have ever given myself. I approach it as I would the consumption of any other product. Price of course is an issue, and inflated fees have often prevented me from pursuing the course of therapy I would prefer. So I shop around. I lucked out with my very first therapist and benefited from working with a wonderful woman who had a large house by the lake, and a heart just as big. Feminism helps me appreciate the benefits of therapy if properly applied. I had grown up with the concept that talking about "problematic" behaviour was something positive, sacramental even.

When I was a kid we used to have contests to see who could make the fastest confessions with the least penance given. You'd never, never confess to impure thoughts or deeds or you would certainly lose, the priest pressing for details, your face flaming, you mumbling, "I forget, Father." And yet there was something comforting about it all, traces of incense, secrets, the box always cool, purple or red velvet curtains—sinful themselves, surely. Then forgiveness, redemption, a clean slate—unless you got Father Kelly, who was old and deaf and yelled at you to speak up. With him, the game was to confess to murder, adultery or robbery just under the decibel level that he could hear, but audible to the other sinners in line. God help you if Sister Mary Pieta came along, because she would haul you out of the box and pull the ear right off your head, and you'd be saying the Stations of the Cross on your knees for a week.

Feminist warning

16:

DID I tell you that I am a feminist? Card-carrying, with capital letters and without apology or equivocation? Did you just roll your eyes? It's okay, this won't take long.

I understand feminism to be a social justice movement that has served more people, effected more progressive change in its first and second waves, than any other documented social justice movement before or since. Feminism resulted in the vote for women, property ownership and business management by women, reproductive choice and freedom, daycare, improved health care, fewer child mortalities, education, legislation, the recognition of violent crime against women and children, and a higher standard and quality of life for everyone affected by it.

There are many feminisms, many practices and applications. Feminism can be radical, socialist, liberal and postmodern. Well maybe it can't be postmodern . . . but it can be, and is, defined differently by academics, legal practitioners, front-line workers and women who do not work directly under its umbrella. It is neither a new concept nor one that can be considered redundant. Its objectives have not been met. It's not dead and it's not going away, although it has been wounded and held captive at different times. While often not successful at either, feminism implies an analysis that is anti-racist and anti-oppressive. It works to free women from historical patriarchal bonds and strictures. It would free men, too, if they wanted it to.

Oh sure, there are a lot of feminists who bother me, and I know that I am seen as a nutbar by others, but in the larger scheme of things, feminism is a practice, a way of being, that is about five minutes old, barely a toddler really and continuing to evolve in its form and understanding of the world it inhabits. It is quite capable of excess and error. But it is evolutionary, revolutionary and dedicated to social, political and economic equality. So what's the problem? Why in the last decade has feminism come to generate so much backlash and fear?

I have a cousin who is the superintendent of all the school boards in his province. He is an educated man and interesting, interested. In conversation with me, he claimed that feminists have no sense of humour and need to lighten up. Not take things so seriously. I agreed and suggested that this sometimes might be a little difficult when three women are murdered by their male partners every month in my home province and a woman is raped every seventeen minutes nationally and that women as a group remain severely economically and politically disenfranchised. I asked him if the political leaders he generally supports are known for their sense of humour, and whether that affects his decision to vote for or against them.

Okay then.

From the beginning of my relationship with the legal system, I was committed to working with feminist lawyers. When I decided to have my own lawyer represent me during the criminal trial of the man who raped me, I pursued women lawyers. When I decided in the summer of 1987 to file a civil action against the police, I knew that it would be with women lawyers. Great leaps had recently cracked the glass ceiling of the legal profession, and I was damned if I would further subject myself to the paternalistic treatment afforded me during my rape trial. How, I reasoned, could a male lawyer understand the realities of a woman who had been raped?

I became aware of the existence of a group called LEAF, a group of feminist lawyers mandated to support and argue cases within the boundaries of the newly minted Canadian Charter of Rights and Freedoms. They were looking for cases like mine: good, clean rapes or other gender-based criminal offences that they could shepherd through the judicial system as Charter violations, specifically under section 15 of the Charter with its gender-equality guarantee, thus establishing the concept within the law.

For weeks I attempted to contact LEAF, repeatedly checking under L and under the acronym section in phone-book pages, yellow and white, but without success. Intermittent calls to directory assistance, hoping that the last operator had not searched properly, were fruitless. Weepy calls for assistance to women who assured me that LEAF existed. Finally, someone gave me an address and I wrote to them. The letterhead of their return mail explained it all. They were the Women's Legal Education Action Fund. The "Women's" was silent. LEAF with a *W*. I arranged a meeting.

AS perhaps in no other country in the last twenty years, Canadian legal feminists have worked to progressively reshape the judicial code. The Charter became the primary vehicle with which to drive that agenda. In 1982 women and First Nations peoples were victorious in their quest for special standing within the newborn constitutional guarantees being drafted to officially separate Canada from the remaining vestiges of British Empire rule and obligation. It wasn't easy. Neither group were welcomed to the table of Canadian sovereignty. In fact, it took a huge national fight to make the Charter address women's issues. The strategic battle, led by Doris Anderson is known as "The Taking of 28"— the section of the document that speaks to the distinct and equal rights of the women of Canada. (The lobbying for the Equal Rights Amendment is the unsuccessful U.S. parallel.) In 1984, the Canadian constitution was repatriated and the Charter became the law.*

Those were salad days. A ripe economy, a liberal government, responsible social programs and a new Canadian identity. This is why I think of myself sometimes as the right woman in the wrong place at the right time. The Charter was newly formed and LEAF's task was to ensure that it was applied to women. The prevalence and nature of crimes of vio-

---

* From the beginning, there were feminists and others on the left who thought the Charter as a whole, and the gender-equality section in particular, would do more harm than good to the very groups it was designed to protect. I was not aware of this criticism at the time. Twenty years after its birth, those worries have been borne out in some Charter precedents that have *reinforced* unequal participation and representation for marginalized groups. Civil suits have been brought against women-only groups and presses, equity hiring practices have been challenged as discriminatory, and the Charter has been used to dismiss sexual assault charges if the case does not come to trial in a timely fashion.

lence against women and children had just entered the public consciousness and newspaper headlines. Only a few years earlier, incest and rape were hidden crimes, seen to be the problems of bad girls and the uneducated. Until 1982, women's crisis centres in the province of Ontario were prohibited from using the word "rape" during phone counselling for fear that clients who sought their services would be induced to make false accusations just by hearing the word. So great was our historical resistance to acknowledging the crime, it was feared that feminists could and would, through mass hypnosis I guess, implant the belief that a rape had occurred.*

But by the eighties, the feminist movement had placed rape into a new criminal framework. And then I came along, or to be more precise, my rapist came along.

BACK WHEN LEAF began, it was a coalition of women lawyers—heavy hitters from across the country—who came together to secure women's rights in the law through the Charter. Many of them were the risk-takers of their generation, women who questioned traditional roles and stereotypes. Women on whose shoulders other women forged legislation and political change designed to guarantee equity and economic stability for this generation's daughters. At least for some of them. At least on paper. Nancy Jackman, the daughter of one of the country's wealthiest, most conservative and most influential families, was and still is LEAF's fairy godmother (she is now known as Nancy Ruth). Nancy waved the golden wand of funding, which, combined with a hefty grant from the federal government, established LEAF. It was a legal force to be reckoned with, and it came to represent for me both the highs and the lows of feminist politics.

Like stern but loving parents who want the best for the child in their care (not a biological or even adopted child, more like a stepchild or a close relative's runaway), LEAF struck me as both troubled and blessed, authoritarian and revolutionary. At first we were all happy to find each other: our agendas seemed similar, our politics aligned. To this day I

* This was a funding rule set by the federal Justice Secretariat; some centres ignored it but others obeyed.

credit LEAF with making the victory of Jane Doe possible. I could not have done it without them.

So it's 1987 and gender and race politics are on the social and political agenda. You could still talk about them without the death-knell rhetoric of "special interest group" or "politically correct" boomeranging about your head. And you could expect to be heard. Those seem like glory days now. Anyway, I showed up at the LEAF offices in downtown Toronto in early summer. I was nervous, depressed, suffering from insomnia. Excited, also, to have this new opportunity, this second chance, this good fight to turn to, to lose myself in, to find myself in. But who were these women? What would they make of me? Remember who you are and what you want, I decided.

I wanted a retelling, a re-framing of the crime of sexual assault. I was—I am still—a woman who was not afraid, who knew what had to be done and saw a way to do it and grabbed on and didn't let go. Even though I didn't fully understand what I had hold of. Even though I didn't have a clear articulation of who I was and what I wanted all of the time. Even when the act of holding on was breaking my arms. Sometimes it was all I could do.

It turned out I had a brief and positive history with one of the LEAF founders. In the seventies I was a waitress at the El Mocambo, a famous bar on Spadina in downtown Toronto. Talk about your glory days. At that time the Elmo was the place to be seen and to hear the established and burgeoning music acts of the day. Everyone played there. Name an act: B.B. King, the Rolling Stones, Todd Rundgren, Gato Barbieri, Wayne Cochrane, John Lee Hooker, Mitch Ryder, Buddy Guy, rock, jazz and blues greats—they all played the Elmo. It was always packed, and the waitresses worked hard, looked good, had fun and made money. My friend Margaret Barnes worked there with me.

The problem for a lot of us was that waitresses had to piece off the managers every night with a percentage of our sales (versus tips, which is the common practice) just for the joy of working there. And sales were high. The money didn't go to bouncers or busboys, it went right into the pockets of management, who then made decisions about which waitress got which section on which shift. It felt like a form of pimping. I stayed there for about three years, revelling in the friendships, music and social scene, but suffered increasingly from degrading and greedy management. Margaret and I and another woman decided to approach a labour lawyer, Beth Symes, who agreed to represent us in court, where we sought an end to the practice of piecing off and the return of our working-girl money. Well the whole issue of tipping and minimum-wage laws got a good going over; the minister of tourism and the hotel and restaurant association waded in. The judge agreed that we had a point, and newspaper editorials proclaimed our moral victory, but we lost and were banned from the El Mocambo for life. A few years later, Margaret and I, determined to see, hear and meet The Damned, wore black wigs and the best of her fashions from New Rose, the punk clothing store she owned at the time, and we returned to the El Mocambo. Reggie the Doorman (and poet) recognized us and ushered us to the best seats in the house.

It had been a good fight, and Beth had treated us respectfully. She was now associated with LEAF. I viewed this as a good omen.

IT SEEMED to me that my case against the police was pretty clear-cut and winnable. The negligence and sexist discrimination practised by the officers in their investigation of the Balcony Rapist was evident. After meeting with me, LEAF, a group of powerful, connected women, was telling me it could be done, that we would work together to make it happen. At the beginning, my civil case was a flashpoint, a convergence of politics and idealism and justice. It was about hope and a good fight, a logical extension of my beliefs and of the work I had been engaged in. It filled me with pride and purpose. It was also about $1.6 million—the amount of damages LEAF thought sounded right.

Within weeks of signing with LEAF, another of those lovely moral victories occurred. The way LEAF worked was they helped me (the client) find a lawyer, whom they paid and with whom they consulted and advised. (This triangular construction would be a source of many tears to come.) We immediately secured the services of McCarthy & McCarthy, a large and powerful Bay Street firm now known as McCarthy Tétrault. Everyone was excited. That same week, Mary Jane Mossman, a feminist professor of law, sued her employer, York University, for discrimination in the hiring of a less senior male professor as dean when she was the acknowledged front-runner for the job. York University hired McCarthy & McCarthy to represent it. In one of those grand moments of righteous political solidarity, I (we) dismissed McCarthy, stating that they couldn't have it both ways. If they were going to stand up in court for women's rights on my behalf then they must do so consistently. Try that in today's political climate and you would be laughed out of court and into scorn. Of course as a result, I had to find a new lawyer.

Often when people refer to my trials, they say, "Oh yeah! She's the one the police didn't warn even though they knew she could be raped." Media reports almost always focused on the issue of failure to warn and, as my civil action wound its way into our legal system, police negligence in the single form of failure to warn became the legal focus. But for me, *Jane Doe v. the Metropolitan Toronto Police Force* has always been about sex discrimination. The second, less celebrated component of my lawsuit was the violation of section 15 of the Canadian Charter of Rights and Freedoms, which guarantees us all, at least on paper, freedom from discrimination based on our gender, race, origin, religious affiliation and sexual orientation. My case argued that a woman is raped by a man every seventeen minutes in this country.* If any other identifiable group was the object of a major crime of this proportion, the state would devote substantial resources to remedy the situation. Since it does not in the case of sexual assault, we argued that women's right to freedom from discrimination based on gender has been violated. The issue is equality.

You can also think of it this way: If, for example, a member of the identifiable group called lawyers were beaten in the halls of the court every seventeen minutes, or if a doctor were attacked every seventeen minutes, the army would be called in to find the wrongdoers and stop them in their tracks. Probably dead in their tracks.

Oddly, the gender specificity of sexual assault remains a complicated and contested area. Despite research, statistics and lived experience of adult women to the contrary, detractors insist that the crime is not gender-based and that women rape too. In fact I have rarely taught or lectured

* Statistics Canada.

Woman sues police over probe of rapes

BY ANN RAUHALA
The Globe and Mail

Metro Toronto Police Chief Jack Marks and two of his officers are being sued for negligence by a woman who says that police handling of a 1986 rape investigation amounted to discrimination against women.

about the legal response to sexual assault without hearing the defensive comment that "men get raped too." Yes, they do. The reported sexual assault of adult men comprises about 3 per cent of rape statistics. (We must also take into account that the majority of men who experience sexual assault do not report the crime either, and that the the incidence of the crime is much greater than is acknowledged.) In more than 99 per cent of the sexual assaults on adult males, the perpetrator is an adult male. Male rape is often motivated by homophobia and is experienced differently by men than by women. Adult men who have been raped are generally being disciplined for stepping out of a pattern. They are being treated like a woman in a misogynous society that regards this as the greatest insult you can give a man. Listen to the schoolyard insults shouted at boys: sissy, pussy, bitch, cunt, homo, fag. Rape is personally devastating for a man, but it is different from the rape of women, which takes place within a social, political, cultural and economic context of historical disadvantage and oppression. This distinction determines the manner in which police respond to women and also the attitudes of friends, families, employers, co-workers, media, medical personnel and the judicial system. While women have mobilized to act on their own behalf in this area without trying to distract from the problem of male-on-male violence, men have not, except by trying to undermine the efforts of women.

I find it heartbreaking that almost forty years into the second wave of the women's movement, women must still struggle to address the crime of rape on our own terms. Oh, I can hear the critics now: "The book often digresses into feminist political rhetoric." If that's how you are reacting to this, perhaps you could skip ahead to another part. But I hope you will stay. Especially if you are male, because without you, without your commitment to change and to understanding that crimes of male violence against women are no accident, that they work to maintain the status quo, nothing will change.

I HAVE been referring to my attack as both a rape and a sexual assault, and I want to address that before I continue, address the language of rape, the very word we use to describe the crime. In 1984 the legal definition of rape was amended and the crime was renamed "sexual assault." The intention was to focus on the violent nature of rape, which historically has been undermined in our courts and through public perception (think of the judge's direction to me to answer that my rape was non-violent). The new definition included a wide range of acts from fondling—an interesting word in itself, as it suggests affection—to forced sexual intercourse. Forced sexual intercourse was divided into three levels.

At the time this was seen as significant. Let's have a look at it in 2003.

A level-one sexual assault can be a date rape. It can also be a stranger rape. Or a rape by your husband or doctor. The common denominator is that there is no accompanying physical violence—or none that can be proved. A level-one rape charge can be fast-tracked through the legal system with no preliminary hearing, and no jury trial. The maximum sentence is eighteen months. Known as a summary-conviction offence, this fast-tracking is at the discretion of the Crown, who can also opt to indict. If the level-one rapist is indicted he faces a maximum of ten years and has the right to a prelim and a jury trial. So a strange man who breaks into your house and rapes you could face a level-one summary conviction. As long as he doesn't "hurt" you.

The level-two rapist carries or uses a weapon, threatens bodily harm to you or to a third person (your child for instance), inflicts bodily harm or is a party to the offence (a gang rape, for example). The maximum sentence is fourteen years. (If he has a gun he faces an automatic minimum sentence of four years.) Level-three sexual assault involves wounding, maiming, disfiguring or endangering a woman's life. The maximum for level three is life in prison, which used to be the maximum for all rapes. The thinking in 1984 was that by establishing these new definitions, more men would accept responsibility for the crime, plead guilty and avoid lengthy trials.

Contrary to its original intent, the term "sexual assault" has been hijacked, once again, to minimize the violent nature of forced sexual intercourse or rape. The definition focuses instead on the presence or degree of bodily harm or injury that accompanies a rape. It makes a date rape or a rape by your partner or co-worker, where there is no physical violence, less serious or violent than, say, my rape was. Moving up (or down) the sexual-assault scale, the crimes of the Balcony Rapist were seen as less violent, and investigated with less diligence, than the crimes of the Annex Rapist, which took place that same summer and in which four women were sexually assaulted and "seriously" physically injured. Ultimately this "new" legislation has allowed the police, lawyers and judges to decide the level or degree to which your specific forced penetration belongs, outside of an understanding of the act of rape itself and often contrary to how you experienced it. The current definition places acts of unwanted touching, molestation and other assaultive or degrading sexual behaviour that women experience solely because of their gender at the bottom of a hierarchy under the rubric of sexual assault.

It's time to revisit those definitions in order that the violence inherent in sexual assault is named again and made apparent. Until it is, let's call it what it is: Rape. A word that speaks for itself, that implies extreme violation and the use of the penis as a weapon of power. And whether it's a strange man with a knife, your boss, boyfriend or doctor, the nature of the harm that is done by rape is the same.

So you ask, I ask, we all ask, "What exactly is the nature of rape?" Good question, and it needs a good answer, one that doesn't get stolen or appropriated, one we won't abandon or run from because it becomes dangerous or locks us into a singular interpretation. An answer that includes a multiplicity of women's experience. A definition that probably can't fit into the law. Because rape is too many things. It is an annihilation of bodily integrity, an imposing of one person's imperatives and fantasies on another through a violent act that rewrites and rewires that person—even if you do not think it does. Rape removes volition, it traduces what sex is, defiles the very act of sex, uglifies it as much as it violates and objectifies the woman who is raped. And it makes her not matter a bit. She is just a projection, a screen on which rape is acted out to the degree that she is separated from the rape, and it becomes the property and business of others. And she is instructed on how to define it, cope with it, recover from it, live with it. Rape is a social issue and an economic issue. Rape is a form of social control. Rape is a crime against society, against humanity, against life. You cannot be a little raped or not

114

seriously raped or non-violently raped. To claim otherwise, to have laws that say otherwise, is to legalize rape. That's what I think, or at least some of what I think. We need to think about it some more.

I HAD had a crash course on the traditional positioning of raped women within the legal system during the trial of the man who raped me. I knew that if I were to enter that system again with a Charter challenge, I would need to clarify my role and status. In writing. With witnesses. LEAF agreed that as the client, I would give direction and make final decisions on my case and that I would have input and final approval on any and all media or public information that we released. I asked that all legal arguments and briefs concerning the issues of sexual assault be written and delivered in language that was clear and accessible. I bargained with them to include a political remedy or codicil in my claim that would require the police to upgrade training and protocol regarding their investigation of sexual assault. LEAF signed on the dotted line. The understanding was that my action, like any civil case, would take several years, maybe even five. It took eleven.

Mary Cornish was my new lawyer and I liked her a lot. She has a fine sense of humour and thinks smart and fast. In our nine years together, Mary was always accountable to me. She never shut me down or cut me off even when I fiercely challenged her law with neither the eloquence or the reserve of a law graduate. "Fuck the law and fuck the judge" was my most common refutation of legal directions or barriers with which I did not agree. Susan Ursel worked with her. Together we forged Canadian legal history.

AMERICAN prime-time television has familiarized us with the term "statute of limitations." It means that an individual has a certain amount of time to file charges regarding a criminal act (or civil action, as was the case here), or else it's too late, no one goes to jail or trial. In Canadian law, the statute of limitations regarding actions against the police is six months—that is, six months from the date of the harm done. My rape, took place at the end of August in 1986. By the time I understood the concepts of a civil trial and decided to proceed, found and hired LEAF who in turn found me a lawyer, eleven months had gone by. One day I got a letter from LEAF's executive director that read, in essence, Oh my gosh! Your lawsuit falls outside of the statute of limitations, and LEAF cannot continue to offer you its services.

I quickly met with her and made it plain that I had a contract with them, that any failure to file my action within the legal time limits was theirs and that if they walked away from me now I would slap a lawsuit on them faster than you can say, "How could you feminists do this to a poor rape victim?" Before I went to that meeting, though, I completely flipped out. Cursed, wailed and then called upon a number of women, some of whom I barely knew, for advice. They all agreed that LEAF was way off base on this one and needed to be coached back home.

The legal argument regarding the statute of limitations seemed obvious to me, and I never understood why they let it trip them up. The limitation period itself was unconstitutional because six months was too short a time for the private and public consequences from interactions with the police to be felt. Legally there had been no harm done to me until the courts ruled on my rapist's guilt or innocence. Until then, it was an alleged crime. The crime was confirmed in February 1987, which meant that we were still within the six-month time limit.

LEAF liked this reasoning, and we kissed and made up.

TAKING a civil suit to trial takes much more time and effort than is represented in the movies. It's also much more boring and High Church than the Hollywood versions. You don't just get to say, "I'm going to sue you." Especially not when you want to sue the police. As with any civil suit, it was first necessary to get a judge to pronounce that there was what is called a "cause of action." That took four years—just to be legally granted the right to go to trial. The police strategy was to fight my suit on every front, drag it out in the expectation that I would either get tired or go bankrupt. Without LEAF, that might have happened, even though by the end LEAF wished I would go away too.

The legal term for the document that contains the essentials of a case is the "statement of claim." Mine, filed in August 1987, was revolutionary. Mary Cornish agreed that input from women working in the area of sexual assault would make it a better record of the issues involved. The result is a statement that is readable and fine. Its content is clear and not disguised in codified language designed to make you weep, sleep or wealthy. The intention was that women coming after me, hopeful of mounting similar challenges, would understand my claim. I love my statement of claim. Even though it contains some (apparently inescapable) victim-labelling, it is an accountable reflection of progressive, feminist language and politics. For years, it has been part of bar examinations as an example of how to write a fabulous claim. Not only is its format considered superior, the very idea that the state, in the form of its police officers, could and should be challenged for its actions in the investigation of a crime is heralded by students and professors of law. Remember, too, that this was in the province of Ontario, where historically the police are rarely found guilty when charged with assault, manslaughter or other crimes, or in internal discipline hearings.

It felt like the odds were beginning to shift in our favour.

Court File No. 21670/87

SUPREME COURT OF ONTARIO

BETWEEN

JANE DOE

- and -

Plaintiff

BOARD OF COMMISSIONERS OF POLICE FOR THE
MUNICIPALITY OF METROPOLITAN TORONTO,
JACK MARKS, KIM DERRY and WILLIAM CAMERON

Defendants

AMENDED STATEMENT OF CLAIM

(NOTICE OF ACTION ISSUED AUGUST 10, 1987)

The ultimate rape victim

17:

I DON'T really know how to be a raped woman. I didn't in 1986 and I don't today. I just have never completely figured it out. Being a raped woman has come to define me in some ways, but I struggle still to understand and define it personally, as opposed to the stereotypes. But I own those too. Trauma and despair have been mine. Depression and pain have marked me. Yet there is more. And less.

A raped woman is framed socially and within the law as something broken. Neither Madonna nor whore but somewhere in between. The carrier of bad luck. There is a general but grudging acceptance that it isn't really her fault, but if she had done something else, gone in another direction, not had that drink or worn that dress or smiled that way, it might never have happened. And thank God it wasn't me or anyone I love. If it had to happen to someone, thank-you-God it was her.

Raped women make other people uncomfortable. Try talking about your rape with friends, at a dinner party or with family. The subject jump-starts every socialized and biological instinct to protect, to seek revenge, to contain, to minimize or to deny that the human psyche stores. The nature of these responses requires the woman to carefully select, when, to whom and how she will recount her experience. Or to decide if she should or can recount it at all. Ever.

Raped women are fallen women. Pushed really, but the shame is on them. A stain like original sin, not of their making but never to be removed or forgotten. Raped women cannot display their rage or joy or sexuality. They cannot be glamorous or successful or funny. They certainly cannot be agents of social and political change.

There are many reasons for this present and historical construction of the woman who has been raped. They are as intricate as political systems, as revered as sacraments.

IT just so happens that I grew up in a Roman Catholic parish that was dedicated to the veneration of St. Maria Goretti. My grade school was also named after her. She was our patron saint. Maria Goretti was a twelve-year-old devout Italian girl who was stabbed to death in 1902 when she refused to succumb to the man who tried to rape her. The miracles required for her canonization were testified to in the years following her death. They included her appearance in the prison cell of her murderer and his subsequent spiritual redemption (and early parole). She was beatified, and attained sainthood in 1950.

One of the best things about a Catholic childhood is the stories of the lives of the martyrs and saints. They are romantic and horrific both, laced with sexual innuendo, braced by bloody murder, torture and vengeance. Good lord, the saints were crucified upside down, burned alive, ventilated with arrows, eaten by lions, ripped apart by juggernauts! Their blood was slowly drained, their skin flayed. And they got to die for a larger good. They died for God, to uphold his one true faith. Upon their grisly deaths they were delivered immediately and whole unto heaven and in rapture. It was all fabulous and Grimm. Often much more than a young soul could bear.

Maria Goretti's story was a little different. It contained the requisite bloodletting (she was stabbed repeatedly), but the truth that her resistance to her rape was the motive for her murder (and canonization) could not be spoken aloud. That part was too horrific even for Catholic ears. Instead we were introduced to the codification of female purity as holy, and female sexuality as sinful. We were taught through her example that it was better to die in a state of purity and resistance than to live defiled as a raped woman. The spinning of her murder upheld the religious doctrine common to all denominations that female sexuality is problematic, a sinful lure

St. Maria Goretti

that few men can resist and that must be cloaked in oppressive tradition and law.

Unlike the stories of the former saints George and Christopher, whose lives and saintly deeds (dragon-slaying and marine navigation) were erased by twentieth-century papal decrees, the real story of Maria Goretti is more firmly located in human rather than heavenly design.* The man who murdered Maria was, in fact, just a boy, who was well known to her family. After thirty years in prison, he claimed that Maria had appeared and forgiven him. He entered a Catholic order of monks and lived out the rest of his life in the protective custody of the Church. Maria was not rewarded for her purity or goodness by deliverance into a position of power or respect in the religion she died for. She lives on rather as the ultimate rape victim. Her canonization occurred at a time when women in the West had achieved increased economic status and liberation but under a pope whose motives and morals continue to be the subject of public debate.

Pope Pius XII did not elect to situate Maria in a powerful position within the faith after her death, as happened with Paul, who hated women, or John the Baptist, who thought women impure. These guys are bigger than saints. Bigger than life. Instead, the pope extolled Maria as a girl whose sexual identity precipitated her death and who was better dead than raped. Amen.

I HAVE never allowed anyone to refer to me as a "rape victim." Certainly for the time that buddy held a knife to my throat I was his victim and I cannot deny that. But every time that term is used to define me, I feel I am returned to that moment, that night of terror and helplessness. Nor am I fond of the label "survivor." Like everyone else, I was already surviving the normal pain and hardships of life before I was raped, thank you very much. "Okay. So what do we call you?" you ask. Call me a woman. Call me a woman who has been raped. Call me a woman who has been raped by a man.

---

* In 1969 the Church decreed that George, who killed dragons and rescued beautiful women, and Christopher, who carried the child Jesus across a swollen river, were no longer saints and that their deeds are mythical.

RAPE victims are supposed to be helpless. We require assistance and must play a passive role while the good men, the police, lawyers and judges, punish the one, isolated bad man who committed the crime. Mass media reflect on and report their version of the raped or beaten woman as victim. Rape victims are othered, viewed as less than normal, unraped people. The term, its use and purpose, is not particular to the legal system and its players or the media. It is commonly used by members of the medical and helping professions as well, and by feminists.

A more appropriate language to describe these crimes of violence was developed by feminists during the seventies and eighties but has been all but forgotten. Look at terms like "wife assault," "partner assault," "domestic violence" and "family abuse." Statistics overwhelmingly support the fact that these crimes are committed by men against women and children. And yet the language we use is gender-neutral. Listening to it, one could logically assume that the wife or partner had assaulted herself, that the children of the family were fighting with or abusing each other and that the violence referred to was homegrown as opposed to imported.

Not so long ago, women working in rape crisis centres and shelters developed language that identified the nature and perpetrator of the crime. Meaning men. Rape is about men. "Male violence" and "violence against women" were the terms we used. After a few years of this, and as we began to work with legal, social and government systems in the hope of effecting change, after we accepted their money to pay our wages and signed on the dotted line of institutional bureaucracy, we were requested to alter our language, to cut back on the perceived "rhetoric" so as not to alienate or hurt the feelings of the men who were sensitive to our issues (and signed our cheques). The long-term effect has been the un-gendering of sexual assault. But what is its cause? What are its other components? How does it end? Who benefits? Why do men rape?

If rape hadn't existed by now, we would have invented it. The rape of women has immense economic, social and legal advantages that are seldom articulated. Put plainly, rape works. It is a tool of sexism, and like racism, it exists because it "works." Stay with me, don't go away, this gets interesting. As a white woman who is anti-racist, I work hard to understand the causes and effects of racism. I understand that I benefit socially and economically from racism, especially the systemic, institutionalized, polite form that Canada has perfected.

As a white woman, I am more employable, better paid and less fetishized than Native women or women of colour. My menfolk are not incarcerated or stopped by police at the same rate. My children are not taunted, bullied or subjected to discriminatory treatment based solely on their skin colour. I can move a little more freely, hold my head a little higher, because I am not a visible container for racial intolerance. In these ways I enjoy privilege based on my racial origin. This acknowledgement does not by itself make me a racist. It helps me to understand racism and how it works.

Similarly, men benefit in systemic and obvious ways from a society that is inherently sexist. Men earn more than women, hold more positions of power, are not responsible for the unpaid work of mothering, walk freely and are free to walk alone. They need not worry about unwanted pregnancies, body image, aging and financial security with anywhere near the same intensity as women. They do not consciously fear the stranger rapist or feel compelled to monitor the actions of strange women around them. They are not taught at a very early age that there is a damned good chance they will experience a form of male violence staved off only by their lifelong vigilance and the curtailing of certain actions, pleasures and freedoms they might otherwise enjoy.*

In Canada, the government statistics are that one in four men would rape if given the opportunity. This is unacceptable, frightening, outrageously high. But let's flip that stat for a moment and look at the inverse proposition: three out of four men would not rape. Indeed there are many more good men than bad. Where are they? What are they doing to address the rapes of their mothers, daughters, sisters and wives? How do I differentiate them from the bad guys? Sure, they're against rape, but do they understand the ways in which it maintains their privileged

* Again, the incidence of male-on-male violence is high and rising. Young men today, especially youth of colour, think twice about walking alone at night. Their mothers certainly worry about it. The subject I am addressing, however, is the rape and sexual assault of adult women by adult men, and how that works as a tool of sexism.

status as males? If rape is an extreme tool of sexism used to maintain the male status quo, doesn't it work for all men?

In lectures I have given, this is where good men redden, their brows furrow and they start to disengage. They don't understand and they ask what they can do, what they should do, but mostly they want to go home. At another time—and appropriately so—I might have said, "Read a book. Don't expect me to take responsibility for your consciousness-raising." But this is what I say here: It's hard to be a man. I shouldn't like to try it.

Men are still socialized from a very young age that to be emotional, delicate or tender is to be a girl, and that that is the worst they can be. They must not cry or play with nurture-based toys or wear pastels. They are overwhelmed with male images that drive cars, leave the house for the majority of the day, and return only to mete out discipline and to enjoy the labour of the more home-based female parent. Traditional family values do not require that men prepare food, clean, organize, schedule or provide health care at the same level as women or at all. Their leisure pursuits are sports or technology-based, their literacy level is lower than girls', their demonstrative signs of affection limited.

Our baby boys, whom we love and cherish and who are born to us free from malice or ill will, are conditioned to understand human sexuality as singular to their individual wants and needs, to translate "bitch" and "ho" as labels of both affection and contempt, to mistrust anything that "bleeds for five days every month and doesn't die," and to appreciate "gay," "faggot" and "queer" as variations of the greatest, most final insult of all.

A good friend of mine, a man who is sweet, smart and pro-feminist, has pointed out in more than one conversation about the meaning of life that his instinct, his motivation, is to follow his dick. To be true to it. I have challenged him on this, suggested that perhaps these are not quite the words he is reaching for when he discusses his life. But he stands firm, and I retreat, fearful that he really means what I think he means. Fearful that I really do—or don't—understand men and the cultural divide that distances them from me.

Every few decades and recently so, the tired sociological saw that men are biologically predetermined to rape is dressed up and trotted out to explain the eternal and rising incidence of the crime.* Women are cautioned to govern themselves accordingly given that the boys simply can't help it. The books, articles, columns that tooth the saw are well received and become the subject of circular logic and debate. What I cannot understand, am fascinated by, is that men themselves do not rebel against such a limited definiton of their ethos and are not insulted by their group equation to molluscs and amphibian life.

Good men don't do it. Our men don't do it. What to make of the fact that 75 to 80 per cent of reported rapes are committed by men known to the women involved. The woman has no problem making an identification. The lighting is fine. She can provide you with her rapist's address and any other identifying information you could imagine. Some you could not. There is no need for a profile, criminal, geographic or artistic. Computer experts, criminologists, DNA and forensic scientists are not called in. They will not be part of the investigation into a crime that escalates yearly and has the lowest reporting rate of all violent crimes. That job goes to the uniformed officer who catches the 911 call or takes the report at the station. That officer has received a maximum of five days' training in a workshop called Family Violence, which blends the rape and sexual assault of adult women with similar crimes of violence committed against youth and children. The training is delivered by other police officers. A rape victim may talk about how well her assault was investigated, she might chide (never challenge) or horrify the cadets to attention with her story. The necessity for adequate diversity training to assist these young men in sexual-assault investigation—which cops themselves will tell you is the most murky and difficult crime to investigate—is ignored. Directives to increase the numbers of women and non-white police force applicants have failed or fallen far short of their projected marks.

Instead, increasingly significant portions of police budgets are designated for the purchase, maintenance and upgrading of computer technology to investigate and solve crime. VICAP and VICLAS, the systems

---

* *A Natural History of Rape: Biological Basis of Sexual Coercion*, by Randy Thornhill and Craig T. Palmer (2000), is the most recent manifesto of this sort.

used in Canada and the United States, are compatible with European and other international policing instruments. They are effective in dealing with international espionage, corporate and white-collar crimes, and auto, credit card or jewellery theft rings. And that's a good thing. Their efficacy in infiltrating prostitution, sex trade, pornography and child-abuse networks is heralded by law enforcement officers. I'm sure they have been helpful in other violent crimes. But if you have not been raped by a stranger or an "anger retaliatory rapist" (who constitute only 25 per cent of the rapist population), your crime will not be compatible with computer technology. These tools and the information they store are based on faulty conclusions about empirical evidence. Which means they can be as racist and as sexist as the agents who design and interpret them. Only now they get to call profiling "science," so it acquires a whole new, if undeserved, credibility.

In the majority of rape cases, consent is the issue. The accused has agreed that there was sexual intercourse but it was, he swears, consensual. If the woman involved has prior activity that registers on the VICLAS system, it is used against her in a court of law. For instance, if the woman involved was raped before or if she did time for a crime she did or did not commit. If in the past she was apprehended by police under the Mental Health Act,* if she was hospitalized for postpartum depression or protested against government policies resulting in police apprehension, or if she whored to pay for college or drugs, fled her country of origin because of police abuse or was part of a Native roadblock, it will show up in a VICLAS search. (If you don't believe that this kind of information is collected and stored and available for some to access, take the time to file an Access to Information Act application on yourself. There is probably a file with your name on it.) Next, an "expert" witness will be hired to testify that you are a slut, addict, terrorist, deviant or other form of miscreant, and your rapist is free to rape you again or otherwise complicate your life. Actually, it probably won't even get as far as the expert-witness scenario because the rapist's lawyer can ask questions to elicit the information him-

---

* The Mental Health Act gives police the authority to arrest and incarcerate individuals they deem to be mentally ill who are held (but not charged) until the diagnosis is confirmed. The record of the arrest is permanent.

self, or he can get it through his own computer search and not even have to pay for expert medical testimony.

One of the things we need if we are to encourage women to report is increased and ongoing training and education on rape and other crimes of violence committed against women by men, delivered by women who are professionals in the area, meaning women who work in shelters and rape crisis centres. This will only happen through police policy and operational changes in law enforcement practices. Changes that will also benefit policing. Changes that women have been suggesting globally. For decades.

Women who work in anti-violence, who write about it and educate others and have first-hand experience of it, are the experts in the field of rape—not some Eliot Ness clone or computer nerd with a PhD. Hire us. And by the way, we will expect to be paid for our work.* The escalating focus on "stranger danger" by police through the media and with the assistance of so-called victim's rights groups has worked to maintain a climate of fear that ensures a large degree of control over how and where women live. Current warnings issued by police to alert communities of a serial rapist are fear-based and hysterical in language and nature. Instead of factual warnings that give us information about the dangerous men in our midst, they issue "don'ts" directed toward women, the people most at risk: The don'ts include:

> Don't go out alone. Don't go out alone at night. Don't go out alone or at night unless accompanied by someone (male). Don't open the windows. Don't open the doors. Lock the windows and doors. Don't talk to strangers (men). Don't assist strangers (men). Don't take shortcuts. Alternate your daily routine and routes to work or school.

---

* The point of payment for work done by professional women who consult with police departments on rape or wife assault is one of the hottest hot-button issues I have encountered in my work as Jane Doe. Even other women working in the area take issue with it, claiming it will further alienate police. Since 1975 anti-violence workers in Toronto have left their paid work to sit on panels and committees or go to meetings with police without financial reimbursement for wages and time lost. And to no effect. Would consultants on helicopter use and purchase or stun-gun efficacy in crime fighting work for free? Should they? The practice of not paying people for their work results in that work being undervalued or ignored. Not to mention poverty.

Don't take elevators by yourself (or with strange men). Monitor the motions of the men around you. Don't ride the bus alone. Don't get off the bus alone. Leave your lights on. Don't use underground parking. Don't park on the street. Walk in pairs. Walk on the road. Walk down the middle of the road. Carry a cellphone. Don't struggle. Don't resist. Don't fight back. Don't arm yourself. Eat grass.

Hey! We already don't do those things! Tell us something we don't know. Give us adequate information that does not interfere with your investigation. Give us dates, times, locations, any description you might have, and let us work in community to craft solutions and to support you and each other.

And stop using the fear of strange men to deflect the bigger problems of sexual assault, beatings and other inhumane atrocities committed against us by men we know.

A LOT of women have told me that they think it would be "worse" to be raped by a stranger than by a man you know. Personally, I think that in the larger sexual-assault lottery, I lucked out by being raped by a stranger. For one thing, I was not assaulted by someone I loved or trusted or otherwise chose to let into my life. I did not have to deal with that level of emotional betrayal. For another, there was never any question of consent or introducing my past sexual history during the rapist's trial. Oh, his lawyer would have done it—in fact, there is even a pamphlet called "Whack the Sexual Assault Complainant at Preliminary Hearing," which advises defence lawyers on how to get women's past sexual history introduced at trial. Defence lawyer Michael Edelson wrote (originally in an article published in a professional journal called *Lawyers Weekly* in May 1988):

> You have to go in there as defence counsel and whack the complainant hard ... get all the medical evidence; get the Children's Aid Society records ... and you've got to attack

with all you've got so that he or she will say, 'I'm not coming back.'

The fact that I was raped by a stranger who was a serial offender with a history of identical crimes actually worked in my favour in court. It predisposed the police and the courts to believe that I was telling the truth and not making a false allegation. As a result, there was no legal basis to introduce my sexual history. (I did not dream that it or my medical and family histories would become issues in my civil trial twelve years later. In fact, if I had known it would come to that, I probably would not have proceeded.)

It is easier (but not a foregone conclusion) for the courts to establish lack of consent if the rapist is a stranger. The justice system is less likely to think or believe that you agreed to sex and then changed your mind or just made the whole thing up to get attention. It should be relatively safe to assume that if a strange guy has a knife at your throat, the issue of consent is not to be debated.*

Mind you, if you change the picture just a bit and make the man with the knife at your throat your husband, boyfriend or date, well maybe he thought you liked it that way because he'd done it before and you didn't call the police that time, or it was just a little fantasy so he's not guilty. Not really. If he doesn't have a weapon but hurts you with his hands or threatens to, drops something in your drink or withholds money or food or shelter unless you succumb, then your consent does become the issue. The only issue that matters. The fact that you had prior sexual relations with him (or others), had been sexually assaulted before, consumed drinks or drugs that night (or ever), the very fact that you knew him can be used against you in a court of law to raise doubt about your consent and to determine that he is not guilty.

And they wonder why more women don't report . . .

---

*The film *The Accused*, starring Jodie Foster and based on a true story, is an example of the courts believing that a woman consented to a gang rape by strangers, even though she was sure she did not. We need not go as far as Hollywood to find examples. In Canada see *Regina v. Wald, Hockett and Girt*, Alberta Court of Appeal and *Regina v. Sansregret*, Supreme Court of Canada.

Living with it

18:

I HAD been seeing a psychiatrist, Vince DeMarco, for about a year when I was raped. I remember how angry he got when I told him and how he said he wanted to kill the guy. I was a little disappointed. I knew dozens of men who would gladly have killed my rapist, including a few cops, but that wasn't what I needed just then. But Vince quickly snapped out of it and maintained his place on my list of good men. It's a short list that includes my father and Nelson Mandela, among others.

I wasn't as fortunate with another male therapist. In the early eighties I decided to try the Clarke Institute of Psychiatry, which is the local seat of medical research and thought on what and who is mentally ill or unstable and how to deal with it. (It has recently amalgamated with the Addiction Research Foundation (ARF) and other local madhouses, all now affectionately known by some as the CLARF. Together they receive scads of money for teaching and research, and they probably help some people.) I knew that I could find a psychiatrist through the Clarke whose work would be covered under the provincial health insurance plan, and so I approached them. They matched me temporarily with a student who was strictly supervised by a staff psychiatrist, and placed me on a waiting list for a "real" therapist. Nothing real huge was going in my life at the time—I was still a good (fallen) Catholic girl in a relationship with a bad boy whom I adored, and I didn't know what I wanted to be when I grew up. The intern's name was Norman Doidge. He was young, too, and very proper with a beard and a rather nice face.

I've always been dramatic in my physical presentation and dress. I like fashion and have always worn shoes that raise me above my documented diminutive stature. I used to own a vintage clothing store, and at the time I was mixing punk attire with office chic and fifties vintage. It worked. But I don't think Norman had ever met anyone quite like me, let alone delved into their innermost thoughts. After a few months, our relationship ended when he returned to his studies, and I was referred by the Clarke to Vince DeMarco. Norman told me he admired Vince greatly.

I saw Norman Doidge one last time in a lineup at an ATM. We chatted briefly. I was teaching by then and happy with my life. While I was always aware that I freaked Dr. Doidge out a bit, I assumed that he had my best interests at heart and that he wished me well. I was wrong.

In a two-page assessment that he sent along with his referral (and which was later used against me in civil court), Norman Doidge wrote that I was sado-masochistic, spoke in a breathy Marilyn Monroe voice, wore miniskirts and go-go boots. And he didn't mean any of it in a good way. He went on to become head of psychiatry at the Clarke. He writes a column in the *National Post* and has published a memoir and some poetry.

My reasons for pursuing therapy were not traditional. Depression or torment did not rule my heart before I was raped any more or less than for anyone else, or out of proportion to the circumstances of my life. I can't say that I knew what I needed after I was raped or that anyone could have "given" it to me. The point of therapy was to figure that out for myself. For me, for many, therapy is a form of life maintenance, like working out at the gym or pursuing other health care; it interests me, helps me to challenge myself and to grow. It is not specific to what is difficult in life but helps me to better appreciate what is good. The manner in which therapy has been twisted and diverted by clinical practitioners to become a medical practice that dishes out pharmaceuticals or other forms of control (for immense economic profit) is deeply troubling, although individual cases can be made for medication. The failure to differentiate between the two forms of practice is just that. A failure.

Although Vince was a psychiatrist (and went on to become head of psychiatry in two Toronto hospitals) he understood the limitations of his profession, and he incorporated holistic concepts of health care and harm reduction into his practice.* He thought far beyond the confines mandated by traditional models of psychiatry. Therapy with him saved part of my life.

After my rape, part of my work with Vince did involve making a decision to take antidepressants. I resisted for a long time, but I had barely slept for two years. I'd get a night in once in a while, skim the surface of sleep, but I averaged two to three hours a night. I spent the rest of the time thrashing, reading or watching TV, listening to the city and pitching from my skin if the wind caught my drapes, a neighbour used the incinerator, my sheets rustled, or lovers or fighters met noisily in the park behind my apartment building.

I went to work every day. Operated, coped, but in a dissociative state, eyes dry and scratchy, heart leaking. I could fall asleep okay, especially in the blue embrace of a quarter of a Valium, carefully bitten in half and then half again. It's a lovely fall, Valium, blissful moments between life and sleep. I remember it still, that free-falling into sleep. And then bolting awake at the witching hour with bloody pieces of heart in my mouth, adrenalin gushing, toothpicks in eyes, someone is here, somewhere, wake up wake up. And then I do and it's okay, it's just the fridge growling, just a door closing, just a knife placed on the pillow against my cheek. More blue, but it doesn't take and then new panic that I will oversleep, be late, screw up, and just as I swallow my heart back to centre and drift off, the clock radio comes on and jolts me into the day, and I am exhausted and full of the drug, and I read the paper, eat and go to work.

You can only take so much of this.

I have an exquisite intolerance for drugs. I know this because I came of age in the seventies, in that moment before drug experimentation became abuse, those few years when young women could have sex for pleasure and without negative consequences—just like men—and you could save enough in a year to hitchhike without fear and with joy across the country or through Europe. I was part of all of that. I did it all. I am frustrated with the useless doctrine that drugs are not glamorous or do

* Harm reduction models of health care are most common in the areas of drug and alcohol addiction and imply a holistic approach to illness that does not separate physical, emotional and psychological symptoms.

not make you feel good. The problem with drugs is that they are exactly that. They are modern-day idols, false gods, phantoms that seduce you with pleasure. They relieve pain, sadness, boredom. They can invoke brilliance and goodwill. What's not to like? But there is a catch. Drugs also present castle-in-Spain delusions, beautiful lies. They are agents of apathy. They will abscond with your day, pilfer tomorrow, rewrite yesterday, thieve curiosity, usurp energy. It's a package deal. Drug use is like a loan, a debt against your life. Addiction is the mortgage.

Drug use softened the edges of my life in ways that I often did not appreciate. Small amounts caused my body to attack me with headache, exhaustion or nausea, which meant I couldn't function at work or attend classes. Still, I was enamoured with the lifestyle, the glamour, the excitement, the bad boys, the bright girls and good music, the wild rush of it all. And I managed to navigate between both worlds for a while. Many of us did in our youth. Many died or now live burdened by addiction, trapped in their lives. I have never been certain what separated us.

So here I was, older, smarter and raped. Without joy or rest. A man I trusted was offering me drugs, and I had said no for two years, fearful of addiction, mindful of the stigma and the dangers attached to antidepressant medication. But the water was at my head and rising, and nothing was any fun any more and finally I said yes. I tried a number of treatments and settled on trazodone, which is an anti-anxiety medication that acts primarily on insomnia. I still take it today, more than a decade later. Every few years I panic, shamed by my addiction, fearful of accumulated side effects, and I decide to get clean, but then I remember what it used to be like and the fear is too great. I'm not going back there to insomnia, night terror, anxiety. So every night I take a quarter of one. I bite a pill in half and then half again. And if I am jerked awake, I take a little more and I sleep.

Although blood tests indicate there is no buildup of the drug in my system, and a psychopharmacologist I consulted assured me that my dosage is so low I might as well take a placebo, I have developed a twitch or two in my face and hands. But no one ever says anything, putting it down to my naturally expressive ways.

No means nothing

19:

SINCE the early nineties, I've watched the flourishing of considerable mythology, even in the women's movement, regarding the No Means No legislation passed by the federal parliament in 1992, and its impact on women who file rape charges.* We like to believe that women's sexual histories aren't used against them any more, that this behaviour is a thing of the past. Well I'm here to tell you that no means nothing. Here's why.

Seaboyer and Gayme were a couple of accused rapists whose lawyers had Canada's rape-shield law struck down.** That law stated that a woman's sexual history could not be introduced as evidence of consent. In 1990 Seaboyer and Gayme, with the help of Louise Arbour and the Canadian Civil Liberties Association, argued that, under the Canadian Charter of Rights and Freedoms, their right to a fair trial would be compromised if the women's past sexual history could not be introduced at trial. They won. They won because one of the women who had been raped had previously worked in the sex trade. The other one knew her rapist. The minimal protection previously afforded women by the rape-shield law was removed. Guidelines were issued to supposedly curb the judge's discretion under this decision but they in fact widened access and reinforced rape myths, which allowed defence lawyers greater latitude to introduce a woman's sexual history into a court of law.

* Officially known as Bill C-49, the No Means No legislation defined consent for the first time ever. It includes a lengthy preamble that sets out its purposes in terms of protecting women's equality rights.
** The rape-shield law had barred cross-examination on the sexual histories of raped women (except in certain circumstances!) and had been on the books only since 1982.

Criminal Code
PART VIII OFFENCES AGAINST THE PERSON AND REPUTATION
Assaults

Evidence of
complainant's sexual
activity

276. (1) In proceedings in respect of an offence under section 151, 152, 153, 155 or 159, subsection 160(2) or (3) or section 170, 171, 172, 173, 271, 272 or 273, evidence that the complainant has engaged in sexual activity, whether with the accused or with any other person, not admissible to support an inference that, by reason of the sexual nature of that activity, the complainant

(*a*) is more likely to have consented to the sexual activity that forms the subject-matter of the charge; or

(*b*) is less worthy of belief.

Idem

(2) In proceedings in respect of an offence referred to in subsection (1), no evidence shall be adduced by or on behalf of the accused that the complainant has engaged in sexual activity othe

Meaning of
"consent"

273.1 (1) Subject to subsection (2) and subsection 265(3), "consent" means, for the purposes of sections 271, 272 and 273, the voluntary agreement of the complainant to engage in the sexual activity in question.

Where no
consent
obtained

(2) No consent is obtained, for the purposes of sections 271, 272 and 273, where

(a) the agreement is expressed by the words or conduct of a person other than the complainant;

Portions of the Rape Shield and No Means No legislation

Political women revolted. They lobbied then minister of justice Kim Campbell to stop the insanity.* Campbell knew an election wouldn't be too far away and consulted with other academic and legal feminists to draft counter-legislation. They called it No Means No. Initially it stated that the responsibility was on the rapist to prove in a court of law that he had full, conscious, sober, willing, go-ahead, yes-this-will-be-fun consent from the woman involved. But by the time our members of Parliament got through with it, the bill was considerably altered to state that the rapist had to establish that *in his honest belief* the woman

* In 1993 Kim Campbell served for three months as Canada's first (and only) woman prime minister.

had consented. He must also show that he took "reasonable steps" to ascertain consent—which could be radical if women were defining what was reasonable instead of their rapists and if the definition were applied appropriately. And if there were justice.

Instead, we're right back to where we began. The woman's word against the rapist's. Only now it's worse because we've got Seaboyer and Gayme, which struck down the rape-shield law, giving rapists' lawyers even clearer shots at introducing sexual history than previously existed. Get it? Believe me, any defence lawyer worth the cost of a law-school diploma gets it and will find a way to use it.

In my opinion the only thing that the No Means No legislation accomplished was to influence public thinking about sexual assault. It educated us a little about the horrors women endure when we report our rapes. But it was not successful in terms of stopping the use of a woman's sexual history in court; it only added a few more hurdles the defence has to surmount. No Means No is not much—and yet we had to fight to get it. In terms of actually changing anything, ask yourself this: Why do 90 per cent of women who are sexually assaulted still choose not to report?

A FEW years after this turn of events, my friend Kelly called and asked if I would speak to a friend of hers who had been raped by two men whose trial was about to begin. The friend's name was Maya.* She was a very young, Black single mom who lived in subsidized housing and had plans to pursue a career in L.A. or New York as soon as she completed her diploma in fashion design. Maya was smart, talented, beautiful. Her look was glam rock/punk. She understood that presentation was everything, though, and for court made a conservative, three-piece black suit which she mixed with a few cotton shirts.

The rapes had taken place in her bedroom. Her child was asleep in the next room. She had invited two male friends in to smoke some dope after they drove her home from a local bar called Sneaky Dees. The guys were holding the dope and had made the offer. She knew them well

---

* I've changed her name to protect her identity.

enough to say yes and feel okay about it. Once inside her apartment, she sent the babysitter home, got high, chatted for a while and called it a night. The men raped her on her bed before they left. Terrified that her daughter would wake up, Maya did not cry out, although she resisted and repeatedly pleaded with them to stop. She sat alone until dawn, took her child to daycare and called the police. They believed her and laid charges against the two men Maya had thought were her friends.

In preparation for the trial, Maya sought assistance from the TRCC. She was assigned a counsellor who committed to supporting her through trial. By the time the court date rolled around, the counsellor had stopped returning her calls and Maya was terribly afraid of what was about to happen. I get a lot of phone calls from women in similar situations. Whenever I lecture, I am approached by at least one woman who is seeking assistance. I never say no. I dive in. It can be problematic, exhausting. Especially when there are no services to refer them to, which is often the case.

I had worked for years with the women at the rape crisis centre. The woman counselling Maya had been a student of mine. I was confident that given all of my power, politics and righteousness, a call from me would get the support process back on track. It didn't. Neither did the second or third calls. None were returned to Maya or myself. By now I really liked Maya, and she was my friend's friend and all alone, and so I accompanied her to court and called her at night and told her not to cry too much. I was also interested. Rape trials are fascinating spectacles, though predictable. Since my own, I had monitored dozens.

Each accused rapist had a lawyer. As they should. Maya had the Crown and the investigating officer. Neither had told her much, certainly not what to expect. Only that she must tell her story, answer questions and leave. The first thing the rapists' lawyers did was to request a dismissal as the poor guys had been forced to wait an inordinate amount of time (one year) for their day in court, and as per their Charter rights, justice must be done in a timely fashion, so would the judge please throw the whole thing out and let these men get on with their lives? The judge said no. They often say yes.

Then Maya was on the stand. Her single parent status; her economic status; her designing career; her rock-star associates; her late night partying; her invitation to the lads to come on up, smoke dope, drink wine; the presence of her child in the next room; her relationship with a friend of the accused; the name of the bar they had been at and the music played; the fact that she had not screamed, fought, resisted enough or called the police immediately; or suffered any bruising, bleeding or other physical harm were used to discredit and malign her by both lawyers. Neither the judge nor the Crown objected. In the halls that afternoon and the next morning, I approached the Crown to suggest that she lead expert evidence that would supply the judge with a definition of sexual assault that included Maya's reactions and excluded her behaviour before or after the crime. She didn't exactly tell me to fuck off, but on the next day she ignored me completely.

In their testimony, both men swore that Maya had said yes. They were found not guilty. The judge believed that they believed that Maya had consented to their charms. I cornered the Crown and asked why a case like this would ever come to trial when clearly it was a no-win-for-Maya situation. She told me to fuck off and walked away. A year later, I was reading the newspaper and there was Maya with her designs spread out over two pages of the *Toronto Star*. "Creative Success in L.A.!" the headlines announced.

After the trial, Maya moved her daughter and her talent to California, where her work caught the attention of an internationally renowned rock star. He hired her to design his costumes for his last tour. She even went with him.

Which is all to say that there is life and glamour and success after rape and that you can't keep a good woman down.

⁜

Maybe a foreign city will help

20:

WE didn't have books when we were kids. My mother subscribed to magazines, though. I took to reading them, scouring them for information, any information, for escape, for allusions to sex. There was a short story that appeared, in several incarnations, in these magazines. A beautiful woman, not so young anymore and with a secret, a past, a broken heart, saves all of her money from her waitressing job and moves to a big city where she finds a high-paying job, adventure and love before it is too late. I loved that story. In 1989 I lived it when I moved to Montreal.

I am a Toronto girl through and through, make no mistake. Although I have lived in other places, I believe that no city can surpass mine in art, progressive civic legislation and diversity. But Montreal! Montreal cannot be compared or contrasted to other cities in North America for there is not another one like it in pride, in culture, history and style.

People *look* at each other in Montreal and flirt casually. And who could not watch and appreciate such women, especially the old dolls in the east end where I lived—their hair pincurled to perfection, their fur collars for everyday and the shopping carts they pushed home like plows, through snowbanks and ice, baguettes flopping, and God help you if you got in their way. Hadn't they birthed five, seven, thirteen children and raised them all? These streets, this city, distinct and winding, were theirs and they hadn't forgotten the struggles that are still waged to maintain their culture. They remembered.

I moved there ostensibly to work at the National Film Board (NFB) although I had no promise of a job, just the idea that I would. I had worked for years in the promotion and distribution of Canadian independent film, and a friend who was an NFB board member made a few phone calls on my behalf. I began as a publicist, moved to marketing and made my way into the jackpot, the motherlode: Studio D. Which was my plan. Studio D was the women's studio of the NFB, famous for winning Oscars and other prestigious awards for documentaries made by women about women. My extra secret mission: I wanted them to support my proposal for a film about Jane Doe.

Kathleen Shannon, the studio's founder, was still there when I arrived. She was semi-retired and attended programming meetings where she knitted and nodded, each motion of her head signifying the death or survival of another woman's political and artistic vision. She was a brilliant person, beautiful and lonely, who made many wise decisions, but as she grew older, her political and artistic concepts seemed blurred by personal tragedies and disappointments. (She found some peace living in the mountains of British Columbia until cancer claimed her. She died in 1996, apparently forgotten by many whose work she made possible.)

I was very happy working at Studio D. Although I felt the visual style and general content of their films to be soft or dated, I worked with women I grew to love. The feminism they practised was liberal in nature but was not diluted to appease those who were uncomfortable with feminists, or for funders who feared that men were being left out. And every once in a while something radical and extraordinary was produced. And celebrated.

Known affectionately as the "jewel in the crown" of Canadian filmmaking, Studio D gave unprecedented access to women artists and produced films that made progressive statements on subjects ranging from nuclear armament to sexuality. More than jewels, the films were a gold mine on which the NFB prospered. I was privileged to work there in its last days, for it exists no longer. It was disbanded in 1994 by new management whose revisionist thinking was that equity in art, and indeed in all representation and cultural work, had been achieved, and therefore the existence of a studio devoted to women's film was discriminatory.

But in 1990 there were still a few treasures to be seen. A series of fifteen five-minute films, called Five Feminist Minutes, was made by first-time women filmmakers from across the country. It was the brain-child of Rina Fraticelli, who was briefly Kathleen Shannon's successor to the Studio D throne. Her idea was to hold a contest, put out a call for proposals for short films by first-time filmmakers about a variety of women's issues. The prize for fifteen winners was ten grand in cash and lab costs. The result is a visual ride across the country and into female gender.

It's bumpy and exhilarating and encompasses dancing vulvas, murder, puppets and whoring. Whenever these fifteen films are screened, women rise cheering from their seats.

One of my tasks at the studio was to arrange a benefit screening for Montreal's rape crisis centre. I cut a deal with the local downtown rep house to show the series on one of their dark days in winter. It was a huge, old theatre that could not hold the mass of women who lined the impossibly cold street for hours to pay the few bucks admission. The raucous laughter and applause from the enormous crowd reflected lost revenue potential for the cinema owner. He summoned me into his office, away from the adoring crowds, and announced that the price had changed and I owed him a percentage of the gate versus the flat rate we had negotiated.

As he spoke, I was being called on to the stage to take my bows as the event organizer. I informed him that I was going down there to announce his thieving ways and that I would suggest that women in the audience rip the seats out of the floor and throw them onto the stage. He said I must have misunderstood him and offered me some compli-mentary passes. I missed the standing ovation that ended the night. Unfortunately, Five Feminist Minutes is no longer in distribution.*

I mended a lot in Montreal. Just like in my mother's magazine stories, glamour and love and work did that for me. Finally though, I had to come home. After almost three years, it was clear that if I was going to stay in Montreal, I would have to upgrade my passable French and become bilingual, and wear proper boots and a parka in the winter. But

---

* Individual films can be rented or purchased from artist-run distribution centres in Ontario and Alberta. One of the segments of the reel, *We're Talking Vulva* by Shawna Dempsey, Lorri Millan and Tracy Traeger, was screened in the United States and became a subject of Senator Jesse Helms's censorship crusade. It was also banned in Calgary, Alberta.

my lawsuit, now four years old, was heating up. I also missed my sister and my parents and my other Toronto family. Before I left Montreal, but after I had quit the Film Board, I submitted my request for funding to develop a Jane Doe script, and I received a small grant, which felt huge at the time.

Back home I was Jane Doe again. Raped again. Being Jane has always interested me, but the rape victim thing continued to grate, to tear the scabs away. I began shopping around for a new therapist. I wanted to see a woman, confident that my work with Vince was complete, although I did see him a few more times. A female therapist and I had done some good work in Montreal, and I was interested in continuing a feminist model of therapy that allowed for greater depth and broader under-standing/understanding of broads.

Some of the women I interviewed for the position of my therapist made me sad. If they bothered to call me back at all, they were nervous about the directions I wanted to pursue, or that I would even presume to have a direction. One even told me she didn't like me very much. When it comes to discussing your rape in a therapeutic relationship, there is a standard approach that commonly results in a form of re-victimization. It sort of begins and ends with helping the woman, who is a "victim," get over the apparently never-ending damages she has experienced. The therapist defines the damages for you based on her own socialized and learned response, which is locked into limited aca-demic and clinical understanding of the crime. Some of this thinking is valid to a degree, but the whole set-up is not very conducive to new explorations of women's experience of rape and other sexual assaults. I couldn't put up with that approach.

I persevered until I found the right woman. Two women, actually. The first was Alys Murphy, who is a goddess. She charged thirty bucks for ninety minutes and was free to women in conflict with the law or who worked in the sex trades—although, as Alys soon found out, you can forget about women in the sex trades not paying. Payment up front is part of their code.

She had wrangled some free office space and was committed to pro-viding economically accessible therapy. Alys had worked as a counsellor in rape crisis centres and with women in prison for ten years before she established her own practice. After a few visits, it was clear to us both that we were becoming friends and we each preferred that relationship to a professional one. We made the transition and remain friends and allies to this day.

Another friend of mine then referred me to her own therapist, Julia Grey.* The problem with Julia was that she charged what for me was a lot of money. Immediately after the criminal conviction of the man who raped us, the investigating officers suggested that we, the five women involved, file for criminal injuries compensation. I didn't trust anything the police were saying and decided I would wait. Shortly after that, I filed my civil suit with LEAF and felt that filing a compensation claim was not ethical and would be used against me. But now I was out of work, borderline poor and feeling lost and crazy. So since there is no statute of limitations under the legislation, I decided to file.

The compensation board makes financial awards of up to twenty-five thousand dollars. You pretty much have to be dead to get the full award (I know of one woman who did. She was in a coma for three days after surviving a hammer attack by the man who raped her). The average award for rape by a stranger is ten to fifteen thousand.

My case was heard by one woman who decided I should have ten thousand dollars and an additional five thousand dollars in therapy fees that would be billed directly to the board. My memory of the hearing is not a kind one. A man in military costume greeted me and asked me to be seated. I was then called into a large boardroom with windows facing the elevator, which allowed anyone travelling in the building to get a good look at you. There was no Kleenex, water, tea or sympathy provided. The adjudicator was passionless, removed, and required me to retell, to relive the details of my rape verbally, despite the written accounts I had already submitted and the police reports she had on file.

Patti McGillicuddy accompanied me, and my experience went relatively smoothly. Which is not always the way, as the legislation has since been radically changed to ensure that the perpetrator is notified of your claim. He is supplied with a copy of your submission for damages and

* Another changed name.

permitted to witness the proceedings from behind a one-way mirror. Any testimony you give can be used against you in a court of law. Any judgment may not be used against him, or viewed with prejudice or as an admission of guilt. The small window of opportunity the Criminal Injuries Board used to represent—the chance to get back on your feet financially, or just to be heard and believed—that little window that was opened for victims of crime is broken, and it's closing fast.

In my case, I told my story, went home and waited. About six weeks later, I was notified by mail of the compensation board's decision. I did the rape-victim dog-and-pony show and got my money and therapy fees and began my relationship with Julia Grey. She challenged and supported me in my quest to find myself, to better understand my work and my world. With her help, I finally left Johnny. I was productive, making friends with my pain, moving through it, leaving it behind. And then she made a mistake. More about that later.

The right to take the police to court

21:

MEANWHILE, on March 31, 1989, Judge Walter Henry ruled, with great fanfare, that *Jane Doe v. the Metropolitan Toronto Police Force* could proceed to trial. I had a legal and meritorious cause of action to sue the police for negligence and Charter violations in the investigation of my rape. The decision set a legal precedent as it meant that police officers could be held liable for their actions in the investigation of a crime. Any crime. Prior to *Jane Doe*, it was seen to be entirely within the scope of police discretion to do what they had to do to catch a criminal. Well the moaning that went on after that decision—you'd have thought the police budget had been questioned. Coppers across the country prophesied crime escalation because police now had to second-guess the way they conducted an investigation for fear of being sued; lawyers bellowed about floodgates opening. Some predicted that everyone ever arrested, raped, murdered or ticketed would file similar lawsuits.

When Judge Henry pronounced that in his considered opinion my case was feasible and could proceed to trial, he added kindly, "Good luck, you're going to need it." Faster than the writ could be dropped, the police lawyers—members of the Bay Street firm Weir & Foulds— appealed his decision and the matter was kicked upstairs to the Ontario Divisional Court.

You know how in those courtroom-drama movies and TV shows the lawyer is as distressed as the client when the case is appealed to a higher court? Well, that's not really accurate. It is every lawyer's goal to argue in front of appellate courts, all the way up to the Supreme Court. It means you have arrived, been presented, debuted. Add to that the opportunity to argue and possibly establish new law under the Charter, and you've got a lawyer's dream come true.

When the appeal to Judge Henry's ruling was heard in 1991, three judges reinforced his decision that I had a solid, viable (legal even) cause of action and that I could finally proceed to trial. I was in the courtroom of course, and while I couldn't understand much of what they were saying, the jubilant faces and warm embraces of my lawyers communicated victory. As a result of the decision, it is possible to sue the police for their actions in the investigation of a crime. But like the judge said, good luck getting a judgment in your favour.

The next stage in my legal odyssey was called "discovery" and, with stops and starts, it took seven years to travel through it.

BECAUSE I was involved in a threesome with LEAF and my lawyer, Mary Cornish, it took three times as long as it usually would to make a decision, file a motion or prepare a brief. Multiply that by the number of LEAF board members who were located across the country—five or six—and there is another reason why *Jane Doe v. the Metropolitan Toronto Police Force* took so long. The triangle was the cause of what evolved into my inability to continue to work with LEAF. The relationship was made even more complicated by LEAF's mandate, which was to represent women as a group, not Jane Doe the individual woman. In a normal client-solicitor relationship, directions come from the client (at least in principle). The women of LEAF took my case on without analyzing the muddied ground on which our triangle stood. As a result, the legal code of ethics, which holds above all else (at least on paper and on TV) the sanctity of the client-solicitor relationship, was violated.

I had assumed that I had control over my case. But it turned out that any decision to proceed with specific strategies had to be discussed and signed off on by the LEAF board of directors, or its legal committee, who would convene with Mary Cornish and me at regular intervals. I found these meetings to be excruciating ordeals. Often one or more board members participated via the telephone, their input ignored, talked over or heard as gospel. Which was pretty much how I was received, except for the gospel part. I tried to always bring someone

Court lets rape victim sue police for 'neglect'

Continued from page A1

who were at risk less important than catching the balcony intruder.

☐ Potential victims weren't warned because officers, allegedly accepting an unfair stereotype, believed women would be hysterical if told of the serial rapist.

Cornish argued that the failure to issue a warning violated Section 7 of the Charter of Rights, guaranteeing security of person; Section 15, guaranteeing sexual equality, and Section 28, requiring Charter rights to apply equally to men and women.

Yesterday, police lawyer Bryan Finlay argued that to sustain a claim of negligence the police conduct must be proven irresponsible, arbitrary or unreasonable.

Jane Doe and her lawyers failed to show any evidence of such

could have driven the rapist other areas of Metro, poli opted for a quiet investigation sulting in 〜〜〜's arrest in 198

"The decision not to warn w a policy," Finlay said, to the fr quent interruptions of appe judges.

"You can't convict the poli for making that policy decision

Greg Richards, another lawy arguing for the police, said Ch ter arguments had no place in t matter. Officers were in no w responsible for what happened Jane Doe, and their conduct c not place her at an increased ri of rape, Richards said. The pi pose of the Charter is to prote people from state interventic not to protect people from ea other, he noted.

"The plaintiff must demo strate that state action gave r to her injury," Richards said.

Three Supreme Court judg

Rape victim can sue police, ju

By Lisa Priest
TORONTO STAR

Rape victim Jane Doe can take Metro po-

"It may open a floodgate," said Christie Jefferson, executive director of Women's Legal Education and Action Fund, a

of the rapist.

She is seeking damages for pain a fering, inconvenience and loss of with me, a friend, a supporter, who could witness what was going on and with whom I could debrief after the meetings.*

It's important to provide a backdrop and some history to explain the problems that developed between the women of LEAF and myself, problems that escalated over the years and eventually led to our unfriendly parting of ways. The legal barriers that LEAF used to keep me distanced from my own case were not of LEAF's design but originated in the male legal culture. While they and other women had made significant advances in reforming that culture, they did not hold the power to define either the terms and conditions by which reform might be attained, or what areas of law might be in need of it. I cannot imagine the difficulties of attempting to be feminist and to survive in legal culture at the same time. I did not have that burden.

LEAF lawyers engaged in the battle of my lawsuit for reasons and in ways different from mine. Sometimes opposite to mine. Within the structure of LEAF's membership were additional political divisions. While primarily liberal or reform-from-within oriented, LEAF also included radical and socialist feminists, which resulted in much disagreement about how to do the work. Feminists and other progressive or revolutionary groups often have trouble forming a true consensus. Within LEAF, I am not sure if there was consensus at all. Which affected me deeply. While it would be easy to say this was the "fault" of the LEAF women, such divisiveness is really a predictable and natural stage in political development and a direct outcome of standing in opposition to power. Since its formation, LEAF has been continuously threatened with cuts to its funding. During my time with them, they were almost completely defunded, and they continue to face the constant possibility of their demise. Consequently, the LEAF board and staff made decisions and chose directions with caution, aware that a misstep could be used against them.

I was not party to this reality when LEAF signed on to work with me.

---

* Two women worked most often with me to develop my case and to assist me in understanding legal codes, language and ramifications. They were Elizabeth Pickett and Patti McGillicuddy. I cannot stress enough the importance of the support, wisdom and friendship they lavished on me during the twelve years I was involved with the legal system—and which they continue to lavish on me today.

They forgot that I was the client, and they separated my rape from me to use as artillery in their battle. I forgot that there is a cult or culture and language of the law that places itself apart from and above others. Above me. I forgot that I did not belong.

LEAF women were attached to achieving equality through constitutional law and had achieved a bit of power through that. They did not have a lot of other political experience and were not living life as I was. As a result of the anti-violence movement, I had some credibility to talk about violence. But I was only one person and we were not a solid or equal alliance, and mistakes came out of that. Mistakes rooted in serious differences of interest—politically and personally.

IN 1990 a litigator named Charlie Campbell was hired by LEAF as co-counsel and to advise us on aggressive strategies in dealing with the police, an area in which neither Mary nor any of the LEAF women had experience. In the early eighties Charlie represented the family of Albert Johnson, a man with a psychiatric history who was shot to death in his home by police after he waved his garden hoe in their direction. Johnson was a Black man. His family settled out of court for undisclosed damages. Although Mary and LEAF were crackerjack Charter and labour experts, they thought it wise to seek testosterone-based co-counsel when swimming with police sharks. I agreed.

I have rarely spoken with Charlie Campbell, but he has a good reputation. When we met, he was distant in a traditional lawyerly way and wasn't great on eye contact or including me in the conversation, although the young man who worked with him was. When it became evident to me that LEAF was not always acting in my best interests, I approached Charlie for advice, since he was also my lawyer but had less of a political tie to LEAF than Mary did. I travelled from Montreal to Toronto to meet with him. In his office he informed me that he was accountable to me and to LEAF and could not confer with me about my case in their absence. Then he walked out of the room. I stumbled from his office, cut to the quick, furious that he hadn't made this clear on the phone or in writing before I had made the trip to see him.

Shortly after that meeting, Charlie called me to say (unclearly) that he was on a shortlist to represent the police in another civil action. Since my case presented a potential conflict for him, would I consider granting him a moral dispensation that would allow him to represent both parties— me in my case, the police in theirs? Shades of Mary Jane Mossman! When I suggested he approach LEAF for such an exemption, he clarified that the decree must come also from me, his client. My reaction in these situations is to give no quarter but to try to take a relatively high road. I responded that perhaps Charlie was giving me more power than I held and that I could not take responsibility for his political decisions.

Charlie withdrew from my case but was passed over as police counsel. (That prize went to Todd Archibald, the Crown attorney in the criminal trial of the man who raped me. The police won their case, whatever it was. No big surprise there.*) I ran into Charlie a few times after that, most notably at an anti-censorship forum I organized. Although he cites his brief involvement in my case as one of the many progressive credentials on his resumé, he never says hello. Many years later, during final preparations for my civil trial, my new lawyer showed me a memo addressed to Mary and LEAF, signed by Charlie, advising them to reconsider the pursuit of my case.

THE reasons for my rocky relationship with LEAF kept piling up. In the early nineties LEAF intervened in an infamous case known as the Butler Decision. Their argument, formulated by Catherine McKinnon, an American feminist legal guru, was that pornography promoted, and was directly linked to, the murder, rape and degradation of women and must be eliminated. The Butler Decision, successfully argued by LEAF members, is used today by customs officials at the Canadian border to defend their right to seize any materials they deem pornographic and to initiate criminal charges.

I was one of many feminists who were alarmed by the presumption of such authority and unpersuaded about the direct linkage between violence and pornography. The granting of such powers to censor is discriminatory, liable to abuse and a threat to artistic and individual freedom of expression. In Canada, criminal laws were already in place to

* Todd Archibald is now a judge.

address violent and child pornography. Education and the production of porn that does not debase female sexuality make such regressive, Big Brother decisions as Butler unnecessary. These are old arguments in an old fight that continues in its umpteenth round with the potential of remaining forever unresolved. Why, if I thought that burning *Hustler* magazines would have prevented my rape, or any rape, I'd set old Larry Flynt on fire myself.

Who is looking instead at the images of women as unpaid or under-paid workers, domestic chattel, clothes hangers, multi-taskers, victims—without individuality, economic security or sexual identity? As proof that the power the Butler Decision conferred could be abused, the very first material seized by customs officials as criminally pornographic was a lesbian text on sexuality. Followed by a feminist book by long-time anti-violence activist Andrea Dworkin titled *Woman Hating*. Meanwhile, the murder and rape of women has escalated. And here I was, as were many feminists, fighting amongst ourselves about dirty pictures as opposed to collectively addressing negative representations that are historical, systemic and sanctioned by Church and State.

Another critique levelled against LEAF by women's communities at this time was that although it claimed to operate on behalf of the whole category of woman, it declined to consult with a broad spectrum of women, especially Native women, women of colour and lesbians in its deliberations.

While Butler and LEAF played itself out on a national or macro level, I was interacting with them on a micro (miniskirted) level that was per-sonal. And personally, I was having a hard time. I labour now to recall it all. I prefer to remember LEAF in victory, to include the women of LEAF in what was accomplished, to understand the factors and influ-ences that drove all of us at that time and to learn what we might have done differently. On my part, I should have dumped them a lot earlier. On theirs, they misrepresented their abilities and intentions. With the exception of Helena Orton, who was my conduit to the ruling Leaflets, I was generally perceived as a fly in the ointment, a thorn in their side, a pain in their collective ass. I was the necessary but unsightly pivot upon which their case swung. Which is not to say that they did not often find me amusing, challenging and occasionally even bright, but it was convenient for the lawyers of LEAF to consider me as an impediment to their work. I was the flighty younger sister who could not be satisfied no matter how many times you lent her your clothes or what you did for her—she just wanted more. And it wasn't personal as far as they were concerned.

But it was about class. About their power in a client-solicitor relationship, as well as socially and economically. When added to the difficulties I've already discussed, it became easy for LEAF to categorize our problems as all about me. (No doubt the women of LEAF would not agree with this interpretation.) As time went on, the negligence or failure to warn argument overcame the political or sexual discrimination argument in the strategies LEAF was pursuing in *Jane Doe*. I believe this conservatism on their part resulted in an internal decision to pursue the piece they thought they could win in order to establish their legitimacy and to create a legal precedent. Very few people think it's worth it to make a purely political argument in court, which is what I wanted to do. I was the one who didn't fit, not LEAF (although there were legal feminists who saw it my way). I cared more about the political integrity and content of my case than its winnability and made that clear from the beginning—in writing, and many times.

But LEAF did know that our relationship was skewed and that (if they were going to continue to receive government funding) they could not deliver on bargains they had struck with me about the direction of my case. To be fair, I believe they wanted to deliver, but any naïveté that I brought to my legal proceedings—and I initially brought a lot—was exceeded by their ingenuousness, intended or not. To be clear, I got a lot more out of them at that time than I was going to get from any Bay Street legal practitioner. So how could it have been different? Better? Certainly we all wanted, tried, hoped to accomplish something. Were we blinded by light, hope, dreams, greed—what? Something prevented LEAF from seeing the fundamental source of our problems. Maybe they were completely confused, too. Maybe they thought, "Shit, we've messed this up!" Maybe they thought, "Okay, let's try and negotiate between representing Jane the individual and the collectivity of women;

after all, it's impossible to represent all women and we are under the gun regarding money and resources. If we lose, this one case could wipe us out. If we lose, we're liable for costs."

But I never knew what they were thinking. We never sat down and said, "Here are the things we have to agree on. Here are the implications. This is how we will operate." They idealistically signed a contract with me that said I was to give direction. I tried to address it all once. I asked them, and they agreed, to convene a meeting of women from across the country to brainstorm about the direction of my case and legal strategies. Unfortunately we never got past the first point on the agenda, which was to determine roles and responsibilities.

As time passed and the legal bills grew, LEAF, like any good manager, decided it might be time for some cost-cutting and a new business plan. It came in the form of a decree from the president of the legal committee (and on her firm's letterhead). It stated that because of depletions in LEAF's litigation funds, it might be "necessary to advise your counsel (Mary Cornish) at some point that LEAF can accept no further responsibilities for fees. At that time, your counsel will have to make a decision as to whether she is willing to continue with the case on a pro bono basis. If she is not, LEAF will of course make every effort to assist you in making alternative arrangements, but obviously no guarantees can be provided." I could hear the shot as it whizzed past my head. I was being warned. I couldn't believe it, but wait—there was more: "As you know the relationship between you and LEAF has not always been an easy one …. [W]e agreed to indemnify you if costs were awarded against you by a court …. this commitment makes LEAF liable for such costs …. This may have serious implications for the approach LEAF will be able to take in your case." She ended by writing this was a painful realization for them and that I better get in there and sign a new deal about the liability and obligations LEAF would have to me. Which I did. Although it never came down to LEAF actually backing out on me, the threat had its effect. I was never able to regain any sense of power or control in my relationship with LEAF. The next three years were the continuation of a long waiting game without a clear end ever in sight.

After the judges ruled that we could proceed, we began the pretrial discovery process in which each side gains access to the evidence and witnesses of the other's case. But my lawsuit went into some kind of legal limbo, and I didn't know what to do. I would get letters from LEAF women I'd never met; by now the board had changed its membership entirely, except for Helena Orton. She took me for lunch one day and suggested sincerely and with affection that if I wanted to drop the case, she would help me. I remember telling Helena that I would drop dead before I dropped the case. I remember marvelling that we could be so far apart in understanding each other and yet so close in our mutual regard.*

I HAVE to stress here that becoming Jane Doe and engaging in this long legal battle, sometimes with my allies, never meant that I hung around just being Jane Doe. For most of the twelve years of the legal wars, being Jane was about third on my list of things to do, although "she" was never far away. My work as a teacher, a culture and community worker and in public relations helped me to be a savvier Jane.

Being Jane Doe assisted me with the other things I did. There was pain and despair (also part of being Jane Doe) but I was never bored, always interested, and I began to find myself again. Loneliness tinted things, anguish and rage stormed about me. But I was living my life. It often felt normal.

---

* Helena Orton died of cancer in 1997, leaving a husband and two daughters whom she adored. Her work on my case, and as a litigator and scholar, is reflective of a brilliant mind and a sweet nature. The Helena Orton Memorial Scholarship is awarded to women working in the areas of equality rights and workplace issues.

A Jane Doe who couldn't live with it

22:

IN 1991 I read about another Jane Doe, another woman who had been raped and who claimed anonymity as she spoke out. Her story began in 1989 and ran concurrent with mine, although it ended sooner. This Jane was a little different. She had been raped by a police officer. And she worked as a prostitute. She wasn't asking for much, just an apology from the Toronto Police Services Board and an acknowledgement that she had been screwed. By the time I heard of her, I had secured the support of LEAF, the women's community in general and the media in my fight against the police. And it was still hard. Here was this other Jane, doing it all by herself and from a place that is so marginalized, so stigmatized, that it's seen as illegal. Even though prostitution is not. I am familiar with the political issues of women who work in the sex trades. I have friends who work there, and they have supported me in my work as Jane Doe. So I made a few calls and sent out the message that I admired and hoped to meet this other Jane.

She got in touch within a few days, and we made arrangements to get together. When we saw each other we both laughed. Fiona Stewart was dressed in sweats, her hair was pulled back in a ponytail and she had a fresh scrubbed face. I was wearing black, high heels and red lipstick. She looked like a librarian or someone's mom. I looked like—well I looked like the bad Jane.

Fiona came from an upper middle-class suburban family but had street credentials. In 1989, as a long-time housing activist who worked for the city, she had read the newspaper accounts of yet another Jane Doe, named Robin Gardner Voce, who charged two police officers with rape. After a police investigation into her claims, criminal charges were dropped, but the officers had to face a discreditable conduct hearing in front of an internal police tribunal. Robin Gardner Voce was found hanging in her parents' garage a week after she gave evidence against them, and after her death, the disciplinary action against the two officers was dropped. Despite the testimony of her father that she had not, would not, take her own life, and evidence that cast doubt on the coroner's reconstruction of the act, an inquest declared Robin's death a suicide, and the case was closed.

Robin's life remained an enigma; her unprosecuted rape and death linger still in the city's memory. Fiona decided that Robin would be more than that. At the time of Robin's death, Fiona was developing plans for a new housing collective for women and children who were fleeing abuse, and she decided to name the project the Robin Gardner Voce Non-Profit Homes. She set about organizing its funding with energy and determination. Fiona charmed, bullied and persuaded. She became close to Robin's parents. Fiona was laid off from her job with the city shortly after the ground for the building was broken, a victim of political funding cuts. She exhausted her savings quickly and found herself unable to pay her bills or find work. Recalling her limited success earning excellent money during university as a call girl, she decided to try it again.

Her past experience as a prostitute had been in another city, where she had been a highly paid worker who had clients referred to her whom she serviced in their homes or in hotels. Unfamiliar with the protocols and hierarchy of the Toronto sex trade, Fiona dressed up and ventured out onto the streets of Parkdale in the city's west end. Parkdale hookers are regularly harassed by police officers and are considered the lowest caste of prostitute socially and within their own community. The first john who picked Fiona up was an undercover police officer named Brian Whitehead who knew a good thing when he saw it and threatened Fiona with arrest and incarceration if she refused to have sex with him regularly and for free. They trysted several times at Fiona's house, always with menace and with increasing violence. After a few weeks, Fiona overcame her fear to report Sergeant Whitehead to his fellow police officers. Internal Affairs placed a wiretap on her phone, and Whitehead was arrested while in her home. But the Crown attorney decided that Fiona would not be a credible witness, and criminal charges were not laid.

A man named Bill McCormack was police chief then. He and his board were investigating the criminal activities of another police officer, Gordon Junger, who had been accused of running a prostitution ring to supplement his income. In the subsequent internal investigation, McCormack rolled the two cases together, and it became known as the Junger-Whitehead Affair. The ensuing scandal almost brought Toronto policing to its knees. But not quite. Never quite.

Fiona began receiving mysterious phone calls and visits to her home

Inquiry flays police integrity

'Serious mismanagement' shown in misconduct cases, report says

Officer keeps job despite guilty plea

Policeman used badge to pressure woman into sex, tribunal ruled

BY SALLY RITCHIE
Special to The Globe and Mail

transcript of the disciplinary h...
for then-Sergeant Brian Whit...

No more 'Junger deals,' police told

By Andrew Duffy
TORONTO STAR

Chief William McCormack and the Metro Police Services Board must act quickly to ensure there are "no more secret deals and no more sweetheart deals," the chairman of a provincial inquiry says.

Toronto lawyer Frank D'Andrea, co-author of a scathing report on mismanagement of the

Junger panel lays it on the line

Christie BLATCHFORD

late at night. She reported them, too. They were of such a nature that the police whisked her into protective custody and relocated her to a motel in Kingston, Ontario, a few hours down the highway from Toronto. She was not allowed to take her beloved dog. Afraid and alone, Fiona did what she knew best. She got out of Kingston and came back to Toronto and organized, which included going public through the media. She provided a political context that identified the larger picture of systemic vice and violence in policing, which she argued was what allowed officers like Junger and Whitehead to break the law. She framed the crimes committed against her as crimes of power further enforced by her identity as a sex trade worker, and his as an officer of the law. The shit hit the fan, but eventually it blew back on her. She was, after all, a whore. What exactly did she expect and from whom? How exactly do you rape a whore? How many police officers does it take? While none of this was precisely articulated, the media did not include her long-time community and political work in their stories.

I asked Fiona if she had considered a lawsuit, but she was quick to respond that all she wanted was an apology from Toronto's finest. Over the next few years, we became friends. She kept me updated on her story through telephone conversations when she, too, moved to Montreal for a while. Fiona was a wonderful woman, generous and bright. But police investigations can take a long time, and her economic condition continued to decline. She was traumatized by her experience and shamed by a police department that characterized her as a hustler. Her epilepsy, long under control, flared up. Efforts to manage the pain of her life with alcohol further exacerbated it. She could barely feed herself and her dog.

Attempts to find employment again as a housing advocate resulted in a few contracts, which then petered out. Around 1994 she turned again to prostitution. Largely ignored by the broader women's community, Fiona found support from sex trade workers who assisted her in establishing herself. But that track is often mined with drug use and dependency, and she suffered those work-related hazards. For a while drugs comforted her, as narcotics will do.

I appeared with her and other advocates in front of the Toronto Police Services Board to demand again the apology she was due. Although two of the members voted in favour of apologizing (Susan Eng and Laura Rowe), the board refused to acknowledge any of the crimes that had been committed against Fiona, from her repeated rape by a police officer to the anonymous death threats and subsequent relocation. Junger and Whitehead received conditional reprimands from the board (which basically translated as "Don't do that again or you'll really get it"). Junger resigned his position. Whitehead was demoted to constable but remained on duty until he retired with a full pension in the late nineties. What had initially been seen and reported as a criminal and moral scandal in policing, requiring broad and extensive operational change, was eventually reduced to the dilemma of a few bad apples, now corrected. Toronto cops remained tops.*

Fiona was found dead on the floor of her co-op on October 19, 1996. Her death was ruled to be the result of an epileptic seizure. There were narcotics in her system. She had arranged for her dog to be with friends that weekend. She was thirty-four years old.

Her memorial service was packed. Poets, politicians, musicians, co-workers and friends filled the community room of her co-op. Testimonials made us laugh and cry. Her mother was present for a while but grief overcame her. Police Chief Bill McCormack and the Police Services Board did not mark her passing. Two years later, I was asked to speak at the first anniversary of the opening of the Robin Gardner Voce Non-Profit Homes in Scarborough. Members planted a tree on their front lawn to honour Fiona. There was lots of food, and babies cried and played. Robin's father cried, too. The complex stands today as a testament to the lives of two extraordinary women.

---

* The absence of a civilian or external review mechanism for police wrongdoings results in the time-honoured tradition of police officers investigating themselves. The story and the lessons of Fiona Stewart and the Junger-Whitehead Affair have been disappeared not just within the institution of policing but also among activists and legal bodies who continue to seek police reform. For further information on Fiona's story visit www.walnet.org.

The damage done, and a new leaf

23:

YEARS passed. My case was still stuck in discovery in preparation for trial. The biggest reason for the delay was the police strategy to stall us, to make every request for notes and records seem impossible to fulfill. Their lawyers changed dates, cancelled meetings, took other cases to trial. The result was to successfully hold up the proceedings. My relationship with LEAF deteriorated to the point that we rarely spoke. It was like a failed marriage, neither party willing to pull the plug because of the children, not understanding that the kids were suffering the most. I finally realized that I had to find new legal representation. There was no big dust-up or confrontation. Our nine-year relationship ended in a telephone conversation I had with the new executive director of LEAF, a woman I had never met. I informed her that I no longer required LEAF's services, and I followed it up in writing. And that was it.*

I found my new lawyer, Sean Dewart, through my friend Rita Davies. Rita knew that my case had seen little movement between 1991 and 1996 and that I was distressed about it. Rita finds solutions to move situations forward. It's what she does best. If she doesn't have the information or skills necessary to move things along, she finds the person who does. It has made her a great leader. I worked for her when she was the executive director of the Toronto Arts Council, the city's arm's-length funding body for the arts. The government was planning to move the culture ministry away from its logical home in the biggest cultural centre in the country to the tourist zone of Niagara Falls. I was

---

* Well not quite. I received a letter from them shortly after requesting that they be reimbursed for all legal costs in the event that I won my lawsuit.

hired by Rita to coordinate a plan to stop them. We did. And we became friends. Mindful of my legal woes Rita invited a lawyer she knew, Frank Addario, to a dinner party I also attended, with the intention of asking his advice regarding my case. Frank is a superior lawyer who loves his job and has effectively litigated Charter and criminal cases that other lawyers wouldn't touch. (I was in court when he successfully defended artist Ely Langer against charges that his art was pornography, charges made possible by the advent of LEAF's Butler Decision.) He knew my case and asked what I needed. "New lawyers," I said. "Let me think about it," said Frank. "I'll call you. Would you like more wine?"

He called the next day and recommended Sean Dewart as a brilliant litigator and a personal friend who worked for a large firm (Blaney McMurtry) that could afford to commit to more pro bono cases.* Which meant that my legal costs, covered by LEAF to this point, would now be covered by them.

By this time I had come to realize that I was not likely to get a feminist political remedy through the legal system and the cost of trying had become emotionally and physically debilitating. LEAF lacked the expertise necessary to take my case through to trial. I needed a male Bay Street lawyer who was better equipped to deal with other male Bay Street lawyers in the pissing contest that is the law. I decided to stop pursuing Jane Doe as a political act, to step back and let the lawyers go at it.

I met Sean in his office. He was wearing shorts, a T-shirt and an earring. He needed a haircut. I figured he was about twenty-five. I was sure I used to babysit him. We sat down in a huge boardroom, and he asked me to describe my case. I thought, "What the hell," and it all came out: rape mythology, sexist practices leading to negligence and Charter violations, requiring system challenges and political remedies. Sean got it and he loved it. All of it. And I was back on.

I asked for his age (he was thirty-five), resumé and references, and then I asked why he wanted my case, why I should work with him (it was a trick question). "Your case is important," he said. "We'll make new law. I'll get you two hundred grand in two years." It took him three.

---

* From the Latin *pro bono publico*, or for the public good. Or in this case, for free, although in pro bono cases, all legal costs are recoverable if the case is successful.

He told me later that other deciding factors for him were that his spouse, Lori, would have killed him dead if he turned the case down and that I had the same unusual first and middle names as their three-year-old daughter, whom I came to know.

Sean had the passion and enthusiasm required to kick-start my civil case. He is the lawyer most responsible for the victory of Jane Doe. It helped that he inherited the brilliant legal groundwork laid by Mary Cornish and Susan Ursel. But finally, it was all about him. Sean is smart and funny and political. He's a bit of a snob, can fire off a gorgeous legal response and he loves to win. Eric Golden was his second, or partner, on the case. Eric is equally brilliant although more conservative. They are both good men with normal testosterone levels, which remained that way until the trial began. I liked them a lot.

Practically the worst thing that ever happened to me

24:

IN the winter of 1996 I was on my way to a birthday celebration with friends. That morning, I had given a local street person ten bucks for a strip of transit tickets he was selling. Not such a bright thing to do, I can see now, but I knew him, and for a change he was giving me something for my cash donation. When I told him it was my birthday, he threw in extra tickets.

I left work and used one of his tickets to enter the subway but was stopped by the man in the ticket booth. He asked if I had additional tickets like the one I had used, and I cheerily showed them to him. The Toronto Transit Commission (TTC) was in the process of changing to a new ticket, and I assumed that he was trading old ones for new. He asked me to wait for a few minutes and I did. Quicker than you can say "the better way," I was grabbed by two men who identified themselves as TTC police and handed me over to 52 Division cops.* At the time, I had an outstanding charge of mischief against me for an act of civil disobedience that I had engaged in with other women. (We had blocked traffic in front of the Ontario legislature to protest government cuts to women's services. All charges were subsequently dropped.) Because of this, I was fingerprinted, booked and placed in a holding cell with my name on the door.

The senior on-duty detective who interviewed me ordered that I be held and strip-searched in the event that I was concealing any weapons,

---

* "The better way" is the TTC's slogan. The TTC has won transit awards internationally and is renowned for its cleanliness and efficiency. The high rate of sexual assault of women who work and travel on the TTC is a subject that surfaces every decade or so only to be buried quickly by bureaucrats and politicians, who assure us there is no problem.

drugs or contraband. I was charged with fraud—the tickets were counterfeit—and driven to my apartment, which was searched by two apologetic but diligent uniformed officers. Next I was forced to accompany them as we drove around my neighbourhood searching for the man who had sold me the tickets. Back in the holding cell, I was informed that I would be held overnight. I was sprung by Frank Addario at about two o'clock that morning. No birthday cake for me.

I had to appear in court four times over the next six months before the charges were dropped. Although I did not recognize him or his name at the time of our meeting, I learned later that the detective in charge of the investigation into my supposedly fraudulent ways knew that I was Jane Doe and green-lighted the charges with a notation that I be prosecuted to the fullest extent of the law. Even though there was no case against me.

That arrest and strip search was one of the worst things that has ever happened to me. I got a full taste of what it is like to be completely controlled, every part of you open to examination, your freedom, dignity and agency denied and with no one to call for help. When I resisted the search, a woman officer screamed that if I did not remove my clothing she would do it for me. Further protestations resulted in more threats. I took off each piece of clothing and threw it at her. She let them fall to the floor. She forced me to spread my legs and bend over. I waited to be penetrated but she was satisfied with a visual inspection. It went through my head to leave my clothes on the floor, to remain naked throughout the rest of the process. But I dressed and as I was led from the cubicle in which I had been stripped and violated, the station room grew silent and every officer there turned to watch me.

The police procedure I have just described meets the legal definition of a sexual assault.

In 1998 community groups organized a meeting with then Toronto Police Services Board members Jeff Lyons and Judy Sgro, where women courageously came forward to tell not only of being body-cavity searched, but also of being forcibly stripped naked, required to allow officers to view and probe their genitals, and frequently searched in full view of male officers and inmates. The women characterized the searches as having had the same impact on them as a sexual assault. Most of the eleven women who testified were women of colour, immigrant women and sex trade workers. None had been found to be carrying weapons or contraband. All charges against them were subsequently dropped. It was revealed that strip searches are frequently used by police to intimidate, abuse and humiliate. The force's own record-keeping indicated that over a quarter of the people arrested are strip-searched and that the majority of these searches are gratuitous.

In response, then Police Chief David Boothby emphatically declared that no body-cavity searches had been conducted in the city of Toronto over the past ten years.

Clearly, the reality of police practice was worlds apart from the official story. Caught red-handed, the police adopted a seemingly kinder, gentler strip search-policy. It required officers engaged in the practice to collect and file basic information and to make those searched aware of a complaints process.*

In 2001, citing a police force overwhelmed with reported crime, Chief of Police Julian Fantino requested that the new policy be scrapped. He claimed that an internal study of statistics collected over a six-week period proved beyond a doubt that there is no problem regarding how and when Toronto police conduct strip searches.

Although the practice continues to receive legal and media scrutiny, and despite the continued protests of women working in the anti-violence sector, strip searches (of men and women) and sexual assault are never equated.

But I'm getting ahead of myself again.

⸭

---

* Despite its name, the Ontario Civilian Commission on Policing Services has no civilian representation or oversight, meaning the police investigate themselves. They are rarely found guilty and immense public pressure exists for the provincial government to make the agency accountable to the public.

25:

I DISCOVERED a lot in the discovery portion of my suit.

By the time you reach the discovery phase, which is the final step before trial, both sides have pretty much prepared their cases and amassed all of the evidence they think they will need. Discovery requires that the opposing legal teams show their evidence to the other side. They then have the opportunity to assess the strength of their opponent, to calculate legal strategies designed to reduce or nullify that strength, and to shore up their own positions. This is accomplished by interviewing the witnesses on both sides and submitting the anticipated written testimony of other witnesses you plan to call (psychiatrists and other experts). Mary Cornish had partially discovered Bill Cameron in 1992, and she had discovered him well. We also relied heavily on transcripts of his and Kim Derry's testimony during the trial of the man who raped me.

The police defence strategy was to prove that the damage I claimed had resulted from my rape actually predated the crime—meaning that I was nutty (psychologically and emotionally damaged) before I was raped. They also wanted to prove that I had a pre-existing feminist and man-hating political agenda when, fortunately for me, I got raped, which fit into my deviant political leanings and provided ammunition for me to attack the state through the police.

I paraphrase of course. The linguistic stylings of the legal system are much more loquacious and less flowery than mine, but it all comes down to exactly the same meaning.

The damaged goods theory or strategy of defence is a common one.

It is often all the accused party can come up with. The only shot they've got. And it is frequently successful, especially when the accused is an institution of governance with immense social support and finances.

Bryan Finlay was the police force's lead counsel, but after making an appearance on the first day of my discovery, he handed the process over to his associate Greg Richards. I, of course, had Sean, who asked me if I was okay with him wearing shorts to the sessions. I suggested that it would be better if he appeared in a suit. He wore one on the first day but then reverted to Bermudas and a dress shirt. There was no judge present, although I was under oath. Everything was taped and transcribed by a courthouse stenographer whose lower face was covered by one of those dictaphones that look like gas masks, but she had nice eyes. Richards is a slender, careful man with apparently no personality at all, who always wears a suit. He struck me as shrewder than Finlay; he carried out his second-banana duties in a professional if somewhat somnambulant manner, rousing himself every now and then to what to me seemed arbitrary and unnecessary exercises of power. On the one occasion on which he spoke to me as a person rather than a witness, he asked to see copies of the women's magazine *Fireweed* on whose board of directors I had served. He said we could have tea while we talked about it. Sean thought he was being sarcastic but I am still not sure. I declined his proposal. Happily, he was only slightly less out of the loop than Finlay in terms of understanding the negligence and discrimination claims we were arguing. It often seemed that they were defending a completely different case from the one we were bringing.

My personal discovery was a hellish experience that lasted four days and took place in the summer of 1996, a year before the trial began. Discovery allows lawyers much more leeway to humiliate, trick or confuse than is allowed in an open court of law. You are warned that failure to answer or answering too much can be used against you. They can't tell you how exactly, because they don't know yet. Your own lawyer colludes in the bared and veiled threats of the game. It was in discovery that my past was first introduced and minutely examined.

I was obliged to submit my health and social insurance numbers to the police lawyers. They used them to access all of my health and

22.　　　　The Defendants deny all allegations of negligence
deny all alleged breaches of the <u>Canadian Charter of Rights</u>
<u>Freedoms</u> (the "Charter") contained in the Amended Statement
Claim.

5.　　　　While a substantial number of sexual assault victims
are women, as alleged in paragraph 12 of the Amended Statement of
Claim, a substantial number of sexual assault victims are not
women. Such offences are frequently committed against children
and, in some cases, against men.

Excerpts from Police Statement of Defence

employment records. As I was under oath, I also gave up the names of
therapists I had seen whose fees were not covered by our provincial
health plan. They were all subpoenaed to supply notes they had kept of
interactions with me. Richards collected all of these files on my life and
went fishing among them. He trawled about for the big ones, cast his
net for evidence of past sexual assaults or child abuse, time spent in a so-
called mental institution or behind other bars. I was one of those lucky
kids who grew up healthy and safe, and there are no damaging criminal or institutional records of my behaviour. He discarded reports that
spoke well of me. But then the buried treasure of therapy notes surfaced.
He read of my long relationship with Johnny, which included abusive
behaviour, and of his time spent in jail (he was actually in jail at the
time). He read of a brother's chronic depression, a worry I carry still,
and my father's use of force when disciplining my brothers in the 1950s
and 1960s. He learned of my troubled relationship with my mother,
whom I adore. He learned that I had been unhappy as a teenager.

He manipulated these normal, common unhappinesses in order to discredit me. He read about my drug experimentation—not abuse—and my flirtation with heroin. My civil disobedience arrests (dismissed in court) and the trumped-up TTC ticket fraud charges (dismissed in court) were additional personal history he carefully mined.

He loved the opinions of poet and son of Freud, Dr. Norman Doidge (I'm a doctor! I'm a writer!), who had characterized me in his referral note, now disclosed to all and sundry, as attracted to playboys and mother-hating. Taken alone, his diagnosis was almost laughable—the isolated, narcissistic ramblings of a student misogynist, unsubstantiated over many years by his peers and betters. Combined with the more mundane yet potentially sensational stuff (Depression runs in her family! Her daddy beat the boys! Her boyfriend! Her drug use! HEROIN!!! WE CAN'T LOSE! SHE SNIFFED HEROIN! THANK YOU GOD, I LOVE THIS CASE!), which was submitted to the court by my progressive and feminist therapist, we had a seminal case to (a) illustrate the abuse of therapy records by the legal profession and (b) use a raped woman's past to discredit her.

Remember I mentioned earlier the mistake that my beloved therapist, Julia Grey, made? Well her notes were part of the required reading list that was produced by the discovery process. I actually picked them up and delivered them to Sean. Neither Sean nor I read them. A page was missing and Richards asked that it be produced. She willingly faxed it over and it was the very page that talked about my drug use. Neither Sean nor I read that one either. I have never stopped kicking myself for that. Having feminist lawyers had its drawbacks but having a male Bay Street lawyer had problems too. Sean should never have passed on those notes without reading them. In his defence, he had never dealt with the issue of therapy records in a rape trial. But he should have known, and not reading them was a massive error, one that LEAF would never have made.

Julia's work with me had been so positive I couldn't imagine her voluntarily offering up damaging personal information about me and not telling me. It was 1996 and the fact that women's personal therapy notes and even journal entries were being used against them to discredit rape or abuse charges was well-known in feminist and therapy circles and in the media. I certainly knew about it, but I hadn't dreamt that my life would be so scrutinized in a civil lawsuit about police negligence and discrimination. Not mine. Theirs.

Richards probably assumed that we had purposefully withheld that particular page of Julia's notes. They were notes she had taken in order to seek her own counsel on a subject with which she was not very familiar. And we're not talking marijuana here. I experimented with heroin. The big one. The drug that dare not speak its name. The one that took away all of my pain. Made me brilliant, witty, safe, irritable, frightened, false, fucked up. And I talked about it in therapy as something self-destructive and dangerous. I moved past it. I cannot turn around today and say, "Oh that was someone else, my evil twin, not me. I didn't like it anyway." Heroin is an excellent pain reliever. Physical and psychological. But it will also wipe out things you need to hold on to and can't survive well without. I never graduated to needles or physical addiction. I do not seek heroin out today, and if someone offered me some tomorrow, I would say no. But listen, addiction could easily have been the biggest, baddest effect my rape had on me.

I was ashamed and horrified that Richards now had pieces of my life, tissue of my heart, in his hands, in his words, open to his interpretations, his law. My drug use was about what I did to myself. No one else. It was about escape, safety, unloading my rape, its corrosion, its realities. It was about not sinking under the legal machine I had set in motion but did not drive. I wanted to smash his smirking face, turn the table over, run, drop the whole thing. But I stayed. I explained that heroin had helped me to manage the trauma of my rape and then it had frightened me deeply. I had pursued and dealt with it in therapy, and it was behind me and none of his bloody business. Everything I said was taped, transcribed, a matter of record, stored for future use. If I had not had the disguise of Jane Doe, I would not have proceeded with the whole sorry mess. I would have dropped the case and walked away.

Richards collected all of these pieces of me, including my chosen and diverse employment history, pre-rape reading material, affiliation with feminist and other left-wing politics, and sent them as fodder to a psychiatrist he had hired named Graham Glancy for his expert analysis.

During discovery, police photos of my bed taken from different angles were placed in front of me. I and the other raped women were all menstruating at the time of our attacks. This perceived anomaly and the fact that we were all raped during a full moon was noted in the police investigation. Our menses were evidence that Sean considered using as an example of the similarities in all five rapes. Clearly it was also relevant for Richards. After three days of being asked to verify if the photos were accurate representations of the crime scene, I instructed Richards and Sean that if they showed me one more photo of the bloodied bed on which I had been raped, I would leave the room and they could discover each other.

In the hallway, I made clear to Sean that my menses were not to be mentioned or displayed again. Ever.* Similarly I refused to answer questions about my brother or Johnny. Sometimes I got away with it. In other instances (my drug use, reading material), Sean instructed me to answer. I did not understand the difference between what to answer and what not to or the logic at play. I have come to realize there was none. I struggled to find ways to answer Richards's prying that would allow me to maintain some dignity. When I could not, I did not. By the end I was so disgusted with both of them and their game, I didn't give a shit about their rules. I realized that I was the only person in the room to whom I had to answer. I understand now that Richards was evaluating me the whole time and making decisions about which issues to attack me on. The problem was I didn't know which subjects he had decided to drop until after I had given my testimony in court a year later. Neither did my lawyer. We had to be prepared for everything.

DURING Sean's turn to discover the police side, we learned of the witnesses the police would call in their defence. Nineteen in all, the majority of whom were cops who would swear under oath that the investigation had been outstanding. The police would also call three expert witnesses to testify to my mental health status and two others to claim that my rape was non-violent.

---

* I really don't know what they were thinking. Women, blood, rape, full moon, madness—I don't know.

It was obvious that we had to deal ourselves a few expert-witness cards if we were to stay in the game. Obvious to some anyway. I became obsessed about it. Remember the game Red Rover? There are two teams. The designated player chants "Red rover, red rover, I call so-and-so over" and that opposing team member must crash through your team's locked arms? Strategically you choose the player least likely to break through, who will in turn choose the weakest link in the fence of little arms. It is a brutal game and had been forbidden in our schoolyard. I was a tiny child but competitive and naturally athletic, and I had three brothers with whom I regularly fought. When called over (I was the obvious first choice) I would run like hell toward two players who would see me coming and strengthen their stance. Seconds before contact, I would deke off and smash through the line a few players down. It worked once or twice. I would hold on for dear life when opposing play-mates made my arm their best crossover point, and in one session my arm was broken in two, placing me in traction for five days and in a cast for months.

I wanted to call over some expert witnesses of my own who could smash through police lines and provide the court with a definition of the crime of sexual assault, its inherent harm and the mythology that prevents us from understanding it. I wanted experts who could describe the sexist, discriminatory practices in policing and present me on the stand as an adult woman with some intelligence who reacted to her rape in ways that were "normal." The use of expert witnesses to deliver such descriptions or renderings of rape victims was completely outside of traditional legal practice. It was much more convenient to rely on the good old psychiatrized versions.

Sean loved the policing expert part but felt that Vince DeMarco would be enough for the rest. I understood that he would not. Sean had never attended a rape trial. I had. I knew what to expect. It was my business to know. Sean finally agreed to consider using experts as part of the case if I found and paid for them myself. I ignored that last part and began the hunt. I knew that he would do it if it made sense.

Women working in the front lines in sexual assault centres were the first obvious choice. The ones I approached agreed immediately to present a definition of sexual assault that would serve as the basis of our case. They were vetoed by Sean, however, as they did not possess the prerequisite doctorate or other professional titles and would be disqualified by police counsel on those grounds. I got on the phone and began to canvass "professional" women across the country. I kept striking out. No one wanted to be on my team. I approached feminist academics, psychiatrists, psychologists and legal practitioners who had forged careers preaching and publishing about the nature of sexual assault. They expressed their desire to help, to be involved, but were certain that what I was proposing could not be done, was not their area, was not appropriate for a court of law as there was no precedent for such testimony regarding the crime of rape.

I don't think I have ever felt as alone, as abandoned, as I did after those conversations. Where was everybody? I wept and wept. What was so difficult, so radical about what I was asking? Was it because the victim was asking? The concept of leading expert testimony about the nature of crime in a court of law was standard. Why did people believe it should not, could not, apply to sexual assault? But then I got angry and more determined than I had ever been to find the right players. Determined because I was confident that I was on the right course. By now, Sean had also realized that we needed to bring on a Charter expert to argue sex discrimination, and better it should be a woman. My national canvass expanded to find her.

I finally found everyone. In my own backyard.

ELIZABETH Sheehy is a professor of law at the University of Ottawa. I had met her through Elizabeth Pickett around 1989 and she has been a friend and ally ever since. She called me one day to tell me that Cynthia Petersen was the best up-and-coming civil litigator in the country and that she also taught law and specialized in equality issues. Cynthia practised with Sack Goldblatt Mitchell, a progressive, decidedly left-leaning law firm in downtown Toronto that specialized in labour and Charter litigation.

I called Cynthia and she said yes, she would be my lawyer. She turned out to be the queen, no the king, of the Charter. Her specialty was section 15, which guarantees freedom from discrimination. Using research provided by Elizabeth Sheehy, she recast part of my negligence claim to clarify that the police failure to warn affected not just one woman (me) but women generally. Cynthia's legal acumen and intelligence were pivotal in winning my case. With less than a year to the trial date, I had my legal team.

I RECONNECTED with Lori and Melanie, my allies of the postering and early days of WAVAW. Melanie was finishing up her law degree, and Lori was now a practising psychologist. Lori would have been my first choice to give expert witness, but since she and Melanie had been central in WAVAW back in 1987, and WAVAW documents were part of the police defence (outrageously, they entered them as evidence of their commitment to working with women), she would be cited as biased if she took the stand to testify for me. Lori had worked with Peter Jaffe, a psychologist from London, Ontario, who was the reigning expert in courtroom testimony regarding wife assault, and she thought he might be our guy, as the physical and sexual assault of women are intrinsic to each other. I asked her to call him and see if he would work with us to prepare a feminist definition of the crime of sexual assault and women's response to it, which he would then deliver in a court of law. He said yes.

Jaffe is best known for his articulation of the battered-wife syndrome in defence of women who kill the men who are beating or attempting to kill them. Beginning in 1990, Canadian courts allowed the introduction of "expert evidence" to explain the impact of wife-battering and how it might drive a woman to acts of self-defence leading to the death of her abuser. Women in cases of sexual assault, incest and wife assault have been successful in criminal and civil forums by establishing that they suffer from battered-wife syndrome, rape trauma syndrome or post-traumatic stress disorder. The "disorder syndromes" have been adopted by our courts and thus reinforced. While these defences have resulted in setting women free, they have also created problems. If a woman cannot establish that she fits within the syndrome or disorder (and there are very specific qualifications dictated by the psychiatric bible called *The*

Diagnostic and Statistical Manual of Mental Disorders, or DSM-IV), she will have a difficult time establishing her damages, much less arguing self-defence and getting a conviction. The problem is that the syndromes and disorders themselves are based on mental-health assessments, which, to be successful, must cast the woman as mentally ill or unbalanced.

This is not to deny the severe and long-term psychological changes that occur in the lives of women who have been beaten or sexually assaulted. However the present definitions of the disorders are based on male models—the most common of which is the war veteran who returns home and commits violent crimes. Current definitions render the woman involved as someone broken who will never regain the status of a whole or good person who is in charge of her life. Would it be too much of a stretch to redefine the crime of rape itself as the disorder or syndrome and the reactions of the woman who has been raped or beaten as normal—coping mechanisms to deal with the violence that has entered her life? That was my position.

But no, I had to be the wilted flower. Damaged, syndromed and disordered beyond anything I recognized.

Peter Jaffe agreed to provide the court with a feminist definition of sexual assault that resisted the compulsion to syndrome me, and focused instead on the crime of rape as one of power against women and consequently against society. He allowed Lori, Melanie and me to help shape the testimony he delivered during the civil trial. It was a very good piece, tempered with big fat scientific and medical terminology and psychiatric blah-blah, which lent it the credibility required to be spoken and heard within the justice system.

NOW I needed someone to apply their expertise to the same tests that the police had asked their mental-health experts to apply to me. Patti McGillicuddy referred me to Rosemary Barnes. Many professional women had declined to be called over by me and by the time I found her, I was getting a little nervous that time was running out. Barnes's mission, should she accept it, was to apply her psychological assessment to the tests administered to me by Graham Glancy and Nathan Pollock, the psychiatrist and psychologist who had agreed to act as expert witnesses for the police. I had been examined by them already, an experience I will describe later. The problem was that in order for Barnes to testify on my behalf, I had to go through the whole painful, humiliating process again. I had to lay bare my life for yet another stranger to scrutinize, prod and uncover. Take more tests. Shed more heart's blood. Honestly, the things I've done for rape.

During her assessment of me, Barnes was as inscrutable as the judge who eventually tried my case. Although I'd been told that she was progressive and feminist, I couldn't get a bead on her. The process was excruciating. I did not choose her for health-care reasons but for political ones, and yet I had to present myself as a patient, a client seeking her medical expertise. I had to come to her as someone damaged rather than as an ally in a political forum. It was only when I read her report weeks later that I knew I had chosen wisely. In her assessment report she writes, "Ms Doe required considerably more time and information than other clients in similar circumstances to satisfy herself concerning the nature, limitations, risks and benefits of the assessment and reporting process."

Of course I did. In the role of her patient, I was interviewing her for a job. And I didn't trust her profession. I needed an unlikely player to crash through the Red Rover line—the fence of medical pathology that the legal system builds around rape victims. Which she did. I regret that I could not be more forthcoming with her about the game, as she is a formidable player, but the legal rules would not allow it. Nor did her medical ones. I had to be psychologized by her in order to counter being psychiatrized by the police defence, and both had to find me damaged—but in different ways and for different reasons. Even though the civil trial was about police negligence and discrimination.

The testimonies of Peter Jaffe and Rosemary Barnes were orchestrated to offset the stylings of the police expert witnesses according to the accepted rules of the game of law. They had to speak the right language, even though the content of what they delivered to my case was a breakthrough in the social and legal interpretation of rape and the ways in which women react to the crime. (Unfortunately, few people heard or read their evidence and the status quo that defines raped women as vengeful, disordered and syndromed remains unchallenged, unchanged.)

My redemption as a raped woman would have to be delivered in the same medical and psychiatric context as my damning. Damned if you do; damned if you don't.

WITH Vince, Jaffe and Barnes secured as witnesses for the plaintiff (that's me), an additional task was to find an expert to explain the culture of policing. We approached several well-known criminologists and professors, who either did not return our calls or declined to be involved. I was finally referred to Ron Stackhouse, a professor at Humber College who had served with the Toronto police, and he told me that the man we were looking for was James Hodgson.

When he was twenty-one, Hodgson became a cadet with the Metropolitan Toronto Police and was trained at the Ontario Police College and at C.O. Bick. He was then assigned to 51 Division in downtown Toronto, where he was involved in the investigation of dozens of sexual assaults. In 1986 Hodgson had worked in the same police division as the officers working on my case.

In 1988, after ten years on the job, he left the police to pursue studies at York University. In 1994 he defended his dissertation on race and gender discrimination in policing to become Dr. James Hodgson. When we contacted him, he was the dean of the sociology department at Longwood College in Virginia. He lectures and writes about the military culture of policing and its systemic nature.

I was suing the police for negligence and gender discrimination. I did not claim that these behaviours were particular to me or the random acts of individual officers. Nothing would be won in my lawsuit without an understanding that the police actions that formed the basis of my claim were part of a system of behaviours and beliefs held by the officers who investigated the Balcony Rapist.

They were simply following police procedure.

They were just doing their jobs.

Just following orders.

Professor Hodgson's job was to show that their actions were systemic. Part of a whole.

"Systemic" is another one of those words that are considered to be jargon or politically correct and therefore unacceptable to many, especially when used to discuss race or gender or poverty issues. Like "feminist," "capitalist," "patriarchy," the word has been all but removed from current vocabulary, on the political left as well as the right. These words are part of a banished lexicon, considered uncool, old-fashioned. Like "groovy" or "album." Jim Hodgson was going to travel from Virginia to Toronto, back into his past, to tell the court the story of systemic problems in policing, and he was going to put his head right into the lion's mouth. As an ex-constable, a grunt, he would do it from the inside of the beast and with the insight of a curious and political mind. His testimony would be one of the anchors that would secure *Jane Doe v. the Metropolitan Toronto Police Force* as winnable.

WHEN it was time to submit my assessment of my damage claim to the courts in preparation for the civil trial, my chiropractic expenses showed up, and my lawyer sent me back to Larry, the practitioner who had treated me for my neck, for official documentation. I hadn't seen him for a while. He had always been supportive and interested in my case. I don't mind talking about my rape and lawsuit. It interests me too. But people usually assume that the mere mention of the word will deliver me into a chasm of grief, and the person who brought it up will feel responsible for pulling me out. And so I suffer these rape silences, aware that people's questions, empathy, excitement, wonder, titillation, simmer just beneath the surface of the conversation. Larry asked questions respectfully, in order to better diagnose and remedy my injury. And he released my physical pain.

Larry agreed not only to submit documentation but to take the stand as an expert witness and testify that my neck injuries were sustained during the attack and were accelerated by the stress and trauma inherent in rape. For years women have argued that the current medical pathologizing of raped women should be replaced by a more relevant diagnosis that includes concepts of body memory and stress-induced physical injury.* Larry told me that as a result of our relationship and the knowledge he had gained, he had augmented his studies and professional development and now dedicated much of his practice to women who had experienced physical or sexual violence. He spoke regularly on the subject and networked with other health-care givers who understood the co-relation between physical pain and emotional trauma. He was transformed. I was pleased for him and of course for myself. My lawsuit was about introducing evidence that would transform existing legal understandings and definitions of the crime of rape. And it looked like Larry was my man.

Then everything got nutty. Expert witnesses are paid for their work. Some much more than others. This was a grey area for us. I was having trouble even finding the expert witnesses I wanted, and there was certainly no money to pay them. A woman I knew had been one, and she told me how much she was paid, so Sean and I settled on a standard fee of $1,500, which would include preparation and delivery at trial. Although my case had been taken on by Sean's firm pro bono, no funds were delegated to pay expert witnesses. So we told our experts that payment was contingent on the success of the case.**

But Eric Golden, Sean's associate and the one delegated to examine Larry at trial, proceeded under the assumption that Larry had been told the fee was tied to our legal success and that his testimony could be a freebie. Larry submitted a good report. Then Eric and Sean decided they would not have him testify after all and instead simply submit his report for the judge's consideration. But they didn't inform him of this decision. Or me. When they finally did, it was clear that Sean was reluctant to overdose the judge with too much new thought on the subject. An impressive roll call of medical mavens was going to take the stand and give expert opinion for or against my sanity. I imagine Larry was

---

* Body memory is an accepted medical concept best translated as the occurrence of pain, irritation or other sensations in people who have lost limbs (again the soldier's example is most commonly used), and referred to as the phantom limb syndrome.

** I found out much later that Blaney McMurtry, while generally neutral about my case, were concerned that Sean and Eric were spending too many billable hours working on a freebie and exerted pressure on them to either hurry it up or stop it. Sean, however, was a full partner and he assured them he would try my case, either with them or somewhere else. In the end, the firm was very pleased to have been involved.

keen to be one of them. Who wouldn't be? But neither Sean nor Eric returned his calls. They assured me they had dealt with him professionally, and then they laughed when they received his bill. It exceeded the entire sum I was claiming for physical damages. A few weeks after trial Eric received a notice from the Law Society. Larry had reported him and was requesting his censure for unethical and unprofessional conduct, and three thousand dollars in compensation.

Eric freaked, and now I had two male professionals, one legal and one medical, cussing and cursing the other with a litany of how-dare-you's and who-do-you-think-you-are's. Eric reported Larry to the College of Physicians and Surgeons, and Larry filed a lawsuit for defamation and Eric laughed again and vowed to tie him up in legal proceedings until he was a grandfather—and he could do it, too.

Now I like both of these men, and my nature is to fix things. Eric agreed with my suggestion that I call Larry and leave a message saying that I was available to mediate between them. But Larry taped the call and cited it in a letter (which contained my real name) as evidence of Eric's unethical manipulation of a poor rape victim. Eric threatened to charge him with the criminal violation of my media ban. It was clear that Larry was going to get creamed here, and I insisted that Eric lay off. He didn't want to but he did because I asked him to. Only then Larry wouldn't stop. Over the next few months Eric sent me copies of Larry's correspondence to him and, worst thing of all, Larry was representing himself legally. Eric is a killer lawyer. His clients are banks and other law firms and he was getting annoyed—something I had never seen in him before.

Then one day Larry phoned me and asked if I would agree to testify for him in his upcoming lawsuit against Eric. I told him that I would never do anything against Eric and that he needed to think about settling all of this because Larry arguing a lawsuit was like Eric doing a neck adjustment. I phoned Eric and spoke to him about karma, and then I spoke sternly, and he said he would settle and pay Larry $1,500. Larry sent me a lovely thank-you letter. The next time my neck went out, I called a woman I had heard about.

THERE were two other witnesses I wanted to call as part of my case. As I was suing for damages, I had to prove that those damages were a result of the crime committed against me. It wasn't enough for me to just say so. Nor was it sufficient that decades of documented legal, medical and scientific research and testimony had established that there are life-changing damages inherent in the crime of rape. Nope, uh-uh, each rape, each claim of damage, must be examined individually, isolated from the rest as if each occurrence was the original crime. Devoid of any social or legal history.

In the damages brief I submitted, I included health costs and loss of income. I wanted to call a witness who could testify to my employment ability and potential. About a year after my rape, Peter Mettler, an independent filmmaker, asked me to produce his next feature film. In 1988 I had worked with him to develop his next project; fundraising, scouting talent, promotion—that sort of thing. After a few months, he invited me to be his producer. Peter knew about my rape, and he came to understand that although I wanted the job badly, I couldn't accept it. I simply didn't have the confidence to embark on something new. Although my working life had been a trajectory of new challenges, my rape had beaten me down psychologically, caused me to question things I knew, things I valued. I was in physical pain, I couldn't sleep. It broke my heart to say no, but everything broke my heart then. Every day broke my heart. A feature film credit after my name, especially on a project by Peter Mettler could have established me as a filmmaker. But I thought I didn't have it in me.

After meeting with him, however, my lawyers decided on my behalf that Peter's opinions of me and my abilities made me look *too* good, *too* healthy, hardly the fragile petal at all, and would cause the judge to think, "Why, there's nothing wrong with this woman, she could find work in a second. Obviously malingering . . . Not guilty! No crime! Not a real victim!"

I ALSO wanted to call an expert witness from the women's movement who would prove beyond a shadow of a doubt that the minimal changes implemented in sexual-assault investigation since 1986 worked mainly for the benefit of the police themselves and that no progressive systemic change had occurred. It was an easy bet that the police would claim it had. A number of women could have done an exemplary job of disproving such a claim, and pounds of print material would have supported their testimony. Sean and Eric initially agreed with me but were less forthcoming about their reasoning when they finally decided not to call such a witness. Something about the judge becoming irritated, or unnecessarily prolonging the proceedings . . . Never mind that I entered the trial process believing that Larry, Peter and an anti-violence expert would be called. Never mind that the police defence was going to call nineteen witnesses to our seven. Or that the testimony of other non-traditional witnesses, whom I also had to fight to have included, would eventually become the linchpins of the judge's decision in my favour. Never mind that the testimony of all or any of the three witnesses they excluded would have salvaged some of my dignity. And the dignity of the court. Never mind.

26:

JULIA GREY was devastated by what had happened with her notes. She explained that she had submitted those records of our therapy anticipating that she would then take the stand during trial to defend me, explain my actions, contextualize them—even though that possibility had never been raised between us or with my lawyers. I am certain that she would have done an able job, but a lay therapist would never be granted expert-witness standing in a court of law. My criminal injuries compensation money had run out. Not only could I not afford therapy financially, I could not afford emotionally to continue with Julia, so great was my disappointment with her. And hers with herself. So there I was, preparing for trial, the biggest and most trying venture of my life, and I didn't have a therapist.

The terrifying thing about all of this was that in the process of discovery, Julia's notes had only been a small part of the haul from my past that was turned over to police expert witnesses for dissection. Turned over to people such as Dr. Graham Glancy. (The ha is silent so it's really pronounced Gram, which is what I called my grandmother.) Glancy is a noted, even celebrated, psychiatrist with a large private practice, and was head of forensic psychiatry at the Clarke Institute. Frequently and for large sums of money, he serves as an expert witness in sexual assault and other violent crime trials. Glancy will bear witness for either side. (In 1993 he was contracted to provide expert psychiatric testimony in support of Karla Homolka's defence that she was a battered woman. He dropped out and was replaced by Peter Jaffe.) Glancy was hired by the police to give evidence against me.

The arrangement was that I would meet with him one day, and his colleague, Nathan Pollock, on the next, and they would administer a series of tests designed to create a psychological profile. Glancy's office was in Etobicoke, a suburb of Toronto. Now I'm a city girl, and all I knew about Etobicoke was that it is west of the city, and you don't pronounce the k. Glancy refused my request that I bring a friend, saying only a family member could attend. So I asked my friend Alys to drive me at least, and we made plans to stop for lunch, get pumped and arrive early for my one o'clock appointment. Alys would wait outside.

We got lost on the highways and BiWays of downtown Etobicoke. I knocked on his office door at about ten minutes to one and said I would be a little late as I had to grab something to eat in the cafeteria in his building. I am hypoglycemic—something they neglected to use against me in court, although many shrinks associate it with female hysteria. We began at about a quarter past one.

The first thing I noticed was that there was another person in the room. When I inquired about her presence, Glancy informed me that her name was Cheryl Regehr, that she was a professor of social work and a researcher in sexual assault, and that he had requested she attend in the event that I made any inappropriate allegations of sexual misconduct on his part.

Shock, fear, indignation smashed through me, stopped my breath, drained my blood. My stomach lurched. Here I was in a necessarily adversarial position, facing a man who was paid to demonize me, and right off the bat he suggests I might cry false rape. The best worst word I know is "motherfucker." "Motherfucker," I thought. I collected myself and asked if he was aware that the danger of sexual misconduct was more apparent for me, the client, and that the courts were filled with women who had been assaulted by their psychiatrists and that his entire profession was under public censure and scrutiny. Where was my protection?

His head moved in my direction and he seemed to register some awareness that someone had spoken. The corners of his mouth moved upwards and he bared his teeth and suggested that we begin.

I had done some research on Glancy and knew that Cheryl Regehr was his wife. Her work is progressive although it is disguised in academic language and does not acknowledge the work of women in shelters and rape crisis centres. I noted the ethical dilemma of her presence but was hopeful that her influence would be positive as I entered into combat with a mortal enemy.

Glancy made no eye contact with me as he carefully explained each test I was required to take. The tests were dated and obvious, designed by men decades ago without a thought about the nature of sexual assault. A psychologist friend had let me look at a couple of standard ones beforehand with the caution that they were as sacred as Veronica's Veil and that I might become blind if I looked upon them for too long with my untrained eye. They are named things like the Minnesota Multiphasic Personality Inventory-2, or MMPI-2, the Trauma Symptom Inventory, the Millon Clinical Multiaxial Inventory-III PK, PSS and so on. We could just as easily be talking about motor oil or a *Cosmo* quiz. One of them is fashioned to determine if you are malingering or trying to cheat their system. It's called Liar Liar Pants on Fire (LLPF). They all demand that the test subject be linear and precise in response to each question. The first one required that I match words with definitions, others had me finish sentences, check off true or false, yes or no. Had I been raped before? N.

All were reminiscent of the secretive, equally sacramental IQ testing that the nuns administered one year in grade school. In both circumstances, I could not ask questions or seek clarification, was closely observed and used a pencil. Gram and Cheryl scribbled furiously the whole time, watching me from under hooded eyes. I asked questions between tests, made political statements about their profession, and suggested that the tests would be more appropriate if administered to the chief of police and the officers I was suing. I managed to quote some of Regehr's published work in support of my position. They wrote down everything I said. Glancy's pencil broke at one point.

Then I was out in the parking lot looking for Alys's car, and she took me home and put me to bed and told me not to cry so much or I'd be a mess in the morning.

Which I was. Nathan Pollock consults with Glancy from his office in Riverdale, which is closer to my home. My appointment was at ten but I slept in and awoke in a panic, exhausted, furious and hungover from

too many pills that hadn't even kicked in until about five that morning. I spent money I didn't have on a cab and got there just in time. I knew that being late twice would factor in their diagnosis. "Ms Doe has no concept of time, Daylight, Eastern or Standard."

Pollock arrived at half past ten and made no apologies or excuses. I asked him where his bodyguard was and suggested he reimburse me for the cab fare. He looked at me as if I were crazy. I made some attempts to explain and then surrendered. More tests began. Different tests that were really the same, only there was a larger oral Q and A component. He asked me if I ever felt suicidal. I responded no, that I was more likely to kill someone else than myself—probably a man. (Probably the same man more than once, I was thinking, but my groggy censor activated itself. If only briefly.) He asked me what I thought the police were doing during their investigation. I said that the police were staked out in the same bushes as the rapist but managed to miss him as he climbed the outside of my building at one of the busiest intersections in the city. He asked if I had been raped before. N.

I questioned the logic and clarity of his questions. They were either male gender specific or gender neutral. For example, I was requested to check yes or no to this one: "Are you afraid of people?" Well, no, I'm not generally, but I am mindful of, afraid of, men I do not know. And some I know well. I monitor their actions when I am around them. I fear there is a potential for harm. He explained that the process did not allow for my questions and that I must answer as best and honestly as I could.

The tests were exhaustive and repetitive. It was nearing one o'clock and I was hungry. I had not been offered water or coffee. There were no snacks. His office smelled of mould.

I asked when he planned to stop for lunch and he looked stunned.

"Stop? We'll go right through. It's better that way."

I explained that I had to eat and needed to stop soon. He said we could stop at two. He wasn't happy about it. I think he feared I would cheat somehow, call friends for the correct answer, use a lifeline. I took forty minutes to find a sandwich and coffee and swallow them. When I came back, the testing resumed and we moved on to the Rorschach.

Rorschach was a Swiss shrink who designed what is better known as the ink blot test. We've all seen it on TV. A series of cards imprinted with shapes crafted from ink blots are held up and you are supposed to verbalize the first associative thought or image that comes into your head. Your answers are analyzed and you are determined to be psychotic or not or somewhere in between. Well I'm here to tell you right now that old Rorschach has more vaginas in his ink-blots than Georgia O'Keeffe has in her paintings. More vaginas than in *Hustler* magazine. Fully intact vaginas, some are bleeding. And it's no accident.

So here's this guy, who has been hired with the intent to define me as whacked out, who wouldn't even give me food if he had his way, holding up these pictures of vaginas, and I'm supposed to tell him what they look like. A little voice inside my head says, '*Vagina. Just say vagina.*' No, I think, *bad move. I'm not saying vagina in front of a strange man. It's not safe. Besides, he'll say I'm vagina-fixated, and we all know where that goes. Or that I'm crying false vagina.* 'Vagina, vagina, vagina!' the voice screams happily in my head, and I smile a little. *It would be worth it just to watch his face, see his pulse quicken, his knuckles whiten. No, uh-uh. But he's waiting, think . . . hurry up.*

"Flower," I say and for the next one, "Bird at the flower." *Vagina!* "Map of Canada." *This one's menstruating!* "Artichoke." And on and on, getting into it by the time we are finished, enjoying the exercise of conjuring second and third images, taking care that they have some artistic credibility. Good thing, too, because he's written it all down and we start over again, only this time I have to show him, outline with my trusty pencil where I see the flower, the bird, et cetera. I nearly had a heart attack. And then I was out on the street again. And I went home alone and put myself, weeping, to bed.

During the civil trial, Glancy testified that my interpretation of the Rorschach tests lacked creativity and imagination.

I ALWAYS anticipated that the police defence would include their best attempts to defame my character and that they would do so from a variety of positions. I'd had a lot of time to think about it and concluded, what else were they going to do? I just never thought they would get so dirty. But what was I thinking? Although my lawsuit was about police negligence and discrimination, the issue was rape. And when rape is the issue, the character of the woman involved is always an issue. The new mythology is that it is not.

I had told Sean all along that the police might bring up stuff about Johnny, about my brother, about the TTC ticket bust. Sean said they couldn't do that, don't worry, it wasn't relevant to the matter at hand. And I wanted to believe him. The thing about Sean is that before he met me, his clients were insurance companies and other conglomerates. He didn't see the attack coming and couldn't warn me, didn't prepare. In law schools, sexual-assault law is sometimes addressed within criminal-law courses. Often it is not. Existing curriculum is developed and delivered by legal academics and does not touch on the issues contained in this book. If we are to encourage raped women to file criminal or civil charges, lawyers must be appropriately trained to represent their issues and rights. Course design and delivery on the subject must originate with women who have first-hand knowledge developed from work in the field. Lawyers should not be learning about one of the most serious of violent crimes while on the job. And at the expense of the women involved.

But Sean was a good man, political and smart enough to know what he did not know and to learn it quickly. I never questioned his commitment to my best interests. He opened himself to my involvement and direction in building strategies and finding witnesses. I marvel now at the luck of finding him, when most other lawyers would not have taken my case at all or would have blown it.

All lawsuits have a pretrial phase so that the judge can canvass the possibility of settlement with counsel for both parties. Mine was held before Justice George Adams, and took two days (they usually take an hour). Pretrials are much less formal than trials. Adams, animated and involved, sat on a table while he listened and attempted to negotiate our legal differences. As is required, I offered to settle for fifty grand and an agreement from the police to work with women to improve training and develop a warning protocol. The police legal team responded that they would not sue me for costs if I dropped the suit. Next stop was trial.

❖

As ready as I'll ever be

27:

IN 1997, in addition to being Jane Doe and preparing for trial, I was working with a small public relations firm that specialized in Canadian publishing. It was work that I enjoyed and it paid relatively well, but I was never much further ahead than my next paycheque. Often the media people I was pitching to, to interview the newest or the oldest CanLit writer, also knew me as Jane Doe and would inquire about the status of my case. This didn't bode well for my career as a publicist. I was also teaching part-time and picking up other contracts with women's groups and arts agencies. By this time, *Jane Doe v. the Metropolitan Toronto Police Force* was part of law school curriculum in universities across Canada. Thanks to Elizabeth Sheehy, who was the first to encourage and invite me, I was lecturing regularly on campuses about my work as Jane Doe (and continue to do so).

For eleven years the media coverage of my case had held the public's interest and provided a focus on sexual assault. The focus didn't really change anything—in fact it reinforced a lot of old notions—but *Jane Doe* was now a relatively familiar story. People were intrigued by my case, engaged by the implications and the legal precedent I had already established. The derring-do of a little rape victim. The *Toronto Star* and the *Globe and Mail* kept my story in their pages. But the telling of it has always been mediated by others, an index of images and headlines signalling other people's versions of my story in language that is so filtered by personal and institutionalized fear of rape that the writers could be talking about something else entirely. And they often were. But they were talking.

One day in 1995 I got a call from a reporter named Heather Bird. She wrote a well-placed column for the *Toronto Sun*, a popular right-wing tabloid. She was their left-wing darling, a tricky position in a truculent journal. Heather had read about Jane Doe in another paper and was reminded that she had lived in the area in which the Balcony Rapist preyed and had seen one of the posters that WAVAW had distributed. She asked if we could meet and I agreed. After that first meeting she wrote fifteen columns about my case, so many that the viciously satirical *Frank* magazine referred to them as her "Bird droppings." She wrote about me with respect and political insight. I believe that her accumulated pieces were critical in providing new readings of sexual assault for a mass readership (which included police officers) who relied exclusively on the *Sun* for their daily dose of news, views and opinion, almost all of which I scorned.

Then the *Sun* editors came on side, too. As the civil case proceeded, their coverage was often the most detailed and least biased. Go figure. On the other hand, frequent front-page coverage of my case was strategically placed next to women in bikinis, Shania Twain and once even a leather fetishist. I leaked documents to Heather and she became acquainted with my legal team. Although we hold different positions on some things (especially sports), I have come to trust and respect her immensely, and I value her friendship.

Before my trial started, Heather got a phone call from a woman named Lori Martin, who was trying to contact me. Back in the summer of 1986, the police had deduced that Lori was going to be number six on the Balcony Rapist's list. They informed her of this and used her apartment, which was located across the street from mine, as a stakeout in their failed attempts to catch buddy in the act of raping. (Lori stayed with a friend.) Her face appeared on the front page of the *Toronto Sun* along with the startling news that apparently some women *had* been warned. Lori agreed to be a witness against the police. The next day another woman who had also lived close by called Heather with the story that a few weeks before my rape, the police had not followed up on her mother's attempt to report an intruder who had tried to break in via her balcony, because they didn't think they fit the profile. The photos of these women also made the *Sun*'s front page. Then Richard Element, whom I did not know but who had lived in the same building as me at the time of my attack, called to say that he had important information. Seems he was persuaded to stop replacing light bulbs at the back of our building because his actions were interfering with an undercover police stakeout. And he was prepared to testify, too! It was wild. Good people were reading the news and deciding to get involved. It was almost as good as it got. (Mysteriously, a columnist named Christie Blatchford was assigned by the *Sun* to cover the civil trial, not Heather. She soon returned the paper's position on my case to its more traditional fifties style of moralizing and victim blaming).*

As the trial date, September 8, 1997, approached, this tentacled, screaming thing that was swirling around me, but in a legal, orderly way, reached tornado proportions. Everything was moving faster than I could see, sweeping me up, spinning me into the centre. It was exciting, but potentially killing. I thought about securing some protection and approached the National Film Board for a first-time filmmakers' grant. My desire to produce a film had never dimmed, and I had written a script about being Jane. I met all of the requirements, and they gave me enough money to hire a small camera crew to document the trial. I would record and tell the story of Jane Doe myself. A friend who taught at the Ontario College of Art & Design arranged for a student to receive a course credit for assisting on the film (and learning on the job) and for two more to attend the trial and produce artist renderings of lawyers, witnesses and myself to play with the tradition of courtroom sketching.

Filming was not permitted inside the courtroom. My plan was to interview people who attended the trial including witnesses for both sides and especially the media, to present an alternative and more accurate record than mainstream media would deliver. I would also give daily updates. It was to be one of the most affirming and powerful actions I would take.

I have never given media interviews on camera. Legally, my likeness

---

* In the year 2000, the *Toronto Sun* and its partner, CFRB radio, named me their Newsmaker of the Year. In addition to the plaque, a fabulous lunch and a standing ovation, they gave me a cell-phone, perfume (Chanel) and jewellery, which remain my favourite awards. One thing about the *Toronto Sun*, they sure know how to treat a girl.

cannot be filmed, and I will not sit behind the shadows and pixillation commonly used to disguise raped women. You've seen them, women whose voices are clear (although sometimes disguised) but whose heads and torsos are in shadow or dissolved into an electronic mass. The viewer moves closer to the screen, becomes focused on her—if only the blind would slip or she'd move out of the shadow, maybe if I tilt my head a certain way or close one eye she will be revealed. Maybe I can recognize her voice, the accent anyway, the level of education her choice of words implies. It is all sensational, mildly titillating. The woman is re-victimized, undone, more invisible than before. Her responses do not fully register (also a result of the dumb questions she is often asked) because you've been concentrating on trying to put a face to her. It's not a fulfilling viewing experience and finally you do not really trust her. Or you feel so bad, are so horrified by the message and its package that you have to go and sit in another room for a while, away from the TV. Those images sadden me, make me angry, and I will not engage, which really pisses some reporters off, and to a degree I do

JANE DOE vs THE METRO POLICE

September 8 ★ 9:00 AM ★ 393 University Ave.

THIS TRIAL IS ABOUT POLICE ACCOUNTABILITY!

★ Demonstrate on Sept. 8 | Attend daily to monitor this two-month trial! ★

not blame them; theirs is a visual medium that can sustain the interviewers' sympathetic nods or patronizing glances only for so long until the pressure builds to show us the victim, why don't ya? When I demur and explain why, I am then asked, "Well, what *can* we shoot?"

That is not my job. Surely I have done enough. "Film the chief of police," I have said, "just his image with my voice. Have his mouth move digitally as I speak." Everyone smiles. They cannot imagine that I am serious. So the opportunity to have my own camera at my civil trial and in the hands of people I trusted and who would follow my direction, was an important thing for me.

I had informed my public relations employer of my Jane Doe identity and requested that my holidays begin on the day the trial began. I worked three days a week and knew that it was important to make her aware of my alter ego, especially as it was about to figure prominently in the media with which she worked. She terminated my contract two weeks before the big day, and I had to take her to the Ontario Labour Relations Board to get the severance pay I was legally entitled to. She even hired a lawyer and began proceedings to fight me for it before she took his advice to give me my damn money. So there I was without a job or other income. I had a few RRSPs and I cashed them in. The good news was that I could now attend all of my trial.

There was one more thing to do. I wanted to organize a demonstration to take place on the day the trial started. The TRCC came through again and let me use their phone, fax machine and other resources to get the word out and to produce posters and placards. Friends helped to plaster them across the city. One night we were stopped by police officers who requested a few copies. I sat up the nights before trial, hand-lettering picket signs.

Very best of all, Elizabeth Pickett had arranged to attend the trial with me. All of it. She had lent her brilliant legal mind to building strategies with me and for me since I had first met her in 1987. Sean was impressed by her, which benefited me more than I could have foreseen. All of that was gravy though, because Elizabeth and I probably used to be the same person once in another life that we can barely recall.*

She is the kind of close friend to whom you do not have to explain what you mean or think, because she already gets it. A single word, a look or smile says it all. She came to court every day. She translated and explained and mediated. And she understood.

And so it began. I felt pretty good about it all, nervous, excited, scared, prepared, unprepared. We had amazing witnesses lined up. I had Sean and Eric, and I had Cynthia Petersen. It was time for my close-up.

---

* I've been blessed to have other friends like that. Friends who are like water to life. Friends like Susan, Anna, Maureen, Sirrka, Beverly, Rita, Patti, Maurice, Goran, Michael, Margaret, my sister. There are more. Look at what wealth I have.

Hello, Police?
I've been non-violent
raped...

Sorry, Wrong Number.

N°4. Such an ending. Silence D the
FBI agent gleefully describing
serial rape cases. His hard-on
the witness not. His balls so
they break through his shirt col

What have I done. Where shall
Who will be there.

Civil trial journal

Civil trial journal
Jane Doe v. the Metropolitan Toronto Police Force

(. . . continued from page 8)

(. . . continued from page 8)

September 9, 1997

I sit alone again. No one to ask questions of, no answers.
My lawyers in a row in front of me. Lots of room there. My
place taken by legal files and boxes. What happened to the
TV version? The lawyer all protective and attentive, the
in-charge client taking notes and sharing information.

I come to court alone and sit alone. Nothing has changed.

Sean's opening statement tells Alice's story. Her letter
(to the WAVAW-police committee) will be submitted as evidence. How will she react? I have made her unsafe. Sean
hasn't met my eyes yet. 11:10 a.m.

I didn't agree with this strategy of retelling/reliving
the particulars of the other women's rapes but we proceed
with that now. So different falling from lawyers' mouths,
so lesser. A little dignity is in order. On order. Order
in the court. Ordure.

Finlay doesn't get it at all. Not even a little bit.
Posturing like a peacock. Great clearings of throat,
swishing of robes, and wordy positioning of anticipated
evidence and precedents. Raising objections that make him
look foolish.

The rapist's picture everywhere.

Security guards with guns behind me.
Plethora, the alleged lawyer, Mr. Hairdo, old clothes men,
words and images as I swallow and swallow to keep the vomit
down.

Visualizing myself at defence table bent over bingo cards
with good luck totems, trolls, dice, etc., as judge calls
out the numbered balls . . .

Sean's law student is more involved, more integral than I am.
I am not being included in the process of the trial. Sean
is acting as if he must indulge a needy client. I don't
understand.

Dreamed of my mom. She was alone and afraid and old. Wanted
me to promise that I would stay with her, look after her.
I did, of course, but also sensing the loss of my future,
of independence and chance to be loved again versus needed.
Wake up, Jane, you're dreaming, wake up.

2:00 p.m. Ignored by Sean et al. at lunch. He is so pumped,
can't hear me, his eyes are closed. Droning on now. Both
of them, about who will witness and brief synopses of the
evidence they will give, upon which the case will be won.
   They will "opine the necessity of assisting the tryer of
fact . . ."
   Depression. Torments my heart.

September 10, 1997

Dreamed I couldn't sleep. The cruellest and most clever of my
recurring dreams. Wrote a letter to Sean, made list(s) of
questions, responders to their experts. Must must MUST have
expert witness to testify to the current police response to
rape versus 1986 and fact that nothing has changed, to
counter the Peacock's claims that Toronto (sexual assault)

cops are tops. Someone from WAVAW or the TRCC.

So tired. Doesn't help that I gave a 7:00 a.m. (8:30 in Newfoundland) radio interview. Thank god they can't show my face. Large boil erupting on prominent left cheekbone. I would frighten viewers. The on-air host couldn't stop staring at it.

We introduce our first witness today. Dr. Peter Jaffe establishes that in his expert opinion "male violence against women is a pervasive social problem that contributes significantly to women's social inequality.

"Male sexual violence, including rape, affects the lives of all women and is an act of power and control rather than a sexual act."

He includes a definition of sexual assault, government stats and a breakdown of common rape mythologies.

A good beginning. The police defence team do not argue or counter any of this except to shake their heads and scowl ferociously.

Next is James Hodgson, professor of sociology, Longwood College in Farmville, Virginia, U.S.A., and former cop, 52 Division, Metropolitan Toronto Police Force. He will further provide the court with an understanding of policing to show how they (cops) cannot—given their good-old-boy training and group mentality—understand the stuff Jaffe just explained. As a result they become negligent in sexual-assault investigations. We are setting the ground here, providing a context for the judge by defining rape and its impact on society versus how the police view it and investigate it. It is a brilliant strategy.

11:15 a.m. Words with Sean. Factoring in that he too is nerved up/biggest trial of his life/just a man, etc. I'm asking for twenty minutes each day with him to be briefed/to clarify/to discuss whatever is going on. Had to chase him

down the escalator to ask for a moment alone. Believe he
was actually trying to get away from me. He categorized my
request as the sulking of a petulant child and feels he is
being forced to indulge me. Informed him that this response
presents a whole new problem aside from the one I wished
to address. Could see in his eyes that he knew he'd just
stepped in shit.

Appears he is not used to dealing with clients in this
manner and perceives my requests as confrontational.
Thinks that my involvement translates into him giving me
support. So I guess that's the way it's gonna be. Again.
But what happened? I've advised him on everything. All of
our experts were my strategies. I'm the one who found them.
I had to fight him for them. He knows that I know. Where
did my friend Sean go?

We're back. Burned my mouth chugging coffee. Therapist
would love that. If I had one. Murder in my heart. Focus.
The Peacock is questioning Jim Hodgson's credentials as an
expert witness. You have to have an alphabet after your
name to qualify. He takes great issue with Jimmy's community college credentials. Interesting class distinction.
Will he stay or will he go now? Up to the judge. Here she
comes now. Yes! Jimmy's in, he's on, he's expert! Begins
his examination in chief tomorrow.

My dad says "tomorry." My dad . . .

September 11, 1997

Arrived at noon. Very upset last night. Red swollen eyes
take gaze away from boil. Evidence introduced that I should
previously have seen. When I inquire, Sean tells me that
I and my testimony are essentially irrelevant, and he goes
into a conference meeting with Jimmy and Eric to strategize about the witness lineup. Sean says he wants me to
testify tomorrow—Friday. I feel unprepared and that I've

been shut out. Had the conversation about briefing versus support. Very stressful. For us both.

Now we're breaking for lunch and Jimmy's still on the stand. That means I won't be on tomorrow after all. Finlay still has to pillory Jim. Great eruptions of laughter from the defence table. Our case amuses them greatly. Finlay and his girl practically guffaw at the evidence Jim presents. I heard her snort. Meanwhile the court clerk guns off anyone who speaks or smiles in the spectator area. She approached several people today and made them spit their gum into a Kleenex she held in front of their mouths. I think she wished it was chloroform. Very stern dominatrix type. No joy there. The courtroom her domain, other court workers hers to command. When a friend passed me a note, she had her removed. The note read, "Courage."

Sean leads Jim Hodgson through his testimony. They are brilliant together. This would be enough, Jim as the prodigal brother analyzing the family of police he left and why, returning only to define them, to explain and understand their nature and culture. He provides a definition of policing, swears that the force does not comply with its own administrative procedures, reveals the existence of a police-only chapter of the Masons cops are encouraged to join, and of course their own hockey league. He decries the efficacy of police training, charges "impression management"—I paraphrase of course.

He is my hero.

PROFESSOR James Hodgson is about forty years old. Perhaps because he lectures to communicate, or perhaps by habit, he speaks a little too quickly and in long sentences. But he is kind and still has his little-boy face about him. When Sean first approached the professor to testify on our behalf, he was not very keen. Then I phoned him one night and we spoke at length about my case. He told me later that our conversation was pivotal in his decision to be involved. He said it was because I talked about doing what we could with the tools we had or something like that. I don't remember.

Jim's first written report for us was almost indecipherable it was so locked in sociological jargon and academic foofaraw. Sean worked long and hard with him, at Jim's expense (expert-witness fees were contingent on winning the case), to modify years of thought and academic position-ing into what became five days of testimony and cross-examination about police culture. In the end, he delivered an incisive description of the insti-tution of policing and exposed its enduring patriarchal nature, especially regarding the cops' attitudes toward sexual-assault investigation. He exposed the militaristic nature of the Metropolitan Toronto Police Force, its hypocrisy and vulnerability. Its sense of valour and vileness both—all mangled within a powerful political bureaucracy that serves and protects us their way. Whether we like it or not. Whether we need it or not.

His testimony was based on his research and writing. He describes his subject as "the organizational structures and techniques that systematic-ally inhibit satisfactory relations between the police and members of the public." Another way to say that is "Why the police are so resistant to change and how they pretend to change when they do not." Or "Why the public needs to believe that the police have changed even though it's clear they have not."

On the stand he talked about the "poison environment" in the police unit that investigated my rape, which was "swamped with cases and laden with deadwood." He spoke from experience as he had investigated numerous sexual assaults himself and worked down the hall from Bill Cameron in 1986.

"Compared to the homicide squad, the unit was extremely poor," he testified. "I would give it a D-minus . . . A number of [the unit] officers were burnt out . . . they weren't being productive." During the specialized training sessions that officers received on sexual-assault investigations, Hodgson said, "officers were allowed to tell sexist and demeaning jokes and to refer to rape as "accidental intercourse," "fraudulent behaviour" or "a business deal gone bad." For female trainers who spoke during those sessions, the experience was like being "fed to the wolves."

September 12, 1997

Jimmy is still on. Media all over. Covering, hovering, beginning to sense that there is even more than rape here. Maybe something important. A bigger story. Christie Blatchford and Rosie DiManno, Terese Sears with the lovely smile, Austin Delaney (Heather Bird says he's really quite nice), an uptight guy

from the CBC—I forget his name—Phinjo (Gorgeous) Gombu and Sean Fine. Radio-Canada too.* Jim is in full stride. The Professor. Very confident, secure in what he knows to be true. Cannot be flapped by the Peacock, who continues to insult and circle, convinced that he is the higher authority. A grand dance. A grand dame. Aggrandize.

Jim's finished. I win.

But so bizarre. No one seems to agree with me, and the judge has not dismissed the court. The media does not report on Jim's testimony in any detail. Despite the language barriers, I thought he was saying such important stuff, shedding light, giving us hope. His best stab at defining the insidious quality of police intransigence. Listen:

> The paramilitary organizational model (of policing) inhibits officers from responding adequately to the magnitude and diversity of requests for service from a twenty-first-century community. It is extremely alienating. It projects a very impersonal quality with strict reliance on rules and regulations with no room for diversity and no opportunity to assess. You take on the characteristic of the organization

---

* Representatives of local and national media who covered the trial, including the queens of personal column writing. Except for Phinjo Gombu of the *Toronto Star* and the *Sun*'s Tracy Nesdoly, who attended every day, they were in and out of the courtroom as their schedules and interest allowed.

you belong to . . . where men of the same racial and cultural background—in the case of the Toronto Police Force, Scots and Irish especially—socialize together, play, pray, intermarry and raise their children in the same homogeneous ideology. The institution of policing presents the clearest exam- ple, the best recipe, for resistance to change . . . This authoritarian model offers no incentive to reward innovation or excellence. It does not encourage greatness or imagination or communication outside of standard operation. It supports a bottleneck struc- ture where those on the bottom are destined to remain there (with the exception of astute indi- viduals who play the game and rise to the top). To maintain order amongst the ranks, police bureaucra- cy must create and maintain a sense of cultural belonging with members (employees) who are detached, isolated from others not inside the group.

Meaning the rest of us. Civilians. It's beautiful.
So how come none of that was in the newspapers or on the news at six? Huh? How come? The police lawyers didn't chal- lenge or question Professor Hodgson on it either. Don't we get it? The police haven't changed. They've only given us the impression they've changed. They're pretending!
Jim is finished before the lunch break. He leaves the court- room, and a bunch of really big guys walk out behind him.

1:00 p.m. Professor of criminology Neil Boyd on the stand, apparently in my defence, although I have never met the man and don't understand what he's yammering about. I don't think Sean does either. Testosterone impulses or something. He seems to have a surplus himself. Apparently he is here in my defence. We are never introduced.

I left to sit with Jim for a while, to keep him company. His plane doesn't leave until this evening. The big burly guys who came in during Jim's testimony and followed him out were cops. I noticed them because they were very unsmiling and trying to cross their arms but could not, the way guys get if they build up their biceps or whatever too much. Jim said they accidentally bumped into him in the hall, then called him asshole and traitor. One of them was his partner when he was in 52, and Jim remembered that he had a wonderful singing voice. Jim said he is glad he came here and to have met me.

September 15, 1997

12:30 p.m. I'm a mess. Sean says I will testify this afternoon! On the only day I asked to be excused. Begged to be.

My first class tonight.* My opening-act outfit at the cleaners. Great disappointment with Sean. He made me cry. At his office until midnight last night. Sunday night. No sleep. No preparation and I teach from 6:30 to 9:30 tonight. I never get home before eleven. He says he will spring for a cab to the college and to bring me back to his office after I finish.

Rise above it. Soon this will be over and there will never be another lawyer in my life again as god is my judge so help me Jesus, Mary and Joseph. Someone better help me.

Give me faith, strength. Fear and bitterness in my blackened heart. What the fuck is Neil Boyd still doing up there?

Okay. Stop. You will teach your class tonight. You will be fabulous and cut early. Students will be thrilled. You will wear your black suit tomorrow and gather all of your power and glamour about you. They can't touch you. Be true. Head up and heart up and let them take their best shot. Breathe.

---

* I was beginning a new semester at a local college where I taught social service diploma students.

AFTER two days of testimony, I decided that if they kept me in the witness box for a third day I would wear red. Fire-engine red. And I would paint my nails and lips to match. I needed to assert myself, to redefine, at least visually, the little rape victim in the box. The courtroom was packed. Jane Doe was speaking at last. I had toned down my hair colour and cut it quite short. It was a stupid thing to have done because it was a bad haircut and added to my distress. Somehow I managed to pull it all back and pin it up. I am a private person and quite vain. Had I been subjected to the unforgiving scrutiny of cameras for eleven years, I doubt I would have carried on.

The artist sketches of me that appeared at the top of the news on every TV station every night for weeks showed me from behind, or with a thin black bar covering my eyes. Although there was a media ban protecting my identity, the sketches were remarkably like me. Good enough that one of my brothers and several acquaintances and students who were not formerly aware of my Jane Doe status were able to identify me. This of course was assisted by additional and repeated screenings of shots of the apartment building in which I had lived in 1986, and radio interviews I agreed to give. My voice is very soft and sibilant. A seductive voice, I'm told, and easily recognizable. It is in jarring contrast to the content and meaning of some of the things I say. My voice, its quality and timbre, became the subject matter of more than one newspaper columnist who covered my testimony:

. . . a baby voice that barely rises above an actor's whisper . . .
—*The Toronto Sun*, September 16, 1997
. . . her voice a sibilant whisper . . .
—*The Toronto Star*, September 17, 1997

Despite the court order, my physical stature also became part of their journalistic observations:

. . . her tiny, fragile appearance . . . she has a sharp, fox face, keenly expressive . . . the smallest adult I have ever seen . . . she has a smashing grin . . . a wisp of a woman, as tiny and fragile as a sparrow, with russet hair and skin that is almost

opaque and wide set eyes . . . an exotic smudge of a woman,
tiny . . .
—A composite from *The Toronto Star*, *The Globe and Mail* and
The Toronto Sun

It was as if they believed that I had deliberately, surgically altered my
physical size and voice for trial. Never were we gifted with descriptions
of the large asses, flat feet and powerful shoulders of the dozens of police
officers who testified in booming voices against me. The balding patterns
of certain expert psychiatric witnesses were not discussed, nor were FBI
agents and criminal profilers described by their soft, Southern drawls
and Scottish burrs. Resemblances to animals were not remarked upon.

But I do understand. The pathology and predictability of the media's
response to rape and sexual assault fascinate me. It fits perfectly with
the broader legal and social understanding that each rape is an isolated
incident, and each raped woman is an agent of her own rape. The media
are the final voice, the blindest eye; journalists and reporters are the
truest ally in the construction of women as victims, and the manipulation
of our fears—real and constructed. And after all, I was Jane Doe, a tiny
little raped woman who dared to hang onto her anonymity as she pointed her finger to direct our gaze to the very agency, the very men, who
were supposed to prevent and solve the crime.

September 17, 1997

Done testifying. Sean says I was hammy and over the top. I
ask him if there were specific places where he observed that
behaviour or if he felt I was consistently so for the entire
three days (years) I was up there. He ignored me. Eric and
Cynthia do not comment.

Man it was hard. Way past hard. Impossible. So impossible
that the only way you can do it is to dissociate. If you do
not, it will kill. Couldn't possibly have survived/tolerated
the humiliation of it all if I had been firmly located in
the room. Fucking witness stand was built for giants. Feet

didn't touch the floor. If I sat back, the mike didn't pick me up, and if I leaned in, I almost fell off. And then everyone is telling me to speak up. Speak up, as you completely expose yourself in a hostile environment. Oh my.

For days (weeks) Finlay showed me newspaper articles printed twelve years ago in papers I have never read and asked me if I remembered what I thought when I read them. They were stories of rape and death, of fear and rape and death. When I asked him to stop, I think he thought I was confessing or something. I could see my sister preparing to throw herself across the room and stab Finlay in the heart. Christie Blatchford with her pen held like a knife.

I waited for years thinking this would be my big chance, the opportunity finally to tell my rape my way. But it wasn't. Again I had to respond carefully, briefly, to questions put to me by men with agendas other than mine. I had to sit and listen and swallow as they tried again to make out it wasn't really so bad after all. Finlay came at me from different positions, parsimonious in his choice of words, parsonical in delivery. His brother is the Anglican archbishop of Toronto, his wife a parson, too. Holy God. What is clear now is that he really doesn't get it, never did. The police defence team is our biggest asset! Who'd have thought? Unless it's a trick, a ruse, a John Grisham plot with Tom Cruise as the lawyer who comes from behind, is much more ruthless, canny than we thought.

But wait, that's Sean! Sean is Tom Cruise. Ours is the John Grisham storyline.

Tom Cruise would never treat me so badly though. James Woods maybe.

Really surreal. Dreamlike qualities, a sense that it didn't really matter as long as I stuck to the script, the lines and questions we had rehearsed in discovery, waiting

Illuminating The Court

for the killing ones to be asked, disguised as something else. Thinking at least two questions ahead. If I move here they will crown me, take my queen, rout my knight. Fighting the compulsion to laugh, leave, scream, sleep, attack, and the paralysis that stops me. As in dreams.

"Can you tell us how your life has changed as a result of the rape?" Sean asks. And my throat catches even after twelve years.

How has my life changed? I am here. Is that not enough?

This was not my plan. I live now in split screen, between dreams, without words. I live in resistance, subversion, I struggle to defend myself to you, to myself. This has its own rewards but I am exhausted, alone. Afraid to stop fighting.

Instead of saying this I open a vein, and bleed for them as is required in a court of law when rape is the subject. And make no mistake, this trial is about rape. We call it Charter violations and police negligence but rape will always out. Even when it is civil.

I can't remember more.
Visual. The courtroom as the set for The Rocky Horror Picture

Show. Pregnant stenographer as Janet, her boyfriend Brad the kindly clerk who kept filling my glass and telling me to drink. The Dominatrix and Finlay as the skanky ones—I forget their names. The judge is Rocky, who else? A chorus of spectators, reporters and cops serenade us along. I play Jane.

When it was over I left the courtroom and walked into an ambush of media scrumming, humming, drumming their own views of what had happened. Pointing their questions at me, shooting them, firing. Surrounded. Worse than Finlay. "Why didn't you lock your doors? Why did you speak with the other women? What did you expect? What difference would it have made? Can't you just admit you made a mistake? Can we shoot your hands, your feet? Other headless body parts? Pixillation? Shadow? Bag over your head?"

I counter. They retreat. I am dead again. I walk home alone. I can't remember more.

September 18, 1997

9:30 a.m. Lori Martin. Eric's first examination of a witness. She is small with the bluest of eyes, wide and far apart. Eric says we look alike but we do not. Earlier, Lori asked if Eric was single, as have many other women. He is the beauty in the room. A cultured Elvis. He's a little nervous, their big date, the flirting done. She is remarkable. Composed, attractive, in a pale green suit. Reinforcing everything I have said, she tells her story, already told on the front page of the Toronto Sun, Sunshine Girl pretty. What do you say about someone like her? That she is true of heart? Noble? Did the right thing? Words that do not nearly speak her.

Tears. If the police had warned me as they warned Lori, I would never have been raped, I would not be here, my eyes would be clear.

1:00 p.m. My lawyers took me to lunch at the Osgoode Hall dining room. A room of black and white and foodstuffs,

lawyers preening and picking the eyes out of their victuals
with laughing mouths. A murder of crows. Pleased with themselves, my lawyers laugh and laugh. No time for questions.
Gotta eat. Apparently it's going well. None of them speak
to me about my testimony.

2:30 p.m. And now it's Richard Element. How many heroes can
you have in one trial? Yes, it's going very well. Going,
Goering, gong, gone.
   Must try and catch Richard in the hall. I want to press
gifts, praise on him.
   Heather Bird to thank for all of this. She would say no,
just doing her job. Wonder why she's not here?

Media reviews of my performance/testimony were in the
paper today:

   "testy exchanges"
   "cry me a river, honey"
   "passive-aggressive"
   "an activist burning to score political points"
   "I longed to give the tiny woman in the witness box a good swift
kick in the pants"

   (You and what army, honey?)

Most of this was from Christie Blatchford. Friends advised
me not to read her columns, as if I could help it. She fas-
cinates me—smart and funny but with a meanness of spirit,
exposing herself so shamelessly, recklessly, cruelly. I
wonder what her story is? Anyway, where is the bitch today?
What's she going to do, drop-kick herself into the game
for five minutes and claim she's a player? Hah.
   I cried so much when I read her columns, I was ill. So
what. Mind your own business.

I wish I remembered more of what I actually said during my
testimony. I know I wanted Sean to ask me certain things
he did not. I wanted to talk about Bill Cameron, his kindness and the fact that I fought against naming individual
officers in the suit. Also, the bastardly balcony door was
locked! There was more . . .

I wanted Sean to do some prep work with my friend, the
psychologist Lori, to better contextualize his questions
regarding sexual assault. He would not, could not. Some of
Sean's questions stopped me, made me retreat even further.
I was not prepared. And why, please someone tell me, for
what reason for whose benefit under what circumstances
were Finlay and Richards allowed to question my work, my
books, my beliefs? Why were they allowed to mock me? Where
was my lawyer? My judge? Must stop remembering.

> "Jane Doe's cross-examination at the hands of Bryan Finlay
> was a walk in the park . . . her treatment was unfailingly cour-
> teous and civilized . . ."
> —Christie Blatchford, *The Toronto Sun*

September 19, 1997

11:30 a.m. Dr. Vince DeMarco. Sean makes a bad beginning.
Asks for Vince's diagnosis of my depression: "adjustment
disorder with depressed mood."
Depressive illness.
Mood disorder.
Nosology? Phenomenologicallylylylylalala.
The scribblers scratching frantically. I should just
show them my tits. Not that it isn't confusing. We are
deconstructing Glancy's report, which labels me deviant,
malingering, delusional, before Glancy testifies. This
trial tells the story backwards. If this were film, real
theatre, the director would have had a stroke by now.
Major depressive disorder as per DSM-IV.

De-realization.

So humiliating. Hey, I said to leave my menses out of this! Okay, I think this is the good part: powerful, good, directed behaviour.

Labile state—that's it, don't go too far!

Even Vince is saying "I" instead of "we," implying that my treatment, our relationship, was not directed by me. Hey Vince! I came to you, remember?

Too clinical. My heart is breaking. But it doesn't hurt as much anymore. And I know that he must present this way. Mustn't move outside of the expert-witness box too much.

Unhinged.

Psychometric testing.

Poor metabolizer.

Jane is not a large person.

Considerable internal resources, bright, friends, hyper-arousal, dissociative states—like now, Vince? When the only way I can stay in my seat is by leaving it a bit? By observing you all dissect me in front of me? Is that what you mean? And it's a negative?

I wish that he and Sean would stop calling me by my first name as if I am a child, referring to my boyfriend as if I am a girl. No one calls the judge Jean, and Vince is referred to as Doctor, not Vince. Shoot.

Unipolar affective disorder, adaptive consequence, psychopathology, deviance, extrapolate backwards. Dysthymia, Dizzy Gillespie, dizzy Mia, Woody Allen.

Marilyn Monroe? Sado-masochistic!? Doidge wrote in his referral letter that I was sado-masochistic with a breathy voice like MM and wore go-go boots. I wouldn't even say go-go boots let alone wear them. Norm, your Freudian slip is showing. Look at the wording in his report. Not very artful, Doidger. But I give up. Really, I surrender. I confess. I throw myself on the mercy of the court. I appeal. This is murder.

Vince quickly slays Doidge for me, a quick incision to the epidepenis: "I believe he [Doidge] was a student in psychoanalytic training and had a supervisor . . . My reaction at the time was that the letter was nonsense and I basically dismissed it [as] the kind of psychoanalytic interpretation that gives psychoanalysis a bad name."

Hah. Take that! Why I oughtta . . .

Now Finlay is cross-examining Vince's interpretation of Glancy's diagnosis, which hasn't been introduced yet. You have to be Miss Marple to follow this. Finlay and Vince are like oil and water. Finlay needing the diagnosis to flow smoothly into a legal defence that I am a nutcase, that I harbour delusional thoughts and deviant behaviour toward police and state. Vince's oil making a slippery slope that Finlay cannot ride, keeps sliding from.

Histrionic, narcissistic, avoidant and other personality disorders.

Vince explaining that depression like mine does not equal dysfunction. Using Mike Wallace as an example. "If you want to get the job done, hire a depressed person."

Sociopath. Deviant. Malingering for financial gain.

"Dr. Glancy's report on Jane Doe is inaccurate, unprofessional, biased and cruel," says Vince DeMarco.

A small stirring from the media who are here, the words like foreplay—visions of headlines dance in their heads.

"Jane Doe would have preferred to sue the police without the claim including money, but the system does not work that way. It is noteworthy that Jane Doe is not suing for $15 million, as one might usually expect," says Vince.

I told Nathan Pollock, Glancy's psychologist colleague—the guy who wouldn't let me eat—that I believed the cops were staked out in the same bushes as the rapist but they missed him as he scaled the outsides of downtown high-rises. Well, it turns out he translated that into evidence of my being delusional under DSM-666. Which means I'm crazy. To refute that diagnosis, Vince uses the analogy of a waitress who tells her co-worker that the ham sandwich at table three wants his cheque. "She does not for a moment believe that the customer is really a ham sandwich. It is merely a metaphor," he says, and the courtroom breaks up—even the judge—haha hahahahahahaha, but wait, even funnier, crazier, I really do believe that those bunglers were out there in the same bushes and missed the rapist as he scaled the walls of downtown high-riseshahahahahahahahahahaha!

American Psychiatric Association, DSM-IV, political injury, anorexia, bulimia, forensic, delusional belief system.

And finally, Vince says, "I suffered along with her but could only glimpse a part of what she went through. It has opened my eyes in a way I should not like to repeat to the general insensitivity in our society to assault against women, and in particular to the key role the police as agents of that society play in perpetuating violence against women."

But then comes Bryan Finlay.

"I'm suggesting to you, Dr. DeMarco, that it's difficult given the long clinical course you have had with Ms. Doe to be objective in this case, to make an unbiased assessment."

I can't breathe.

September 20, 1997

I've asked Sean to meet with me. The tension between us is unbearable. I have to practically tackle him to get his attention. I'm here, Sean, in the room! His table just far enough in front of me that I can't pass him a note without rising from my chair and stretching across my table, skirt lifting, Dominatrix glaring—no, boring holes into me. Everyone watching, aware, but my lawyer.

Sean doesn't read my notes anyway. I should just post them

on his back. Ball them up and wing them at his head.

Rosemary Barnes is in the box now. Her written report is good. Takes the piss right out of Glancy but still characterizes me as specimen, something inspected

poked

prodded

psychiatrized.

Why do I have to fight them with their weapons? Let's see if Rosemary uses any of mine.

I found her, hired her to counter Finlay's position that Vince knew me too well to be objective. She begins by agreeing that familiarity in a psychotherapeutic relationship can affect objectivity. In the name of arse! Here I was all these years thinking cops and lawyers were the problem.

Here we go again with my childhood! Depressive symptoms, unconventional. Johnny, she's talking about Johnny. Leave him alone. Leave him. Alone.

"She re-involved herself with the boyfriend . . . she and he needed to have access to what comfort this relationship could provide in spite of the difficulties . . . "

Fucking Sean just said I was anally penetrated. Rosemary corrects him: "I haven't indicated anything about anal penetration." The judge asks for clarification: "Was there anal penetration?"

"Let's see . . . uhm, no . . ."—a great turning of pages—"I'm wrong," says Sean.

But let's just say it a few more times. Anal penetration, anal penetration, analpenetration. Perhaps they could set it to music.

Now Rosemary describes my rape and how I reacted to it. This is the fifth time we have heard it. Hello? Someone? I'm suing the police for negligence and Charter violations . . . anybody? Then quietly, clearly, calmly, Dr. Rosemary Barnes disagrees with Glancy's personality disorder bullshit. Something very dignified about her. Something true.

She commands us to listen. Finlay's girls aren't laughing.

"The psychological, physical threat (of sexual assault) is worse than (the threat to) the soldier in a front-line combat situation, who is trained to carry out that commitment and prepared for what to expect," says Rosemary.

She's good. The tune is the same but she's changing the dance. Sean falling into step, following her lead. When he is good, he is very very good. And what a lot of big words he knows. Bringing in WAVAW, postering, covering the defence assertions that I malingered, manipulated the system. Softly, cleanly, she rips Glancy and Pollock apart, laughs in Doidge's face.

"In my opinion, Dr. Glancy's report seriously distorts an understanding of Jane Doe as a person, and the distortion is the kind that might be consistent with discriminatory, sexist or stereotyped views of women," says Rosemary Barnes.

and

"I would characterize Dr. Doidge's report at best as extremely traditional, outdated, quite simplistic and not to be taken seriously . . . the formulations of an unsophisticated novice. He signs his report simply as MD and his qualifications to conduct psychotherapy are unknown to me."

I love you, Rosemary, love you love you love you.

"Dr. Glancy's statements don't describe Ms. Doe's above-average intelligence, her social poise, her outgoing personality, her financial independence, commitments to community, responsibility, ability to problem-solve."

Marry me, Rosemary. Sean just asked her, "Whither hence for Ms. Doe?" He makes me laugh. Too bad I hate him.

Now it's Bry's turn. (I call Finlay "Bry" now, sometimes

I feel I know him well enough.) He's still wearing his split-seam pantaloons and it's been two weeks. He begins by thanking Rosemary for substantiating his case. Then leads evidence that only two people out of one hundred would have scores like mine on one of their psych tests regarding attitudes toward social norms and traditions. If that's true, we're in more trouble than I thought.

It's a Very Snotty Bry who trys and fails and fails and fails to make Rosie say it his (Glancy's) way, believing that only his way is credible, believing that we will believe that because he says so. Believing his belief makes it so. My my, what would I do without Snotty Bry?

As Rosemary leaves the stand, people rise, move toward her, even Finlay shakes her hand. No one can doubt the importance of what she has done in retelling, reshaping crude, clinical interpretations of rape into something humane, something normal.

For a moment, even for those who do not really believe or understand what she has offered the court, she graced the halls of justice with dignity and reason.

And we're done. We rest our case. Wrest our case. Wrestle it. Wretched case.

I may never rest again.

September 22, 1997

9:30 a.m. Bill Cameron. He's a mister now. Retired. Mr. William Cameron. Hey Bill! Hi!

You look good. Bigger than you were, paler, same sad eyes, just spilling out of that witness box—he must be six foot six or something. Not overweight, just big. Slightly uncomfortable but secure. He's been here before. Doesn't look at me but I know he sees me.

Let's see how many stories you will tell and whether they will be the ones I remember or the ones police officers must tell. Tell so well. William Tell.

He is the first witness for the defence, and Finlay gets first shot. Leads him through his resumé, high school, police college, Auto Squad, old-clothes man, which included robbery and sexual-assault investigation. Interesting career path. He took a two-day seminar on sexual assault in 1985 and returned to Auto after he'd finished my case. In 1988 he became a founding member of the newly formed Sexual Assault Squad and was involved in apprehending the Subway Rapist. Then back to Auto from 1989 to 1993. The next year he landed in the newly named Major Crime Squad, where he specialized in counterfeit auto theft. He retired in 1996 with almost thirty years on the job and took his present position with the Insurance Crime Prevention Bureau specializing in . . . auto-insurance fraud!

Now Finlay is taking him through the physical layout of his office in 1986, police division boundaries, and how very busybusybusy/tiredtiredtired—but True Blue—police officers are. Especially when it comes to rape. This has been going on for hours.

Feelings of what? Fatigue? Paralysis? Shit, I'm bored. This is boring me. How is that possible? No wait, it's fear, anxiety masked as boredom.

No, it's boredom.

Finlay might as well be saying mass. In Latin. And Bill mumbling answers like the altar boy who doesn't know his lines and just blathers something and no one knows/cares. Or like an awards ceremony where the accountant and president of the academy take the stage in tuxedos and blither on about integrity and vote-counting and the audience glazes over because we just want to get to the good stuff and who are these guys anyway?

Time for a little courtroom surveillance. Hey! Cowboy Junkies in the (court) house . . . Patty Zuver looking like a movie star . . . my film crew. How delicious, ironic, to have David Findlay, one of the best-looking men in Toronto, on camera. His eyes on mine every day, recording my trials, my version of my rape. At first I was nervous, but he is so good, so kind, and I laugh to watch the cops watching him.

He probably doesn't think it's that funny.

There's my friend Windsor, flushed from methadone, nodding just a little (so is the court security guy). I'm glad he is here—one of my oldest friends, a stand-in for my brothers. Lori and Melanie, a group of poverty activists, fists clenched to their hearts in salute. They rotate between my trial and Daishowa down the hall where my friend Kevin is one of three being sued for boycotting a multinational to stop their attempts to clear-cut Native forests. I sit in sometimes when I can't take it here. Gave Kevin a few of my downers. He is not sleeping either.

Elizabeth by my side, in my ear, the only one who understands.

How am I going to stay here? Meeting with Sean tonight. He was too busy on the weekend.

September 23, 1997

More Bill. Getting into it now, the Bigger Awards. Best stakeout. Best supporting surveillance techniques. Telling us that there were thirty officers in old clothes (plain-clothes) staking out nineteen apartment buildings in my (then) neighbourhood and five marked police cars, which did not answer any radio calls except those related to the investigation. Jesus. They also used four unmarked vans as "stationary observation points." This for two weeks.

Telling the story of the arrest—uhm Bill, that's not what you told me. You caught him after we postered. After his parole officer saw the posters in the media. She put the pieces together. You seem to have added a few steps, a few days, a few feathers. Making it appear that not warning was effective. It effectively created a lot of police jobs and career opportunities.

What? WHAT! Buddy had a prior rape in Toronto. In addition to his spree out West. Same MO, an elderly woman, everyone agreed that a criminal proceeding would probably kill her, and he pleaded to three years. 1983. Goddamn. And no one told me. I've got three fucking lawyers and not one bothered to inform me. I spoke with Sean yesterday. Asked him what was up, what to expect. Oh god, am I in the room? Am I visible at all? Is that my hand shaking? Did my head just explode? Will they notice if I leave? Prefer it? This is so hurtful, shaming.

And another thing. Why the fuckfuckfuckfuckfuckFUCK wouldn't all of this info have shown up in a computer check of prior rapists who came in through windows with knives in downtown Toronto? How come no one told me, told us, in 1987 after his trial?

Did I just scream?

September 24, 1997

12:15 p.m. So I left and no one noticed. They preferred it. Arrived late today. Wanted to stay home but couldn't resist the flame. Couldn't stay off the cross. I asked Sean if there was other evidence of which I was not aware. He said he didn't think so.

I had an idea to start sketching, drawing. Doodles of judicial insignia, grape clusters, penmanship exercises, only mildly distracting. So I brought an HB pencil and my eyeliner sharpener to court and here I am. I'm going to sketch Bill. I'll sketch every bastardly one of them. Define them. Erase what I don't like. Tell them visually.

Besides, that's not my Bill. I remember one of the last

times I saw him, just after the arrest. He came to my home and when I opened the door I didn't recognize him for a moment. He was rested, the stress had left his face and he looked different. Calm. With a real smile.

He talks on and on, believing it true. They're referring to me again by my first name. As if I am a child or a rape victim.

He is a stuttering incompetent, vague and evasive in his answers, pathetically trying to rationalize and defend indefensible police conduct. Damn. I preferred a more roman-

ticized version of him. Was he ever so? Have I let my need to believe there are good men colour my memory of him?

Now Bill's saying that women in the area should have hidden their knives to prevent rape.

Hid them in the rapist's back maybe.

Billy billy boyo watch what you say . . .

Sean is taking him through more procedural lalala. Overwhelming caseloads, the importance of maintaining the crime scene. (Jeez, it's good I never told anyone that I cleaned up a little after I called 911 that night—before the police arrived.)

Walking him through all five rapes. He wants Bill to con-
demn the investigations of the other women's rapes but of
course he will not, cannot. Which is okay finally, because
the negligence jumps off the pages of the first three occurrence reports. The ones they didn't believe, didn't connect
until Bill came on.

The investigating officer on the second rape was listening to what the woman's apartment superintendent was saying
and not the woman. Seems the super didn't like her, and he
was a man in authority and that was good enough for the
police. Seems she saw several men, and the super didn't
approve. Then her boyfriend told the police that she had
given him a dose. As if! They considered filing her rape as
a false allegation. Worst of all—something you couldn't even
make up it's too outrageous—there was a bowl of potato chips
on her bed and because they had not been overturned, spilled
during her rape the investigating officer, a Sgt. Duggan,
wrote—he actually wrote the words (we've entered his report
as evidence)—that he didn't believe her! It is to weep. She
had a knife at her throat but because she didn't fight or
struggle enough to upset the chips, he wrote that he does
not believe her. And Bill is defending him. Duggan will testify next week. I am ashamed to be in the same room with
any of them.

Kim Derry sits at a table just across and in front of me.
I turn my head to watch him. He confers with his lawyers,
whispers, reads documents. Older now, a little softer, he
wears vague suits with shirts that do not match and faded
ties. I feel . . . what? A little bit of fear, contempt, feelings that are old, settled, as if I have already had them.
He has said hello, asked how I am, all very civil. A little
too civil, too friendly, as if we share something. To others
he would look earnest, like a nice guy. To me he is without
personality or emotion, acting a part. I bet he does it well.

"Feeling like the fall guy"
(in the voice of Kim Derry)

I CAN'T believe it's come down to this. I'm a superintendent on the largest police force in the country—okay, *acting* superintendent—and here I am the defendant, the fall guy in some pissant lawsuit by a rape victim I knew was trouble the day I met her. What are there, like a million females in the city and he had to pick her? Frivolous and vexatious, that's what the law calls this kind of harassment and cop-bashing. And now I have to sit here every day and put up with these snot-nosed lawyers and some lady judge on a case that should never have made it this far and that there's no way they can win. And I'm the bad guy. Bill's retired and I'm it. All I did was do my job. Does anyone remember that I caught the guy? How come no one's talking to the other women he raped who I helped, who thanked me, who still send me Christmas cards? And what about my citations? I'm the youngest officer to make this rank this fast, and the old man will retire soon and he's encouraged me to think ahead five years.

And now this. Not to mention the other stuff with that do-gooder Girdlestone on the Sexual Assault Squad.*

I told Bill that we needed to take a stronger hand with Jane. I could have arrested her over that whole postering thing. Interfering with a police investigation, mischief, whatever. But no, Bill says he'll deal with her and then goddamn if we don't get another call from that probation officer the day after she posters. I guess I shouldna yelled at her, Jane I mean, but the first time she sort of asked for it, and the other times, what did she expect? That I was gonna listen to her denigrate my work? And we took down the Sunshine Girl posters. Jeez. And every time I opened my mouth she was saying she's not a victim and she's not a girl or a lady and that I wasn't her father. Her father! She's older than I am. And then she tells me not to talk to her anymore!

Anyway, the point is we caught the guy. It was superior police work. I got a promotion for it. Bill did, too. You have to make a choice, and we decided to go with the B&Es. Lori Martin would have been next without us, and

---

* More later, or go to page 321 now.

that mother and daughter. If you go to the media, the perp runs and you've got every women's group in the city breathing down your neck, and then the politicians and everyone is second-guessing us and criticizing. Police work is not a TV show. That neighbourhood had so many cops in it, all crime rates fell. Even the hookers were staying in.

So now I'm sitting here eleven years later and she'll hardly look at me. That one day when she said the armed security made her nervous, didn't I talk to them and didn't they move away from sitting right behind her? The lawyers said I didn't have to be here, didn't have to come every day, but this is about me. My name is on the court documents, I'm cited as a defendant. I make no apologies for what I did. I'm proud of it. I'm a damn good cop. It's all I ever wanted to be.

September 30, 1997

10:00 a.m. Kim Derry on direct.

The Legend continues . . .

Three days off. Heronner was ill.

Again with Sean, I can hardly stand it. If he's going to patronize me he could at least put some energy into it. The last day we were here Finlay entered a huge document, which is a compendium of Kim Derry's notes and views on which he will base his testimony. Sean said he would make copies for Cynthia and Eric, and I asked for one too, so I could follow along, follow his bouncing ball, follow MY TRIAL, and Sean said yeah, sure, and this morning he tells me that my copy was MAILED to me and what's my problem? How can he not know how insulting that is?

Calm down.

But I am so pissed off. I should get out of here. As soon as Elizabeth gets here, I'll leave. She'll tell me what happens, take notes.

I'm gone.

Have fun. Bye-bye.

Okay so I'm still here, shoot me why don't you. Please shoot me. I'll pay you to shoot me. But I'm going soon. How can I not watch Kim Derry's opening act? And it's worth it because get this: Derry has his notebook from the Balcony Rapist investigation but all the other documents, the volumes of working files, profiles and investigative strategies he said he used are missing. So, he will use an aide-mémoire that contains his recollections of these things. Sean objects but the judge says she's going to let it in for now.

I can't stand it. I've got to phone Lee Lakeman. She can advise rape counsellors across the country that the whole therapy notes issue has been solved! Call them aides-mémoire. Why you could write things that would assist the woman you are counselling. After the fact! Kim's entire testimony is an aide-mémoire.*

I like the way Finlay says it: "ayde-memoirrrr."

Kim is more subdued than I thought he would be. As if he's been hauled in. He delivers his testimony although very little he says can be corroborated by any document or by any other evidence. Just his 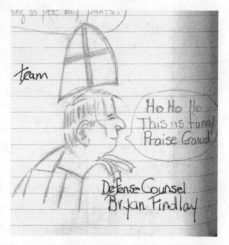 notes and his memory. The judge is to believe that although there is no paper trail, intensive work was going on continuously in the month before I was raped, because he (now an acting superintendent) says it was. Continuous, intensive activity that left no permanent written record, only Kim's

---

* Lakeman works with the Canadian Association of Sexual Assault Centres (CASAC). She is also on staff with the Vancouver Rape Relief and Women's Shelter, Canada's oldest shelter and rape crisis centre. She is one of many women who have fought the seizure of therapy and medical records by the courts.

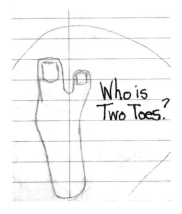

Who is Two Toes?

"recollections," based on his recent "reconstruction" contained in his aide-mémoire. This contrasts starkly with police documents we have that state that in 1986 Derry worked extensively throughout August on a case called Two Toes, until I was raped on the twenty-fourth.*

Bastard.

One of his recollections of the investigation, delivered under oath: "We didn't want to drive him away. We were sort of close and yet far. We had determined that he was in the area but we hadn't narrowed it down to that was the only area of attack."

In addition to his aide-mémoire, Kim has come with a giant blow-up of a map of the area in which the rapes occurred. It is an impressive map that sits at the front of the room as if it belongs there. Must ask Sean if we can have a map. I would like a map of how to get to the cafeteria, which is hidden in the basement, buy a coffee, drink it, and then get back into the courtroom in fifteen minutes.

Kim goes on: "It was a low-key investigation . . . Our feeling was that although the Annex Rapist investigation was successful, he fled . . . so we didn't want to drive this person away . . . we tried to ID him through whatever means we had . . . We were in possession of the Oliver Zink book . . . We pursued the strategy of not moving the rapist. We had this feeling or whatever that if we mounted massive media coverage, he would leave. Think the heat's on. Criminals are not a stupid person."

---

* Two Toes was the major armed-robbery investigation that Kim and Bill completed just before I was raped.

God help us all.*

More aided memories from Kim: "We elected to talk to a specific group which was previous break and enters."

Translation: We went at night to the homes of single women who had previously reported thefts of small objects and who, based on the rapist's MO, were likely future rape targets, but we didn't tell them that.

On the rape of Jane Doe: "The urgency that this suspect has now changed his MO . . . four out of five were near the end of the month. He was dark-skinned but not Negro. If we started knocking on his door, word was gonna spread and he was likely to move and we would put other people at risk . . . By moving him to a new area, people in the Church-Wellesley area wouldn't know that he was in their area."

Translation: It's easier when the criminals are Black. If we put out a warning, the rapist would flee.

"If we could stop the break and enters, we stopped the rapist and that was our plan. We talked to the prostitutes on the track about kinky tricks" and "There were little bits of mud like spaghetti. So I took some of that and put it in a plastic bag." And my favourite: "We just sort of drove around, looked and talked."

Translation: We didn't know what we were doing.

---

* The "rapists flee" mythology rests on the notion that men who rape are transient, live in the bushes and elude detection by teletransporting themselves throughout the city. This excuse is regularly served up by police when explaining their decisions not to issue warnings. The thinking is rarely borne out in stranger rapes and never in the majority of occurrences, in which women know the identity of their attacker. The Annex Rapist actually left Toronto for his family home in Vancouver before a public warning about him was issued.

11:45 a.m. I left. It felt better to be outside. Walked around Chinatown, phoned Heather Bird, went to the gym. Maurice cooked pasta for dinner and we watched a Ken Loach film and laughed out loud. And I don't go back the next day because I am too miserable and sick and tired.

October 6, 1997

Back in court a little restored. Sean needs a haircut and I should know—all I ever see is the back of his head. Don't feel as bad as I feared being back. Seems that Melanie and Lori got me into some trouble with the Dominatrix while I was gone. They wanted to sit at the table reserved for me behind my lawyers even though I was not there, and the Dom was not amused when they argued with her. She asked Eric to warn me about appropriate courtroom behaviour. Great.

Elizabeth filling me in on Derry's evidence. The Peacock has him shored up to Mr. Nice Guy Super-Cop—he should have his own show based on his own true adventures. Apparently he was once accused of stealing three hundred bucks from a guy he had just arrested, and Derry offered to be strip-searched if they didn't believe that he hadn't done it. He was promoted after my case and never looked back. Everyone likes him, he is so nice, and he has letters to that effect.

But Sean has him now. Catching him in contradictions and confusion. His investigation seemed to be based on the belief that rapists drive to the crime scene—"no one ever heard a car." He offers that "the arrest of an individual, and traffic safety are all equal parts of crime prevention." He also says he removed a warning poster from the door of the man who raped me. A WAVAW poster???? Sean doesn't pursue that statement . . . why not?

Oh man . . . it turns out Derry never took the Sexual Assault Investigator training. Squirming around on that one—refers to other prior experience as if he can fool us.

Finally gives the example that once he transported a rapist prisoner to and from a mental health centre.

And here we go: The Oliver Zink Rape Cookbook evidence. Derry actually supplied a copy of it as the basis of his investigation. He said the words "based on . . . supported by . . . in addition to." I'm here listening, writing it down, his exact words. He's proud of it. Standing behind it. It goes to their position of not warning because the recipe my (our) rapist followed fell into the "power reassurance" or "gentleman" category versus the much more serious or organized rapists who are sadistic and ritualistic in their practice.

Derry's use of those qualities as categories into which our rapist does not belong is unbelievable. We experienced our rapist's party chat, his binding of our hands, his covering our heads, his mask, his knife, his use of force as both ritualistic and sadistic. How come Oliver Zink gets to define those terms but not us?

This trial is ritualistic and sadistic.

What are his lawyers thinking? He's awful, argumentative, superior . . . not a good witness for himself. He should have hired an expert. An actor maybe. Ethan Hawke as Kim Derry. Dim Kerry.

Sean is pulverizing him but Derry won't stay down. His aide-mémoire evidence contradicts Bill Cameron's testimony of how they ran the case. Maybe they'll impeach him! That would almost be worth the whole thing.

Finlay is trying to fix him up now although there is blood everywhere. Implies that Derry's present position (acting superintendent) demonstrates his considerable ability and that, working backwards, he was therefore a cop with considerable ability when he investigated the Balcony Rapist.

Meanwhile Derry's rise to the top proves Jim Hodgson's evidence of the systemic nature of the problem! Derry is

testifying now, today, that there were no problems in the
Balcony Rapist investigation, no problems in not believing
the first women, in not making links, in not warning us.

As a reward for his discrimination and negligence, he was
promoted. It's that thing Jim said: "rewarding apprehension
over effective community policing." Using women as bait to
catch the rapist as opposed to serving and protecting.

I just won this case.

Why is it so cold in here?

Eric just came and sat beside me. I asked him why, and he
said it was to emphasize the non-hierarchical nature of my
legal team. Then he got the documents he needed from the
boxes they've piled up on my table (the B table) and he
went back to Table A.

I can't do this. I'm forgetting to breathe. The police are
mounting a defence, giving evidence through the mouth of Kim
Derry, who is quoting Oliver Zink, that my rape wasn't as

serious as some and didn't warrant a warning. Course they
won't actually say that, but my kickass lawyer is drawing
it out and using their own evidence against them. By letting
it all mount up until it becomes a mudslide that will bury
them. Only it's burying me too.

Before we adjourn for the day, the judge hears Sean and Finlay's
arguments re the use of Kim's aide-mémoire as evidence and she rules
that it is not admissable. Meaning all the stuff he said that
referred to it cannot be filed as evidence. I guess I'm supposed to feel good about this but he still got to say it all,
and use it for three days of testimony. I don't get it . . .

I COULDN'T write much during the testimony of Margo Pulford. I
was more interested in watching her, and then too shocked and
amazed at what she said to look away.

She looked lovely. Good suit, great shoes. Finlay introduced her
work history first.

MARGO Pulford, now Superintendent Margo Boyd, was the first female
officer to be permanently assigned to Homicide. She was involved in the
Barbra Schlifer investigation—the young lawyer murdered in the spring
of 1980, when the random murder of women on the streets where they
lived was still uncommon. Margo's career also included tours of duty in
Narcotics, Organized Crime, and Family and Youth Services, where
she held the position of sexual-assault coordinator.

By the time she took the stand, I had withdrawn considerably from
any notion that the civil trial, to which I had devoted eleven years of my
life and work, involved or included me. Outside of the optics, of course.
I was sleepless and isolated. I felt that I had been betrayed and abandoned by my lawyers. Again. I was pierced with despair. Add to this the
weeks of testimony that had pathologized my entire life, the bizarrely
quite legal degradation and mortification I endured every day, the deceit
and lies under oath, and you get a taste, a whiff, of the misery that woke
me every morning and that I pissed out every night. I felt bitterness

approaching now, and that is a really horrible thing. The worst thing. But it wasn't just the trial. There was high water everywhere. I had no job, no money, no intimate relationship, no therapist, no clarity, no hope, no rest, no future.

It was bad. I was having problems living, loving and working, and I knew it was going to get worse. I had to do something. I was sketching the police witnesses and that helped a lot. I was captioning their testimony with little thought balloons—some of the captions were true and some I exaggerated with evil. You would be surprised at the power I drew from it, because people knew I was drawing them, they could see it in the way I sat, how I watched them. But I had to do more than crude sketches. I tried to negotiate a weekly meeting with my lawyers, but it only happened if I forced the issue and it made them resentful, and legally, their resentment trumped mine. I decided to withdraw as opposed to being forced out. A strategic retreat. I no longer expected Sean to speak with me. I did not rush to court to be on time. I did not allow the hateful things I heard to penetrate me too deeply. I decided to try and have a little bit of fun with it. Except every other time I thought about it, fear and anger surfaced, gnawing at my resolve, glomming hold of every bit of me. But it was a little bitter, I mean better.

So when Margo took the stand, I was watching and listening differently, thinking that I was inoculated to whatever she had for me. Besides, our relationship had been respectful and I liked her. Then, right off the bat, Margo testified that in 1986 I had told her that I knew about the rapist in my neighbourhood before the rape and that she had me admitting it on tape. She said that I said that one of my brothers had warned me, and the judge decided to play the tape the next day and court was adjourned until then.

It wasn't that I didn't know this was coming. A transcript of the tape had been introduced as evidence during discovery—I had already explained my brother's comments during my own testimony weeks ago. Sean told me that unfortunately he didn't have a copy of the tape for me—I can't remember why—so I was up all night paralyzed with worry and fear. Have they doctored the tape? Have I forgotten something? Perjured myself? Jeopardized the case? The next day Greg Richards played it and there was my voice telling Margo and Bob Qualtrough that my brother had visited me a week before I was raped and did one of those "there are rapists in the city, you should have more security" (meaning a moat and drawbridge) lectures that substitute for affection and which he delivers every time he sees me even though I have more locks and bolts than he does.

Everyone in the courtroom was expecting this "case closed; she lied" proof in my own voice from the past. Instead it was obvious that I did not say what Margo said I said. But she kept on saying it anyway, and then the judge called for a break (probably just so she could go and shake her head in wonder).

The rest of her testimony was a mixture of Margo supporting police logic and protocol regarding sexual assault, and her remarkable candour in giving up information that worked completely in my favour. The report she authored in 1986, which called for the formation of a sexual assault squad, was entered as evidence and through it she supplied her insider's educated view of the problems in training police to investigate sexual assault. Margo's report included studies published in 1982 that sounded alarms for increased police training and public awareness in rape investigations, and another identical one from 1975.* Her report stated that the Toronto Police Force "is not meeting the needs of sexual-assault victims." There are a "lack of adherence to police procedures and deficiencies in the investigation of sexual assaults, inadequate utilization of resources, and a lack of understanding and support for women who report sexual assaults."

We also entered as evidence a memo written by Margo's supervisor on the project, Inspector John Dennis, which reads, "There is less adherence to the procedure, less investigation into the occurrences [of sexual assault], less resources being utilized and a lack of understanding and support being given to the victim. The object of this report is not to identify individual mistakes as it should be pointed out that the

---

* The Task Force on Public Violence Against Women and Children was ordered in response to a series of rape/murders in the summer of 1982. In 1975, the Report of the Police Committee on Rape was initiated in response to demands by the Toronto Rape Crisis Centre for increased and improved police training. A central demand was the need to form a special squad for the investigation of sexual assaults.

problems being discussed have been seen in every division in each district." In response to Sean's questions, Margo supplied the court with information about police behaviour in WAVAW meetings and Superintendent Jean Boyd's internal memos, which said the force needed to make changes in sexual-assault investigation pronto. "The bottom line is that we are going to get roasted very soon if we don't get our act together," Boyd wrote. "WAVAW has identified and it is accepted that more intensive training is required." In other memos, she recorded the

Cop: Victim was aware of rapes

By TRACY NESDOLY
Toronto Sun

A former Metro Police sexual assault co-ordinator said she had no doubt Jane Doe was

and is serving a 20-year prison term.

"It was always my understanding that she knew about the rapes in the area, she had

OCTOBER 10

Force ill-prepared for rape cases: Cop

By TRACY NESDOLY
Toronto Sun

About a month after Jane Doe was raped, a Metro Police sexual assault co-ordinator called for "radical change" in the way police

were being given specialized training — stating that "rather than the 'cream of the crop' attending the sexual assault investigator's course, personnel that were 'available' (not in court or on vacation) were sent" on courses

problem of constant turnover in SACO and a problem in attracting competent staff to fill the position of sexual-assault coordinator.*

Margo repeatedly did not give Richards the answers he wanted. Instead we heard that although she was the coordinator of SACO, she often didn't know what was going on in sexual-assault investigations. She commented that cops who attended at the scenes would often be unable "to get over the initial hump of rape trauma syndrome" and if they couldn't, the woman would often not be believed and the investigation

---

* Superintendent Boyd and Inspector Dennis were both members of the WAVAW/police committee meetings that took place in 1986–87. Their clear statements in internal police correspondence regarding systemic problems in the investigation of sexual assault were in opposition to the public positions they took in WAVAW meetings, which were that no problems existed.

would not be pursued. Margo acknowledged that even when the police felt that they had investigated a rape well, the women involved did not. She talked about the whole profiling business and said flexibility is crucial when using a profile. I wonder whether Greg Richards even knew what she was talking about. But I did. We did. The judge did. She identified the frequent problem with profiling technology, where police missed patterns because they were focused too rigidly on single characteristics.

She testified that trained sexual-assault officers knew how to get over the "hump" (she said that word a lot) of rape trauma syndrome, whereas officers who were not trained found victim statements inadequate, did not notify the ID bureau, did not submit supplementary reports and did not call victims back or brushed them off. It seemed that even Margo's approach was to treat rape trauma syndrome as pathology, rather than as a normal response to something awful.

This in turn led her into talking in a paternalistic and condescending way about "handling" raped women. But she was steadfast in what she believed and in recounting what she had experienced, and she did not attempt to dilute her testimony or to deny historical problems.

Although she created the blueprint for SACO and shepherded it through its formative stages and mandates to become the prestigious Sexual Assault Squad, Margo was never transferred nor appointed to work there in any capacity.*

SEAN played on her honesty and ambivalence cleverly. It was one of his finest scenes in the trial. Margo's testimony did not break my heart too much. Her performance piece with the tape and her insistence that I was warned were unforgivable. But a lot of the rest of it felt like her gift to me. I went out into the hall to find her after she had finished. She wasn't there but I could hear angry voices coming from one of the witness rooms. I looked through the bulletproof window and saw Margo and Kim Derry standing face to face. He was screaming at her, waving his finger in her face. Superintendent Margo Boyd held her ground and gave him whatever he was dishing up right back. I walked away.

---

* In 1988, however, Bill Cameron became a founding member of the official SACO.

October 10, 1997 (Yom Kippur)

Staff Inspector William (Bill) Blair
Unit Commander 51 Division
Metropolitan Toronto Police
(Kim Derry's best friend)

This is perfect. I can't have friends testify for me but Kim can. And how come Kim gets to stay in the courtroom to hear the evidence? Oh right, this is a civil case, I forgot, and it's not a rape case either. I get so mixed up sometimes.

This Bill is smooth. Kind of a faded beach boy. Doesn't look particularly happy to be here.

And he is here because . . . ?

How odd, he seems to be claiming that he is the author of the SACO report and not Margo, and that he was the sexual-assault coordinator in 1986 and not Margo . . . okay he was, but then he was seconded to the Provincial Inquiry into Allegations of Criminality within the Workers'

Compensation Rehabilitation Centre . . . must have been difficult to be in both places at the same time—and writing a report too . . .

Is he saying that I met with him? Hey Bill! I never saw you before in my life. Wrote Sean a note to that effect. Balled it up and threw it on his desk but it bounced to the floor and the court clerk picked it up and ate it.

Bill says that "things were as good in policing in 1975 as they are today." I somehow don't think that's quite what he means but no one else seems bothered by it. Now he's testifying that he was the one who gave Kim the Zink cookbook! He actually met Oliver Zink. Heard him lecture!

Bill is still up there bleating on. Billy goat, Billy gloat. I have no idea what he's talking about. How come blond men are so often boring?

October 15, 1997.

12:40 p.m.
Staff Sergeant Stephen Duggan

I was going to do some work at home but Elizabeth called, told me to hurry up, that I had to see this, and she wasn't kidding. Sean gave her a copy of Duggan's resumé.

It looks like the police have hired someone to pull together resumés for all the officers. I know this because they are all the same, and I teach resumé-writing myself. Duggan has "married with children" on his, with a specialty in youth violence and gangs. He has been utilized in numerous police services across Canada to implement education programs in schools to confront youth violence. He has been responsible for parades and is presently with Homicide. He has appeared on television shows on CBC, CTV and Citytv including the shows Canada AM and BreakfastTelevision.

Duggan's memo books for the period he investigated the

Balcony Rapist have been destroyed. It is not determined how or by whom. He will give evidence based on his eleven-year-old memory of the events.

This is all especially fascinating as HE IS THE POTATO-CHIP COP! The one who didn't believe the second woman's rape because the chips weren't disturbed and her superintendent and her boyfriend said lying, shameful things to him about her. He wanted to charge her with mischief.

He looks like Mr. Bean.

And he's so mad at Sean right now, if he had a gun he'd shoot him. Sean is leading him through his disgustingly sexist, negligent, hateful report on the crime, and Duggan just screams, "YES SIR!" every time Sean asks him if he really wrote and thought what he wrote and thought in 1986 "YES SIR!" about that poor woman's rape and if he would write and think it again.

I wish she could be here to see this.

The We-Are-Fools lawyer suggests that Duggan didn't pursue her rape because sexist Crown attorneys, judges, jurors would not prosecute diligently and convict, so why bother? But the evidence is clear. It was Sergeant Duggan's own adherence to rape mythology that impaired the investigation. He dismissed her rape as fictitious. Not to mention—and we barely mention it—Duggan investigated another rape that buddy committed in the same building, same MO, just months later, and he still didn't make the links, sound the alarm. And he is defending those decisions today. Would do it the same way today.

"I have come across the problem of attention-seeking women inventing rapes in several other cases during my career," screamed Duggan.

I have a copy of his supplementary report, in which he concludes that the incident "didn't occur the way the victim says." In it he explains that his conclusion was drawn for the following reasons:

1. The woman involved was seeing a man, other than the boyfriend, who took her away for three days following the rape. "In fact, according to the apartment superintendent . . . she saw several men."
2. She was "far too calm in reporting the incident."

3. It would be "very, very impossible for the rapist to have fashioned a towel over his head and cut a hole in it to see through. Curious enough she still had a matching set of towels in her bathroom without any missing."
4. The woman had allegedly given the boyfriend a sexually transmitted disease, which "must go to show her possible sexual activities."
5. She was "an only child with some contact with her mother. She has no immediate friends and keeps to herself."
6. According to the ex-boyfriend, she would "fantasize about persons and people" and "she or her moods would change."

7. There was no evidence of a forced entry into her apartment.

8. A bowl of potato chips, resting on her bed during the alleged attack, was not spilled.

9. Though the medical evidence "confirmed" that she had had sexual intercourse, Duggan was "positive that she knew the person who had this contact with her."

This document was written and submitted by Duggan in April 1986, one month after he completed the sexual-assault investigator course.

I don't get it. Isn't this enough? Ain't it clear? The police don't believe raped women.
     Arrest that man.

Everyone is gathered round looking at my journal, Cynthia is pink from laughing. Sean looks hurt when I will not show it to him, and I feel bad for about two seconds. I want to ask him, I want to convince him, to call a witness who will testify that what the police did in 1986 they still do today, but he will say no. And it is his trial. I speak to them mostly through Elizabeth now and they speak to me through her when they want to tell me why they have no intention of doing what I want.

October 16, 1997

12:30 p.m.
Cross-Examination of Detective Sergeant Eugene Reilly, Chief Investigator/Annex Rapist
Eric is driving.
     According to his resumé, Detective Eugene Reilly left farming in Ireland in 1963 to work as a bricklayer until he immigrated to Canada and joined the Toronto Police Force in 1969.
     His face is the map of Ireland and if you couldn't see

him, his brogue would tell you the same thing. He has one year left until retirement and is presently with Internal Affairs. He started on foot patrol, baton training, Central Traffic and then became a famous detective.

He was the chief investigator of the Annex Rapist, who was operating in the city the same summer I was raped but in a different neighbourhood. In that case the police put out a warning. Now the defence appears to be trying to contrast the Annex rapes as violent and "more serious" than the

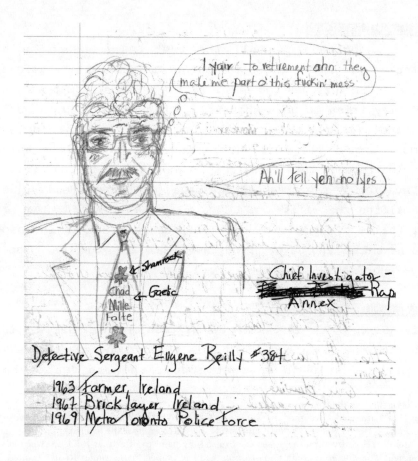

Balcony Rapist ones, which were "gentle" as per Agent Zink. Therefore a warning was not warranted in my case.

But Reilly won't play. He will not bend his investigation

to suit theirs. He will not say what they want him to say. He will not lie. He agrees that the warning he issued DID NOT cause that sorry excuse for a human being to flee, and he agrees with warning the public about rapists.

In response to Eric's question about his thoughts on the strategy followed in the investigation of my rape: "It would have been morally reprehensible to sit around and do nothing and wait for a break."

Hey Eugene! Go raibh míle maith agat!* You're a mensch!

October 17, 1997

Reilly continues to tell the truth. The Annex Rapist attacked one of the women twice. On two separate occasions. I wonder if that was the one I met?** I wonder how they are?

Finlay tries to undo what Reilly has offered up to us in his redirect but the man will not be part of it. His testimony proves our case. There is a tectonic plate thing running through this court case, running down the courtroom, separating my rape from police rape, and Eugene Reilly just identified the rift.

I follow him out into the hall, ask him how he is doing and he smiles and says, "Fine, good, how are you?" He doesn't know who I am.

October 18, 19, 20, 1997

More police officers testify. A platoon of them. Gary Ellis, who took the call from the parole officer who saw the WAVAW poster and said to look at buddy, who was one of her

* Irish Gaelic for "thank you very much."
** In 1987 I attended a group counselling session offered by the Sexual Assault Care Centre at Women's College Hospital. The facilitator made the statement that she had never met a woman who didn't feel guilty about being raped. I raised my hand to offer that I did not feel guilty, never had. The women present, two of whom had been raped by the Annex Rapist, wanted to understand how, why, I had escaped guilt. I could only say that I was clear that the act was not on me but on the man who raped me, and like them, I was not responsible for his crimes. I don't think they understood, although they wanted to. I wish I knew better ways to tell them. I didn't continue the group sessions.

clients. Ellis also worked on the Annex Rapist investigation. He looks like Bob Newhart.*

Others testify—I don't know why, my lawyers are as stymied
as I. Well no, they have the documents in this document-
driven process and I do not. Every once in a while Cynthia
passes me her copy of whatever is being entered as evidence,
although she doesn't always get a copy either, and besides,
it's not for her to do it. It's Sean's case. He is the boss.
She has offered to speak to him about our cold war, but I

don't think it is appropriate and it would put her in a difficult position.

   More officers take the stand. Ronald Piers from the OPP.
A grey, grandfatherly gent who has been in court every day.
We thought he was CSIS or RCMP but he's only OPP.** His
testimony is sycophantic. Mike Sale, who is the police
media spokesperson, declaring in an expensive suit that

---

* In 2001 Gary Ellis was appointed head of the Sexual Assault Squad (now Sex Crimes Unit).
** OPP stands for the Ontario Provincial Police. CSIS is the Canadian Security Intelligence
Service or spy agency, and the RCMP is the federal level of law enforcement, the Royal Canadian
Mounted Police.

there has to be a good reason to withhold pertinent information in cases involving life and death, but he doesn't direct us to what the good reason was in my case. Goes on about media blitzes and public warnings giving rise to false confessions from deranged but innocent members of the public, and copycat rapes.

He just ignores the fact that the Annex Rapist warning did not result in same. As if it never happened.

I missed the testimony of Officer Andy Petroff of Community and Safety Relations. Something about Elmer the Safety Elephant, no doubt.*

October 27, 1997

9:00 a.m.

Jack Marks, Former Chief of Police (1984-89)

A few more days off. Something about another trial. There are other trials? Mine isn't the only one??? And then we had to wait for Jack Marks to fly up from Florida. He didn't want to come. I don't blame him. He is an old man now and just wants to lie in the sun. Forget that he was here. I wonder if he can.

Apparently he can. Apparently he was a cop saint. Saint Jack of Marks. Finlay is like a master of ceremonies who doesn't have the imagination or isn't getting paid enough and just introduces all the guests the same way. Seems Marks's apology to WAVAW back in 1986 wasn't an apology after all—it was a set of speaking notes written for him by another officer, Robin Breen, who is to testify later.

---

* To support their defence that they did warn women about the Balcony Rapist, the police called Officer Petroff, who was with the Crime Prevention Office (CPO). Under cross-examination he admitted that his seminars concerned building safety and were not specific to sexual assault. He said the work of his office was reactive in nature and took place only after members of the public made a request. This contravened Kim Derry's testimony that he had worked with the CPO in the Balcony Rapist investigation.

Feeling remote, stunned, alone, but that isn't unusual. It's okay, I am alone. Even with my platoon of friends, I must do this alone. That is the nature of it. The nature of rape and the legal system. Wept a lot on the weekend. Flowers from Michele Landsberg. Completely unexpected, made me cry even more.* Again, Sean made compendiums of all the relevant documents he would question Marks on. Again no one

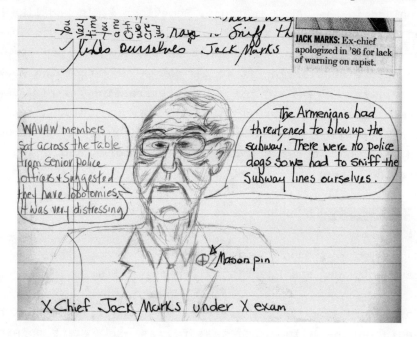

asked if I wanted a copy.

He's really giving it to Marks though. The chief is not used to being spoken to thusly, his judgment judged, his memory questioned, his apologies remembered.

Sean forces him to agree that if internal reports were received stating that the Homicide Squad, for instance, was conducting "shoddy investigations" with "inadequate supervision," "inferior training" and "arbitrary" decision making

---

* Michele Landsberg is a columnist for the *Toronto Star* who writes from a feminist perspective on women's and other issues, and has done so for decades. She is probably the only person who writes consistently from this perspective in Canadian mainstream media.

(as was documented about rape investigations during Marks's watch), there would have been no delay in implementing "swift and effective change to correct the situation" and that "delay would not be excused because of the difficulties in changing people's attitudes about homicide."

Now it's Breen. Another mick. I remember him, he was involved in the WAVAW meetings. Sometimes it looked like he got it. And now they're making him say that he wrote Chief Marks's apology, only it wasn't an apology, it was speaking notes. He's saying it to get Marks away from the hook. These guys will say anything. How embarrassing for him. Sean gets him to admit that if it looks like an apology, sounds like an apology and contains the words "regret," "sorrow" and "I admit it was wrong," then it's more than a set of speaking notes.

October 28, 1997
10:30 a.m.
Dr. Thomas Gutheil,
President, Law and Psychiatry Centre, U.S.A.

Cynthia objected to the presence of Gutheil, said that he should not be allowed to testify, as his expert opinion would be biased and irrelevant and used only to validate the upcoming testimony of Graham Glancy (who is supposed to start tomorrow). The judge ruled that based on the testimony of Drs. DeMarco and Barnes and their critiques of Glancy's diagnosis as NEGATIVE, IRRESPONSIBLE, NOT BALANCED, SEXIST AND DISTORTED, then Tommy Gutheil can do his thing.

Which is basically to say that Gutheil agrees that I am a fluffernutter, although I'm not sure, because between the academic/medical lingo and his American accent (a's for o's and no g's) I can't really understand what he's saying.

Anyway, he's finished now.

Yankee go home.
Glancy tomorrow.

I MADE no journal entries during the testimony of Dr. Graham Glancy.

Don Weitz, a former psychologist and current anti-psychiatry and poverty advocate, came to court during Glancy's time on the stand with a dozen colleagues and dozens of buttons. They were large, bright buttons that read Stop Psychiatric Rape. Everyone in the spectator's gallery except Glancy's father-in-law and the bingo callers (members of the media) wore one. When Glancy entered the room he looked at me and smiled. I think he actually believed I would smile back, which, considering all of the evidence to date, was indicative of someone's delusional beliefs.

Cynthia Petersen was in charge of cross-examining him. It was her most important cross-examination of the trial. She was exceptional. Cynthia is a masterful lawyer, always at least a page ahead of the script. Her reputation for excellence began when she received tenure after teaching law for only five years at the University of Ottawa. In 1994, although she had not yet been called to the bar, she was approached by EGALE (Equality for Gays and Lesbians Everywhere) to argue the case for same-sex spousal benefits in front of the Supreme Court of Canada. She won. Since then, she has argued and won similar challenges under sections seven and fifteen, which have restored or granted constitutional rights to individuals and groups across the country. Sean understood that we needed an expert to argue the Charter component of my case to demonstrate and prove the sexist practices of the Toronto police. Cynthia brought her legal acumen to that argument and, while she was at it, blew Graham Glancy and his expert psychiatric opinions to pieces.

Remember that by now, Vince DeMarco and Rosemary Barnes had already testified on my behalf to discredit what Glancy was about to say (I know, it's confusing). Radio, television and newspapers across the country had recorded my experts' condemnation of Glancy's diagnosis of me before he even delivered it. Newspapers in border towns in the United States were also reporting on the trial daily at this point.

By now it was clear that defence lawyers Bryan Finlay and Greg Richards were the best things I had going for me in this trial. We were like ships passing in the night—they weren't responsive to our arguments because we were arguing different cases. The performance of the Weir Foulds police defence team was a consistent source of hope to which I clung. The performance of Graham Glancy rivalled even theirs. His testimony was based on his expert analysis of his own findings. He had decided that I had barely suffered any damages as a result of my rape, and was already barmy, and he believed he could prove it scientifically.

The wilfully blind manner in which he made himself vulnerable to being seen as a mean prick as he delivered his expert diagnosis in a wilting Manchester accent was astonishing. Rereading his testimony years later, his contempt for me leaps from the page. And is still painful to read. But where did the contempt come from? He didn't know me, had only spoken with me once. I posed no threat to him. What did he think was at stake? How did he benefit? Does being an expert make you that way? Does psychiatry, like other "helping" professions, lead to burnout and dissociation to the degree that you no longer empathize at all with the people you assess? Or was he simply hard-hearted?

Looking like the cat who ate the canary, rubbing his hands, seated on the edge of his seat as if ready to spring, Glancy was nasty, sarcastic and patronizing and appeared quite comfortable about it.

As a result, he didn't see Cynthia coming. Didn't know what hit him until it was too late.

But first it was police lawyer Greg Richards's opportunity to elicit Glancy's expert opinions and testimony. He led him through his CV of published articles and psychiatric practices for a litany of children's, Native, disabled, and incarcerated communities that would choke a feminist PhD student. He had been chief of staff, president and founding member of psychiatric and legal institutions of repute (though Richards did not elicit the doctor's past as a member of Britain's men's swim team). Glancy's expertise established, Richards then led him into and through his diagnosis of my mental health, past, present and future.

Glancy began with this:

> The purpose (of the tests) was to delineate any psychiatric or psychological issues relating to the sequelae of the sexual assault on August 24, 1986; to assess the allegation that police actions, both prior to and after the assault, may have caused psychiatric sequelae; to delineate any antecedent factors which may affect the picture; and to assess whether there's any particular psychiatric issue that may have delayed her capacity to retain counsel and make a statement of claim.

That's the way people talk in court. I don't know why he mentioned the last part about retaining counsel. It probably had something to do with the statute of limitations thing although it was never broached with him.

Here is a synopsis of the personality traits and qualities Glancy assessed as mine, based on his interpretation of the tests he and psychologist Nathan Pollock conducted on me over a two-day period three months before the trial began.

After a brief attack on my father and mother, he lit into me: I was a "vague personality style, who denied any alcohol abuse but admitted to sniffing heroin on occasion." My test results indicated "an unrealistic self-concept, someone who exaggerates her contributions . . . is excessively demanding of attention" and becomes "sullen and resentful when these expectations are not met," which causes "problems in interpersonal relationships." I have a pattern of "suspiciousness and distrust" and "typically poor work histories and problems with intimacy." I have tendencies to "deny personal problems" and to be "overly dramatic with a strong need to be the centre of attention." I am a person who becomes "easily excited with frequent emotional outbursts who may manipulate people to garner approval and affection" and has "strong needs for social acceptance." "According to the computer reports of Ms Doe's tests she is emotionally labile."

"She presented with a . . . hostile and argumentative attitude . . . She frequently answered questions with another question and was personally challenging and confrontive. She had a tendency toward involuntary sniffing and snorting. And when looking at the form of her talk, to trail off at the end of a phrase." She made "sweeping generalizations" and would "become irritated. She had problems with living, was dissatisfied with her financial status. There was no doubt that she had problems living, loving and working. It is clear that there was a severe family discord . . . she was in a seriously unhealthy sexual relationship" which "caused her a great deal of distress." She was "having problems living, loving and working prior to the assault. There are factors which support malingering. She still has some difficulties living, loving and working" although "her activities of daily living such as cleaning, shopping, paying bills and attending to personal hygiene are unaffected" and "there was no evidence of brain damage."*

And then it was time for the morning break, which was immaterial to me because I had reacted according to my labile state and was now a quivering specimen of shame, seated at the front of the courtroom with everyone watching, listening, recording my undoing as a responsible adult woman. I remember thinking that it was a good thing Glancy hadn't examined my trial journal, and I considered burning it in the washroom in case they subpoenaed it.

---

* Glancy was on the stand for two days. The words and phrases attributed to him in quotation marks are taken verbatim from trial transcripts.

When court resumed, Glancy continued: "She candidly admitted to me manipulating the media and using their tendency to sensationalize rape for her own advantage . . . she led an organization called Women Against Violence Against Women and she was able to retain independent legal counsel to gain standing at the criminal trial . . . Doctor Pollock was surprised because her knowledge of vocabulary and abstract reasoning are somewhat higher than expected from her clinical presentation." (When Cynthia later asked him if that meant I wasn't as stupid as I looked, he basically agreed.) "I diagnosed her as a mixed personality disorder . . . I think the important thing for the court's point of view is that here was a woman who experienced subjective distress and impairment in her lifestyle in living, loving and working at various stages in her life."*

On my prognosis he offered: "I just find it embarrassing to recommend more therapy from now on because I think, to a great extent, therapies

---

* While there is no such medical diagnosis as "mixed" personality disorder, the key words "personality disorder" classify the subject (myself) as mentally ill under DSM-IV.

have been tried and it doesn't seem to have made a great deal of difference to her." He did think that stronger medication would help.

Richards thanked Glancy and indicated that he was finished. Then Cynthia began her cross-examination.

In addition to revealing his adherence to the rape myth that women make false accusations, and men must be protected, which Glancy had demonstrated when meeting me, Cynthia got him to admit that the presence of his spouse, Dr. Cheryl Regehr, at our testing session and her purpose for being there were a sexist insult to me and might have resulted in what he then diagnosed as my hostile and defensive behaviour. Before he could recover, she whacked him with a document that contained a psychiatric report Glancy had written in 1991. A client had come to Glancy and told him that he had murdered his wife the night before and left her body in the house while her children slept. He returned the following morning to take the kids to school, and after school he had delivered them to the home of their aunt. Then he came to see Glancy. Who did not call the police. Cynthia suggested that Glancy had contravened his professional standards and demonstrated a coarse disregard for the woman and her children and "a lack of compassion for the female victims of male violence . . . you fell short of your ethical obligations and, at minimum, exercised a shocking lack of sound judgment." Glancy claimed client-solicitor privilege and refused to answer.

We broke for lunch. I did not kill myself.

WITH Glancy back on the stand that afternoon, Cynthia explained that client-solicitor privilege was a lawyer thing, not a psychiatrist thing. Glancy went on too long with defences that made him look kind of pathetic and desperate. With the stage set, my lawyer continued the execution (of her cross-examination strategy).

In preparation for court Cynthia had consulted with my friend Lori Haskell, formerly of WAVAW and now a psychologist with a private practice. Although Lori and I had not worked together for almost a decade, she agreed to help me develop a legal strategy specific to the psychiatric material to be used against me. She came through big time. She sat with Cynthia and tutored her in a crash course in psychological

Jane Doe has a
strong desire to
attract attention. She
is emotionally labile, narcissistic,
denies personal problems
and is over dramatic. She
must be stopped.
Dr. Graham Glancy
Clarke Institute of Psychiatry

tests, research and methodology. It helped that Cynthia is a genius.

Cynthia used her newly acquired understanding to defeat Glancy at his own game. The thrust of her position was that the tests Glancy relied on to make a diagnosis of me did not allow for a gender (or race) analysis and were not specific to the experience of rape. Interpretation was biased and formulated on the interviewer's own belief systems. The tests drew on the novice and sexist opinions of Norman Doidge as a data bank. She also used the published thesis of Glancy's own wife to contradict his testimony and diagnosis. In order to do this, of course, Doidge's opinions of me had to be entered as evidence. Here is an excerpt from the referral letter he wrote to Vince DeMarco in 1985:

In the initial assessment, she came dressed in a miniskirt and black leather. She looked like a 1960s go-go girl who was inviting danger. It became clear that this was an invitation to danger boys so that the two of them could be involved in a sadomasochistic relationship. I became aware that she had no close relations with women but, rather, got together with them to talk about the enemy—man. She tended to involve herself with people who are drug addicts. She had a wish to not think of herself as an adult. She would find babies to mother in the form of a political cause.

I was struck by the breathy Marilyn Monroe voice, the skimpy dress and the dramatic use of language. She had a histrionic per-sonality and a mother-nun-rescue fantasy. She became a secular Mother Theresa of Love looking for Mr. Goodbar. Initially in the transference she tended to play the part of the little girl who uses a breathy voice to eroticize things. She saw the therapist as a sadistic, unpredictable violator. She was emphatic that she proba-bly should have a female therapist. She was violently against hav-ing children—a male plot no doubt—even though she was a com-pulsive motherer.

Her resistance to my maleness began to melt when I became aware that she had no close female friends. Her legitimacy was derived from her connection to religion and there was a sense that she was illegitimate or a bastard. Her idea of femininity was that one needed a man to survive. She is bright and psychologically minded.

I wouldn't print anything from Doidge's letter except to use it as a warning, a caution to those who turn to psychiatry for therapy or as a tool to better understand and enjoy life. It can be used against you. Even if the notes a psychiatrist is required to keep are untrue and fetishistic. We chose not to call Norman Doidge as a witness, certain that by now, with all of the degrees and positions he holds in psychiatry, he has moved beyond such openly cruel and dangerous practice. I'm betting that he is embarrassed by his own juvenile posturings. Putting him on the stand, however, might have given him an opportunity to correct or minimize his sexist prejudices which, perversely, now worked in my favour since we could prove that they formed the basis for Glancy's diagnosis.

As I sat in the courtroom listening to Glancy dissect me, expose and reconstruct me, my heart turned to ashes. Mascara streaked my face the colour of bruises. I was broken and beaten. At the time I did not register that Glancy's testimony had been thoroughly discredited, or that he had left the stand rattled and angry, that he stormed from the room. No judge's decision, no amount of money, can undo what was done to me that day in a court of law. My past had been used against me. To discredit and malign me because I was suing the police for negligence and Charter discrimination. If that's how we're going to do it, I thought, surely the past of the police officers involved would have been more relevant?

Had I not had the anonymity of Jane Doe, I would have stopped the proceedings that day. It was the only time I ever faltered. In hindsight, someone should have told me in 1987 that it would come to this, and I would have walked away then. Of course, the option to walk away was always mine. I was the aggressor, the prosecutor, the complainant. Because I was suing for emotional and pyschological damages incurred as the result of my rape, the police, who were defending themselves, had the right to determine if the damages I was claiming had pre-existed my rape. Everything they said and did to prove that was legal. It was all accepted in law. At no time did my lawyers or the judge make objections about the use of my past, my political leanings, relationships, reading material or work history as police defence material. And they were on my side.

The next morning, national and local papers repeated Glancy's testimony about my mental and psychological problems, including my past sexual relationships, drug use, family history, delusions and personality disorder. Not one word of the evidence mounted against Glancy, which clearly showed his own sexist bias and unethical conduct in failing to report a woman's murder, was reported. And so a message was sent across the country to other women who have been, or will be, sexually assaulted: if you file charges, if you come here, this will happen to you, too. And they wonder why we don't report . . .

Afterwards, Sean commented that perhaps if I hadn't been so hostile in

Glancy's office during his examination of me, if I had "kept it together and played the game," Glancy's evidence would not have been so damning nor would so much effort have been required to restore my good (rape victim) status.

Eric said he felt bad for me.

THE trial still had weeks to go. The police defence still had about five thousand additional witnesses to call. I was on automatic pilot. I showed up, took my seat and was ignored by my lawyers, who by now were in high gear, doing what they loved and doing it well. Their client seemed to have calmed down, stopped her pestering, her need to know and to be involved, which for them was a much better state of affairs. Only Cynthia saw that I was broken and there wasn't much she could do. Being broken was required under the law.

When I think about it now, read the transcripts, go over Glancy's testimony and that of the five other shrinks who agreed to define my rape and my reactions to it for a court of law, I marvel that the danger of such an alliance is not more obvious.* The collusion of perhaps the two most powerful systems we have (legal and medical) to judge rape and assess guilt, when neither is versed in the true nature of rape, has set us down a dangerous path. And not accidentally. Lawyers and judges seek out and rely on the opinion of doctors to enforce the myths supported by religious and social beliefs that women lie, malinger and are delusional about their rapes. The media reports it all to us in bite-sized pieces. Surely we conclude (if we bother to question this confederation at all) they know best, would not mislead us about a matter so grave. And yet the occurrence of the crimes of sexual assault continues to rise. Fewer women report. What is this about? Who benefits here? I certainly did not.

BEFORE I leave Dr. Glancy, his testimony and his profession, a final observation about his two days on the stand and my attempt to defend myself from his attack: As much as I believe he made huge errors in conduct and opinion, the police lawyers who hired him, Bryan Finlay and Greg Richards, clearly made litigation errors in situating the doctor as an

---

* The six shrinks were Drs. DeMarco, Jaffe, Barnes, Glancy, Gutheil and Pollock.

advocate for their side as opposed to an impartial observer. Whatever I might think of Glancy and his profession, he *is* an expert in his field. His lawyers, however, set him up as their advocate as opposed to a witness. They acted as if *he* were their client. Their strategy seemed to be to create a persona for him as a feminist, a pre-eminent expert who understands women. Which is not who he is.

I do not know what the judge thought, as she did not mention the evidence against Glancy in her decision (just as the media did not), but I do know that I wouldn't have trusted him. I imagine the police lawyers would have preferred a female psychiatrist to make their case. When they couldn't get one they tried to make Glancy look like one. They should have objected, questioned the relevance of Cynthia's counterattack on him. Not that there was anything illegal or objectionable about her procedure—it just would have looked better, indicated that they knew what she was doing. It would have defended Glancy better. But they did not object once, and Glancy was effectively blindsided.*

The final irony in the whole sorry episode of my experience of Graham Glancy is that we used his past to discredit him in a court of law.

October 31, 1997 Hallowe'en

10:00 a.m.
Sergeant David Bratt, investigating officer into the rape
of the first woman (Alice) raped by the Balcony Rapist

This guy's name is Bratt. Seriously. His partner was
Officer Lye.

Bratt looks like Brian Mulroney. Oh my god, he's the one!
Oh oh oh how dare they! He's defending what he did to Alice.

Elizabeth is here, Patty Z, Daphne, my camera crew—we
could rush Bratt, pummel his testimony back into his lip-
less gob.

I am definitely in contempt of the court now, the proceed-

---

* Although she does not mention Glancy's biases in her judgment, Justice MacFarland does refer to the testimoney of Dr. Vince DeMarco as biased as a result of his therapeutic history and knowledge of me.

ings, all of it. Again with the pitiful defence that the courts would not convict a man for raping a woman who had multiple sex partners and who used dildos or a little bit of bondage and that's the real reason Bratt didn't believe she had been raped. Nothing to do with his own or police code sexist prejudging and discrimination. No, no, he's not like that, none of them are . . .

Telling now how he photographed everything as if that was not maniacal. He measured the length of her stockings! There was a serial rapist on the loose and he was preoccupied with sex toys. And that's all right with the Metropolitan Toronto

Police Force. Lye 'n' Bratt even moved things around—they actually altered the crime scene in order to take photographs inside a dresser drawer and a closet that had remained closed during the rape.*

* To recap the particulars of the investigation into the first woman raped by the Balcony Rapist see page 81.

SEVEN weeks of this and more to come. *The Pallisers* didn't go on this long.* How to describe the tedium of it all without invoking it? The excruciating, vapid, unextraordinariness of court proceedings. Mixed up with explosions of villainy and daring. And you never know which piece you will be served up. Like an exotic salad made with crummy old iceberg lettuce.

I could barely lift a pen by now anyway, so I will continue with some snapshots of what was left.

CROWN attorney Mary Hall (also known as Maximum Mary) came to defend the police investigation into my rape. For the defence she played the role of strong, independent woman working in the system with the police, who did not experience sexism. She went so far as to say that there was no sexism anymore anywhere and that it was better from a victim's POV for male officers to investigate sexual assault.

Next up were two high-ranking law enforcement officials, flown in to testify to the excellence of the investigation into the crimes of the Balcony Rapist. The core of their evidence was that some rapes are non-violent, and mine fell into that category. Since that was the case, they reasoned, warnings were not necessary and Toronto police had investigated properly and with due diligence and there was no negligence. So help them God.

None of this particular expert-witness testimony was reported by the media. So I will report the evidence for you now. I refer to it as "Jane Doe's Coffee-Table Edition of the Oliver Zink Rape Cookbook," complete with sketches, recipes and diagrams. Sort of a coffee-table cook-book book.** The following are true stories.

OLIVER ZINK was an FBI agent who in the seventies developed and transcribed profiles of stranger rapists to assist in police investigations. The profiles are collections or recipes of childhood, social and criminal

* *The Pallisers* was a twenty-six-part BBC melodrama set in the intrigue and deceit of eighteenth-century politics and with a cast of thousands.
** The working title for this book, the title under which I wrote this book, was *Jane Doe's Coffee-Table Book about Rape*. A survey of major buyers indicated that such a title would not sell, and I was required to change it.

behavioural traits found in common among men who rape. They are divided into sections under the headings Purpose, History, and Social Background. The Oliver Zink Rape Cookbook, as it is known in law enforcement in the United States, culls from the work of psychiatrists and behavioural scientists and the archived investigations of serial rapists from across that country. It has been adopted by Canadian police forces and was referred to by the investigating officers in my case as well as others as an important investigative tool. Agent Zink evolved two categories of stranger rapist, the Power Reassurance or Gentleman Rapist and the Anger Excitation or Retaliatory Rapist. The police defence was that I was raped non-violently by a Gentleman Rapist.

Gregg O. McCrary is a retired FBI agent from Virginia, who was flown to Toronto at taxpayers' expense to testify for the police as an international expert on serial rapes and murders. He is a large, manly man with a rugged face and a big voice. Kind of an aging Marlboro Man. His expertise included the FBI massacre in Waco, Texas, and he assisted the Toronto police during the investigation of Paul Bernardo. McCrary loves to talk. Why, he could talk all day about the cases he has solved. Finlay cued him through a litany of serial rapes he had investigated, each more graphic, more gruesome than the next. The judge had to repeatedly request that he slow down. "I'm sorry, your honour," he apologized, "I just get so excited when I talk about these things."

Then he expounded on the Oliver Zink Rape Cookbook and its efficacy in determining the nature of my rape. I quote from a copy of the cookbook submitted by Metro police as evidence at trial:

> The Gentleman Rapist comprises 81% of all stranger rapes. He has no intent to harm or to degrade the victim but is resolving doubts about his own masculinity.
>
> He will only use the force which is necessary to overcome the victim but will bring a weapon or threaten use of a weapon.
>
> He uses little or no profanity.
>
> If confronted with resistance he will negotiate, desist, flee or resort to threats.
>
> He will demand verbal activity of a personal nature and will

do whatever the victim allows him to do, i.e.

"have oral sex with me"

"no!"

"okay, then play with me"

He is an unselfish rapist and is likely to apologize after the assault.

He is gentle, quiet and passive.

He lives close to the victim. If living with his mother she is a domineering type.

There are additional identifying factors—fifty in total—but it's clear why they call him a gentleman.

The Anger Excitation or Retaliatory Rapist is a whole other kettle of rapist. This fucker will cut, maim or kill you to resolve his masculinity. He says bad words, will not negotiate or apologize and should not be confused with his kinder, gentler counterpart, even though they have dozens of traits in common according to the cookbook.

Under these definitions, McCrary located my rape as non-violent and went on to opine on the folly of issuing a warning. He actually said that men, not just women, would become upset if warnings were issued, because men get raped too. He praised the police investigation as exemplary and spent considerable time issuing his own warning about the danger of provoking the rapist, insulting him or resisting.

Finlay and his team preened and paraded about like cats who have brought home a not-quite-dead bird and expect you to be all thrilled about it, and then it was Sean's turn.

No matter how mad I was at him, I had to admire Sean for being the exceptional courtroom lawyer he is. His direct and his cross-examinations were often works of studied art, performances not to be missed.

Someone once told me that when he was at law school, other students would gather to watch him present during mock court-trials. Like other predators, lawyers study their prey, understand their habits and weaknesses, interpret their psychology. Like a cat, Sean enjoys playing with his natural victim. He moves slowly at first, handsome and polite, gets up close, might ask if you would like a glass of water or if you would indulge

THE OLIVER ZINK RAPE COOKBOOK

ANGER RETALIATORY TYPE

FIVE PERCENT OF STRANGER TO STRANGER RAPES

PURPOSE: 1. To punish or degrade women.
          2. Getting even for some real or imagined injustice
              done to him by women.
          3. Using sex as a weapon.

MODUS OPERANDI

1. Not premeditated, therefore a spontaneous crime.

2. Blitz type attack.

3. Generally attacks in own area due to anger.

4. Offender spends a short time with the victim.

5. Will select victim of the same age group or older.

6. Tears or rips off the victim's clothing.

7. Commits his crimes sporadically, depending on the event
    on him perpetuated by female.

8. Uses a weapon of opportunity.

9. If a sexual dysfunction, will be retarded ejaculation.

10. Likely beats victim before, during and after the sexual
    assault.

11. Uses a great deal of profanity.

12. Anal intercourse followed by profanity.

13. Will attack at anytime of the day.

14. Typically he will not kill, but the assault may go to far.

him by repeating the obvious. Sean looks like Luke Skywalker but he has the cunning and weapons of Darth Vader. Once you have let down your guard a bit, he begins to draw his weapons, which he shields from your view. He will lead you through something mundane and then, just as you are confident that there will be no difficulties here, he unsheathes his sword and plunges it into your neck.

"Oh my goodness," he will cry, "Is that blood? Did it hurt? Let me help!" And then he's got the blade up and under your ribs where he pokes

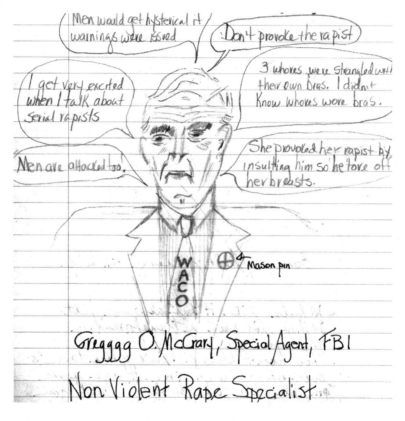

around for evidence of your lying ways. You bleed all over, lies and contradictions spilling everywhere. Before it even registers, he has patched you up, wished you well and returned to his seat. With his robes all black and flowing, he now reminds you of Brad Pitt in *Interview with the Vampire*. The one who harms only those who deserve it and then erases their memory of the harm.

That was my lawyer. The FBI agent didn't have a chance. He rode out of town on the same horse he rode in on and left us with the image of an egotistical cowboy with a dated, unrealistic concept of sexual assault, the men who commit it, and the men who investigate it.

A few weeks later I was at home watching the Geraldo Rivera show, when there on the screen was Gregg McCrary! The caption under his face and his animated conversation with Geraldo revealed him to be a regular contributor to the show. He was lending his expert opinion to the murder investigation of little JonBenet Ramsay (which remains open.)

Kim Rossmo, then a detective inspector of the Vancouver Police Department, another cop with a PhD, was also flown to Toronto as an expert witness for the defence. He is known internationally for developing a new policing tool to find criminals involved in serial murders, rapes and thefts. The tool is somewhat mysterious and is called geographic profiling. Many cops believe profiling to be pretty much the end of the line in an investigation—just short of calling in the psychic. Not that there hasn't been success with both. The thing is, neither are crime prevention tools but both sometimes work to apprehend the guilty after the crimes have occurred. Nonetheless, profiling is gaining massive popularity and credence.

Rossmo echoed the police mantra that my rapist was not violent and that if a warning had been issued, women would have been negatively impacted. His direct contribution to that myth was to say that if women in one apartment building knew there had been a rape in the building next door, they would become *less* vigilant. He also attempted to reinforce the "rapists flee if a warning is issued" delusion.

Less than a year after appearing at my trial and testifying against warnings, Rossmo publicly challenged the Vancouver Police Department for rejecting his recommendation that a warning be issued to alert women of a serial killer in the Vancouver area.* He blamed police resistance on the existence of an "old boys' network."

* As of this book's publication, the number of Vancouver women believed murdered is sixty-three. Their families, their co-workers, and activists had appealed for warnings and a police investigation for years before the case was officially opened. Shamefully, the women are remembered in death only as prostitutes and women with drug dependencies—the same labels that allowed the police to be negligent in following up their disappearances in the first place.

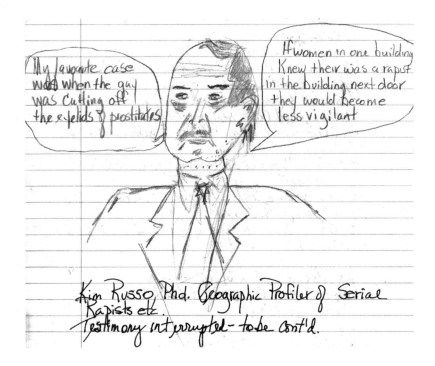

November 4, 1997

Such an ending. Silence of the Lambs FBI agent gleefully describing his serial-rape cases. His hard-on splintering the witness box, his balls so swollen they burst through his shirt collar.

"When you investigate a rape you are in darkness."
— Gregggg McCrarrrrry, FBI ma'am

What have I done? Where shall I go? Who will be there? Boo hoo.

November something, who cares at this point? Is there a final ending anywhere soon?

The police have called a woman to testify that she and other women in the neighbourhood in which we both lived had knowledge of a serial rapist. She is a surprise witness, not on

the list. We waited a while for her to arrive. What came
out was that she had knowledge of a rape that summer. One
rape. Not a series of rapes. It was very confusing. Everyone
is tired. Apparently she had no transportation into town and
no child care, so Kim Derry drove up north to fetch her,
and he played with her baby in the hall while she testified. They gave her bus fare to get home.

And then the police rested their case.

THE last wearying bits.

Sometimes when you are in a difficult situation, the only thing you
can do, the best thing to do, is just hold on, secure in the knowledge that
it will all end soon. Must end soon. And surely this trial without end,
this rape without end, had to end soon. After eleven years of resisting
the rape-victim role, battling with it and everyone who cast me there,
here I was: the silent, passive, raped woman, watching and waiting while
the good men (and some women) saved me from the bad men. Weeping
and unsleeping as psychiatrists and other experts deconstructed what
had happened to me that summer night. Raging and roiling as lawyers
reconstructed their version. It was exhausting. Unnatural. My own
endless ennui was the worst part. I just wanted to lie down, sleep, read,
be with friends who made me think and laugh. Do some drugs . . . just
kidding . . .

I had been hired to oversee a municipal arts grant to agencies working with marginalized youth. I had come to court for the morning but
sat at the back, in the peanut gallery far from the action. The
Dominatrix eyed me suspiciously. Weeks had passed since the last
police witness had given the last piece of evidence. Now it was
December. Gloves and boots. Days that end too soon.

Court was convened once again for each side to deliver closing arguments. Her honour had made it clear that the trial had gone on long
enough and she wanted the lawyers to be snappy about it. So one more
time, we had to go through it all again. Another telling of my rape
would be translated onto paper, perforated and Cerlox-bound, then presented for someone's consideration and judgment. I suspected I had

become one of the most written-about women in the country. A Liz Taylor of the justice tabloids. More like a Tonya Harding probably (whatever happened to her? Last I heard she got Jesus. She got Jesus, I got Julian Fantino. More about him later).

In a civil trial, closing arguments are presented in writing by the plaintiff or complainant (that was me) to the defence (the police). The defence replies with their side and then the plaintiff gets another crack at it in what is called a "reply submission." Both arguments are then presented verbally before the judge. It was the lawyers' show.

I was prepared to sit there and make like I understood, positive that any pretense of speaking in either of the official languages of Canada would be dropped in favour of legalese. But I had come this far and I would see it through. I brought some work I could do.

And then, in this most remarkable of courtroom dramas, something extraordinary happened again.

Cynthia Petersen delivered the Charter portion of our closing argument in a voice and in language as clear as water. She drew a solid line through the jumble of police testimony and evidence to prove their negligence and systemic sexism beyond a shadow of doubt.

"Hey," I think, suddenly back in the room, something stirring in my chest, "this feels familiar, feels like hope or something. I understand this. I can hear this. Cynthia Petersen is putting it all together, quilting the pieces into a pattern, using the police testimony, the very things they believe they did well, to prove they are guilty."

She defines the Charter arguments and their social relevance and lets us see how they apply to rape and how the crime affects us all. She is comparing the Annex Rapist investigation to mine and demonstrates that their rape cookbook is hate literature and that their concept of rape as non-violent is criminal. She quotes Margo Boyd's evidence to declare police policies in sexual-assault investigation discriminatory, careless and irresponsible, despite decades-old recommendations for change. Which resulted in the pretense of change. The impression of change.

She shreds the police failure to warn and their contention that my rape was non-violent by comparing their own officers' testimony about the Annex and Balcony rape investigations.

She challenges Kim Derry's memory and evidence. His and Bill Cameron's involvement in the Two Toes armed-robbery case are proven to have affected their ability to effectively investigate the Balcony Rapist. Despite their sworn testimony to the contrary. She demonstrates the sexist and discriminatory beliefs and attitudes of key police witnesses through their own words on the stand.

After weeks of this trial and years of others, I finally saw the best the law can be. The best a lawyer can be. It was as if Cynthia had become the teacher of everyone in the courtroom. She taught us Charter law. She shared information—which is what a good teacher should do. She shared her understanding of the case in order to assist the judge in reaching a conclusion based on the evidence before her. And her argument was so compelling that there couldn't have been any other conclusion by the time she was finished. That's how lucidly she presented it all.

Sean argued the negligence portion of my suit and was as distinguished and splendid as Cynthia in proving that the police had what is called a "private-law duty of care" and were, therefore, negligent in their decision not to warn.

During closing arguments, the job of the opposing lawyer is to likewise find ways to assist the judge to see why the other guy's arguments are just plain wrong. I can only think that the reason Bryan Finlay and Greg Richards came back with arguments that were weak and easily refuted was because they did not understand the Charter or take our challenge seriously. Unlike Sean, they did not understand the importance of the sexism argument in my case and how it was applied in law through the Charter, and they clearly had not bothered to find someone who did. They did not understand sexual assault. They were so bad and Cynthia and Sean were so good, their arguments so closely reasoned and well thought out, that there was only one obvious conclusion for the judge to make.

The police lawyers could not counter or refute our closing arguments. Cynthia and Sean made the judge's job to rule on a complex issue easier. Which is what judges want and what lawyers are supposed to do. Anyway, that's what I thought about it.

THE problem for me was that I had no faith that the judge would rule for us just because our argument was just. Not when the issue was rape and the police were the defendants. I did not believe that the very system I charged with negligence and systemic discrimination would also judge itself so. And even if it did, what would be accomplished? Who would benefit from *Jane Doe v. the Metropolitan Toronto Police Force*?

The closing arguments ended and the trial was over. I did not approach my lawyers or attempt to speak with them, and they left the courtroom without looking at me. I did not speak with them again for months. A friend took me to Cuba for the holidays, my second vacation in fourteen years. Another friend who worked in a public health clinic gave me two thousand condoms and a carton of Tylenol to deliver to a sister clinic on the island. In Havana, I learned to dance the merengue.

When I returned home, I started working for a labour and arts festival.

I never expected to win my civil case. From the beginning, my goal was simply to access the system that presumed to define my rape for me. To get the thing to trial. And to present a feminist position there that would challenge all of the systems, myths and laws about rape, which have historically misrepresented the crime and women's reactions to it.

And I did that.

I won that.

But actually winning the case? Beating the police? Not in my town you don't. Stronger cases than mine with more substantial evidence (including dead bodies) have resulted in acquittals and wrist slaps for the police. Following which, the officers involved received promotions. But I figured that if we could lay a foundation, present an example that reframed the crimes of sexual assault and social and institutional responses to it, others would follow. And push the envelope a bit further.

A little while into my civil trial I had realized that a verdict against me would reinforce prevailing mythology, and my heart sank to my knees in despair. What had I done? I was trying to change the system from within the system! I don't even believe in that stuff. I think it is a dangerous position to take, but there I was, asking the law to change the law. And I wasn't even the boss of doing it. My lawyers were. It is true that as the trial progressed, it was clear to anyone observing that my team was winning. My lawyers were shinier, brighter, and I was proud of them. Our experts were more intelligent, clearer in their presentation. We argued discrimination and negligence. The police countered with arguments that were confused, cut from another page, pasted from another file. Their defence was their arrogance. They ignored the Charter, thinking it did not apply to them. They presented themselves as the law in front of the law. Which usually worked. So while it was clear that we had won, I did not believe that we would win in terms of a judge's verdict, and I grieved that so few people had witnessed what was presented and denied during those nine weeks. It had been magnificent in its horror and glory both. Grand theatre. Theatre of the absurd.

I grieved that the media representation of what had occurred in the courtroom was not accurate. Women working in anti-violence were not present or involved enough. Legal and academic feminists are not aware of what took place in my trial, what was argued and how. There was no channel to communicate the strategies I engaged in, to repeat or build on them. *Jane Doe v. the Metropolitan Toronto Police Force* was seen to be the property or the business of lawyers and judges. If I were to lose, as was my expectation, it would all have been for nothing (except of course for the millions of dollars spent and salaries paid) and I would be responsible for a court decision that buttressed a rotting system, that strengthened myths and stereotypes about rape rather than exposing them. Sigh. I was deep in depression and could not be comforted. When you know it well, depression can be its own comfort.

Then I won.

⁘

Hull to Dallas, Gilmour a Hawk

WEATHER
HIGH LOW
22°c 15°c

THE SATURDAY SUN

VOL. 12 NO. 39   TORONTO, JULY 4, 1998   80 PAGES

BALCONY RAPIST'S VICTIM WINS $220 GS

- Jane Doe used as 'bait': P. 4
- Vindicated: Heather Bird, P. 15

Jodie VanDerkail breaks down in tears last night after being named Miss CHIN Bikini at the Bandshell, Exhibition Place. Last year's winner, Katie Carbone, offers a congratulatory kiss.

More CHIN party pix: Pages 20-21

28:

JUSTICE Jean MacFarland took seven months to reach a decision on my case. Winter lasts forever in Toronto, spring barely warms us and then suddenly it's too hot. By June, Sean and I were speaking again. I called him and he apologized, pleading temporary insanity and hazardous working conditions as a defence for his behaviour during trial. I dismissed the charges and forgave him for practically everything, but his conduct remained a matter of record.

I asked him to call the judge's office with a request that we receive a few days' notice of her decision date. This would allow us to prepare ourselves and to work on our statements for the media, who were ever-vigilant, as keen as we were for a verdict. Sean thought it was an outrageous thing to do but was so determined to stay on my good side that he went ahead and called her office anyway. The judge said sure, no problem, and also offered to release her decision to us a few hours early, as long as we kept quiet until the public release.

I was deeply affected by how long the judge took to reach her decision. I had already waited twelve years. She gave the impending birth of her partner's child as one of the reasons she was taking so much time, and referred to the due date frequently when legal arguments at the end of the trial threatened to push the proceedings into a new year. I just wanted to be finished with the whole cursed business. What was I supposed to do for the next half-year? Why did the birth of her child put my life on hold? Because that's what it was like. For seven months I just held on, waiting, unsleeping, barely able to work. Mentally premenstrual. Quiet, humid, still. Convinced that I would not win, could not win. Increasingly fearful of the consequences of losing.

But there was another reason for the judge's delay. In 1996, Jean MacFarland had ruled against her colleague, Justice Walter Hryciuk, also known as the "Kissing Judge." She had found him guilty of the sexual harassment of several female officers of the court (witnesses included Crown attorney Mary Hall, who you will recall testified at my trial that sexism did not exist). A few months later, MacFarland's decision was overturned and the Kissing Judge was exonerated after an appeal court cited errors in her decision. A good judge takes a lot of pride in getting it right, especially in a precedent-setting case. Judge MacFarland would have expected an appeal in my lawsuit regardless of her verdict and I imagine she took the time necessary to review the testimony and evidence and to craft a decision that would be strong in law and weak on appeal. And she also took some time to change diapers and to celebrate her most fortunate new child.

For all those long months, we had no idea which way she would rule. MacFarland was the most inscrutable, unreadable person I have ever encountered. In court I couldn't even sketch her, she was so contained. She gave us nothing—no nods, no hints—that she was partial to one side or the other. She rarely smiled, never censored Finlay's audible amusement or nabobery but took Sean to task on more than one occasion.

We got our few days' notice. The decision would come down on Friday, July 3, 1998. We would receive it at eight that morning, when the court offices opened, but would be enjoined to secrecy until it was officially released at two that day. The plan was that Elizabeth Pickett and I would meet my lawyers early in the morning, get the news and work out a strategy for the media conference we had called for 2:30 p.m. I was teaching on Thursday night and decided to sleep in if I could, knowing that whatever the verdict, it was going to be a hell of a day.

IT was all very anticlimactic really. There was no hushed, packed courtroom, no media rushing for phones or photo ops, no pounding of gavels, applause, swelling music. No *Twelve Angry Men* or Morgan Freeman–like magistrates. In a civil case, a written decision is made available to counsel at the judge's office at a prescribed time. It is all very civil. Sean and Eric showed up to find Greg Richards already waiting. They all grabbed copies of the hundred-page document and raced to the last page. Greg got there first, and when Sean saw his face he read his own victory. We had won. On both grounds. Meanwhile, I was still sleeping. I actually slept. At about nine I called Sean's office, hardly able to speak due to presence of stomach in throat and nightmare residue.

"Sean, it's me."

"Get down here," said another stomach-throated voice. "You won and you won big. Over $200,000!"

Silence.

"I won?" Call waiting interrupted us. I put Sean on hold and took the call. It was my sister.

"I won! Hold on, Sean's on the other line."

"Sean, I'm sorry, that was the CBC, they want an interview, can I tell them?"

"You can't! Promise me you won't! The judge will charge you with contempt! Get the hell down here! We won! Elizabeth is here already. Wait, promise me you won't tell anyone, say the words!"

"I won't tell anyone, Sean, I promise. I'll take a cab." We won!

Back to my sister.

"Mary! I won! Yes, it's true, I'll call you right back. I have to call Susan and Maurice."

I took the cab down to Sean's office, wondering why I still felt nauseous. I won! When the elevator door opened on the fourteenth floor I saw Sean. He stopped pacing and looked at me a little blankly. His face was flushed, his manner distracted—I'd never seen him like this. Then he lit up, huge smiling face, fists pounding chest, then lifting me into the air, elevator music swelling. Well, not all of that, but definitely big smiling face, joy, we won! Happiness! All over!

I got a migraine.

SOME assumed I got the decision I did because my judge was a woman. It was one of the first things I was asked after I won, and I have been asked that question ever since. I've decided the question is a reflection on the person who asks it. A statement really. Jean MacFarland was,

Police failed rape victim, judge rules

Toronto force ordered to pay $220,000, called negligent for not warning Jane Doe, other women in area about predator

BY KIM HONEY
The Globe and Mail

TORONTO — A judge has awarded more than $220,000 to a rape victim in a landmark case against Toronto police, condemning investigators for failing to warn women that a serial rapist was stalking their neighbourhood.

The woman known as Jane Doe was the fifth and final victim of Paul Callow, the rapist, who

The judge agreed that Jane Doe was used by police as "bait" in the case of the so-called balcony rapist in 1986.

Yesterday, Madam Justice Jean MacFarland of Ontario Court General Division handed Ms. Doe a stunning victory, ruling that police violated her constitutional rights with their sexist approach to the investigation.

"It is no answer for the police to say women

to look out for themselves," the judgment says. "... The conduct of this investigation and the failure to warn, in particular, was motivated and informed by the adherence to rape myths as well as sexist stereotypical reasoning about rape, about women and about women who are raped."

Ms. Doe, who learned of her victory about 9 a.m. yesterday when her lawyer phoned her,

was accomplished," she said in an interview yesterday. "I won the day the trial started."

The case breaks new ground because it awards a substantive amount — $175,000 — in general damages for a breach of the Charter of Rights and Freedoms, said Cynthia Petersen, Ms. Doe's lawyer. The rest of the money is for special damages, such as medical expenses.

"The judgment clearly indicates that even if

the Charter breach, and that sets a very important precedent in terms of accountability and liability for Charter breachers."

The decision will have far-reaching implications for police forces across Canada, said Ms. Petersen, one of Ms. Doe's three lawyers. Police officers on the beat will now have to conduct themselves in a manner consistent with the Canadian Charter of Rights and Freedoms an

THE SATURDAY STAR

Thundershowers. High 22C.　　　July 4, 1998　　　www.thestar.com　　　Metro Edition

Judge blasts 'sexist' police

Force called 'utterly negligent' in Jane Doe rape investigation

BY PHINJO GOMBU
STAFF REPORTER

The Toronto police force was "utterly negligent" in the way it handled the probe of the so-called serial balcony rapist, a judge has ruled.

Excerpts from judgment, A18

year court battle by a rape victim known only as Jane Doe — the judge condemned police for failing to warn the woman about the serial rapist they had already identified.

It was, the judge ruled, a violation of her Charter rights. And it was fuelled by systemic sexist discrimination across the force as well as a complete failure to understand how the victims of

Doe, now in her early 40s, said minutes after a chaotic news conference to announce the judgment, which was welcomed with cheers by friends and supporters.

"It's been a 12-year journey," she said, referring to Aug. 24, 1986, the day of her assault. "I've been pushing it for 12 years and then one day it's suddenly the culmination of all my work and effort.

"I'm having a hard time absorbing

ing by Madam Justice Jean MacFarland of the Ontario Court, general division — which is sure to be carefully studied by police forces across Canada — also ordered the Toronto police force to pay Doe $220,000 in damages and $20,000 annually for the next 15 years.

Police Chief David Boothby was unavailable for comment but issued a news release in it, Boothby said he had directed the unit commander of

'It certainly suggests to me that women were being used — without their knowledge or consent — as 'bait' to attract a

THE JANE DOE CASE

Police sexist, judge says

This is an excerpt from the 92-page ruling by Madam Justice Jean MacFarland on the Jane Doe case regarding "discrimination" by the then-Metropolitan Toronto Police Force (MTPF)

vestigation to be conducted incompetently and in such a way that the plaintiff has been denied the equal protection and equal benefit of the law guaranteed to her by s. 15(1) of the Charter.

victims.
■ Lack of experienced investigators investigating sexual assault.
■ Lack of supervision of those conducting sexual assault investigations.

is a serious crime, second only to homicide. Yet, I cannot help but ask rhetorically — do they really believe that, especially when one reviews their record in this area? It seems to me it was, as the plaintiff suggests,

ample (Sergeant Stephen) Duggan's occurrence reports in relation to the (second victim's) investigation — clearly "slanted toward disbelieving the victim" to quote (Sergeant) Margo Pulford. It is obvious to

The problems continued are because among adults, wome are overwhelmingly the victim of sexual assault, they are ar were disproportionately in pacted by the resulting po quality of investigation. The r

finally, a perfect judge. As to the issue of her gender, let me say this about that: Five male judges supported and delivered my case to MacFarland for her consideration. Judge Kerr ruled that I be allowed to remain in the courtroom during the preliminary hearing of the man who raped me. Judge Henry ruled that I had a cause of action in 1989, and three male justices upheld his ruling in the Superior Court of Ontario in 1991. I would like to believe that even a male judge would have read the facts in my case and interpreted the law justly and without bias, as did Jean MacFarland. She is an accountable person who rose courageously to the occasion of change and acted responsibly through her position, which is probably the highest praise anyone could bestow on any worker. I wanted to send her flowers, praise, thanks, something, but nothing seemed adequate. Or necessary.

And yes, I am glad my judge was a woman.

But I do regret the doctrines that separate us in the courtroom and outside of it—the same doctrines that allowed my lawyers to separate themselves from me. Were we not all working toward the same end, to create legal and social justice? Even the lawyers from Weir & Foulds? Why, then, were our relationships within the courtroom so unequal and adversarial? I know that shortly before trial began, Sean was advised by his associates to rein me in, to get control over me. While my involvement had been crucial to building the case, people became worried that I would imperil it, and they recast my desire for strategic input and direction as a need for emotional support. Traditional client-solicitor relationships are quite blatantly paternal, and that paternalism is exaggerated when the client is a rape victim. It was not Sean's instinct to follow that tradition, but I think it was easier for him if he did. It was what he was trained to do. As a result I did not function as a full player in a process that could not function without me. The judges and the lawyers were replaceable. I was not. My rape is seen to be the issue over which *Jane Doe* was fought. But my case was about equality, and the victory belongs to the women's movement. It belongs to me. The judges and lawyers were our tools. How sad that we must all perform in a system that will not allow us to be the best we can be. No wonder it doesn't work.

BACK to victory. To winning. To July 1998, when a hundred-page court decision confirmed that the police had been "grossly negligent and irresponsible" and "were motivated and informed by adherence to rape myths as well as sexist stereotypical reasoning about rape, about women, and about women who had been raped." Hah! I tell you it was heady stuff. Intoxicating. Precedent-setting, too. And I breathed it in, my very words and work reflected in the judgment. In Law. *Okay, sort of in law. Okay on paper.* Bound but not binding, because nothing in the judge's decision required the police to change their practices. In fact, within moments of the decision, after they recovered from their group heart attack, the police were spinning the verdict, claiming that all of the bad stuff her Honour had judged them on was from the olden times and they didn't do that anymore. Indeed the Sexual Assault Squad was world-class. A model of its kind. Never mind that months earlier, during my trial, high-ranking officers, many of them present or past members of that squad, testified under oath that the Balcony Rapist investigation had been without fault and they would do it the same way all over again.

Here is the thing, laid out in the language of the court: Judge MacFarland ruled that my Charter rights had been violated. The police did not issue a warning because of their discriminatory belief that women would become hysterical and jeopardize the investigation. This belief caused the police to act in a way that violated my rights to equal protection and benefit of the law. I was also deprived of my right to security of the person because the police did nothing to protect me even though they believed that the rapist would strike again. Therefore the police had exercised their discretion in a discriminatory and negligent way, contrary to the principles of fundamental justice. The judge declared that the police conduct and general policies on investigating sexual assault left much to be desired. She considered me to be the victim of not only a criminal assault but also of bureaucratic and systemic discrimination.*

There was no doubt that this was a victory, and I was wildly happy about it. But even at the time, I couldn't help thinking other thoughts. Civil law had come through for me, but what could civil law really do? I was only one woman with a single court victory. A drop in the bucket. How likely was it that other women would step forward and sue when it cost millions and could take decades? Why should it be the responsibility of the woman against whom the crime has been committed to mount the case, challenge the system and sacrifice her time, money and health?

I couldn't help but look at the damages conceded by my courtroom victory and take the tally of rape's real cost in my life. As a result of my rape, I take medication. I rarely socialize. I sleep with the lights on. I experience insomnia and am terrorized by nightmares to this day. I have permanently damaged my neck by trying to pull myself out of bed when

* The full text of the decision is available (for a fee) at www.quicklaw.com. It can be also read in any law library.

Jane Doe ruling tricky for police

New legal ground broken, lawyer says

BY HENRY HESS
The Globe and Mail

TORONTO — An Ontario judge's decision in the balcony-rapist case significantly expands the responsibility of police to give people the information they need to protect themselves against harm, legal specialists said yesterday.

Madam Justice Jean MacFarland ruled yesterday that Toronto police violated a woman's constitutional rights by not warning her about a serial rapist in her neighbourhood.

The woman, known as Jane Doe, was attacked by the so-called balcony rapist in July, 1986. She sued police for failing to issue a warning so she could have protected herself. The court heard that police thought a public warning would have caused panic and hurt their chances of catching the rapist.

Spokesmen for a number of Canadian police forces said they don't anticipate any problems from the ruling, because they already routinely issue such warnings.

However, Ottawa lawyer Lawrence Greenspon said Judge MacFarland's decision breaks new ground by holding police liable for something they failed to do.

"The case is the first of its kind that way," Mr. Greenspon said in a telephone interview. "Usually, you're suing them for things that they did or that you say they did wrongly."

The full implications will be hashed out over the coming months and years, he said, but it appears to put police in a difficult position when it comes to deciding how to handle potential threats.

"Do we warn and run the risk that we upset the community or scare the community, or do we stay quiet and hope and cross our fingers that our efforts to prevent [a crime] are going to be sufficient without counting on the population to protect themselves?

"When you know that a particular community, be it demographic, geographic, occupational or whatever, ... has a very good chance of being a target of a particular individual, I'm assuming what [the Jane Doe decision] is saying is that you've got a duty to warn."

He also predicted the decision will complicate the already tricky process of deciding how far police can go in issuing warnings about offenders who have been released from jail.

"You're setting up a clash between the collective, community rights ... versus the individual's Charter rights protected under the same Constitution," he said.

"It's a very interesting development in the balance between community and individual Charter rights. It's a question that's going to continue to be litigated, I suspect," Mr. Greenspon said.

Toronto lawyer Marvin Huberman, a specialist in civil law, said Judge MacFarland's decision has huge implications.

"The bottom line is the court basically handed the law-enforcement authorities a stern message that this conduct, whether it be by commission or omission, is not going to be tolerated."

He said the court recognized public protection as a paramount value, taking precedence over other issues. "Do police have an absolute duty of care to warn all those at risk when a dangerous offender is let loose? I wouldn't say that necessarily follows, but it may."

Acting Sergeant Gerry Davenport of the Peel Regional Police said yesterday that although his force has been watching the Jane Doe case with keen interest, "I don't think it's going to change anything we're doing."

He said Peel has long had a policy of issuing public warnings. "The [public's] need to know and investigative strategy sometimes can come into conflict with one another, but you always err on the side of safety."

That sentiment was echoed by spokesmen for several other big-city forces.

Staff Sergeant Gilles Larochelle, media-relations officer for the Ottawa-Carleton Regional Police, said the Jane Doe case was used as an example in his training course.

Years ago, he said, police sometimes tended to hold back information about crimes to try to catch the culprit in the act. Now, the pendulum has swung the other way, toward making the community aware of everything that is going on.

Reasons for decision

These are excerpts from Justice MacFarland's ruling

The police were there to wait and watch for an attack to occur. The women were given no warning and were thereby precluded from taking any steps to protect themselves against such an attack. Unbeknownst to them they were left completely vulnerable. When all of these circumstances are taken and considered together, it certainly suggests to me that the women were being used — without their knowledge or consent — as "bait" to attract a predator whose specific identity then was unknown to the police, but whose general and characteristic identity most certainly was.

◆

It is no answer for the police to say women are always at risk and as an urban adult living in downtown Toronto they have an obligation to look out for themselves. Women generally do, every day of their lives, conduct themselves and their lives in such a way as to avoid the general pervasive threat of male violence which exists in our society. Here police were aware of a specific threat or risk to a specific group of women and they did nothing to warn those women of the danger they were in, nor did they take any measures to protect them.

◆

In my view, the conduct of this investigation and the failure to warn, in particular, was motivated and informed by the adherence to rape myths as well as sexist stereotypical reasoning about rape, about women and about women who are raped. The plaintiff therefore has been discriminated against by reason of her gender and as a result the plaintiff's rights to equal protection and equal benefit of the law were compromised.

◆

[They made the] very serious decision not to warn these women of the risk they faced. This they did in the face of the almost certain knowledge that the rapist would attack again and cause irreparable harm to his victim. In my view, their decision in this respect was irresponsible and grossly negligent.

I dream that the rapist is in the next room and I can hear him ripping up my clothes, but I am paralyzed and cannot move. I don't trust men. Although there are men in my life I love and admire, I don't like them as a group. Sometimes I hate them. I don't believe that I should have to live my life according to their definition of me. Because of their actions, I do not live in a safe or civilized world. I believe that what happened to me—or worse—could happen again. I have immense anger about it. Winning didn't change any of this.

A memory of our goodness recalled

29:

BUT still, I won! And for a while I was a winner. There is something about a raped woman, clearly wronged, fighting back, resisting, winning, that plays to our hearts. Something about taking on the rapist, the cops, the machine. Winning at a time of so much change, so much loss, so many struggles that had failed or continue even today. It was like finding something lost, a memory of our goodness recalled.

I think the fact that I was anonymous helped spark in people a greater appreciation of what had been accomplished. They could examine the events without focusing on the image or the personality of one woman but of women in general. As this convergence of goodwill and triumph played out around me, I had to recognize that these were not notions familiar to me. I do well in battle. What was this winning thing? What exactly had I won and what was it supposed to feel like? Taste like? What was I supposed to wear?

As much as I rail against the stigma of victimhood, it can be a convenient place to battle from. I had just spent a dozen years—most of my thirties and early forties—locked in combat at a time when most women of my generation and background were establishing careers, having children and relationships. My contemporaries were travelling, creating, buying homes, racking up RRSPs. I was suing the police and defending myself. I was attempting to introduce new thought and new law about a political experience that was deeply personal and caused me to relive the crime on a regular basis. By myself. Just as I was supposed to be jubilant when the man who raped me was convicted, I was expected to suddenly feel justified and exultant over this judicial finding.

It's not that I don't know how to be happy. I had planned a victory celebration long before the decision was announced. Win or lose, I was going to dance to the tune of a good fight and honour the people who had been part of it. I booked the Bamboo Club on Toronto's Queen Street West and had matchbooks printed in aqua, which read "Jane Doe: a match for the cops" in an elegant silver script.

When the judge ruled in my favour, word of the party circulated widely and the place was packed. People came from as far away as Montreal and North Bay, a cross-section of ebullient friends, family, supporters and admirers, some of whom I did not know, including a list of notables in the worlds of Canadian art and politics. People said wonderful things about me. I believed that they believed them. Rita Davies was the emcee. Miche Hill of the Unceded Band sang Nancy Sinatra's "These Boots Are Made for Walkin'." In an attempt to put a face on Jane Doe, Anna Bourque talked about our twenty-five-year friendship and revealed my true identity as a doctor with Médicins Sans Frontières who had discovered the polio vaccine. Michael Hendricks, half of the first married gay couple in the province of Quebec, took photos. My sister toasted my friends and guests and wept as she thanked them for supporting me when my family could not. All of my nieces and nephews were there. The late TV newsman and architect Colin Vaughan waltzed me around for a while. Anne Collins said I must write a book. A famous dub poet, an ex-mayor, a national columnist and an immigration judge were engaged by my friend Anna in a conversation about oral sex. Val Scott of the Canadian Organization for the Rights of Prostitutes (CORP), arrived too late to share the stage with me as one of the many people present who had supported my work as Jane Doe. Women from LEAF accepted my invitation to attend. It was a wonderful party.

See? I do too know how to be happy. But I kept thinking, if I was the winner. Who was the loser? What had really been won?

IN a movie I would have been physically and psychologically transformed. Job offers and romance would have come my way. Gruff but kindly police officers would have been transformed too, would have welcomed the verdict. I would have got a lot more money.*

What did happen, though, could never have been scripted.

Five days after the judge ruled against the police in my civil case, Toronto City Council voted fifty-two to one that the police could not launch an appeal. They also voted that the police force and council itself apologize for my rape, and that an audit be conducted into how the police had investigated it and into the nature of sexual-assault investigations in general. These proposals were initiated by councillors Olivia Chow and Pam McConnell and championed by all of the women on council. The men were not far behind.

The notion of not pursuing an appeal in a court of law is pretty much unheard of, not just in the annals of rapedom but in legal history overall. Appealing is the loser's right. That's certainly how the police lawyers saw it. And they reacted with all of the indignation, fury and legal clout of, well, powerful Bay Street lawyers.

Now fast-forward a bit. Dizzy, speedy days. Phone ringing merrily. Media support all over. Germany calling my lawyers. Buffalo, Florida, Australia too. Will the police appeal or won't they? Can city hall really stop them? Should they? Will the police apologize? Should they? Thirty days to decide, and each day new headlines, new outrage, new indignation. On my behalf.

But like I said, the problem was that after MacFarland ruled, it was now up to the police themselves to change their policies and practices. Or not. The ruling did not order them to change their policy on sexual-assault investigation but relied on the good conscience of police to do the right thing.

---

* The total amount awarded to me was $220,000. Court costs were awarded to my lawyers and LEAF. Both amounts and the fees of the police lawyers were paid with taxpayers' dollars. Legal fees for both sides were in the millions.

We like to believe that public institutions respond positively to court decisions. But the evidence is that they greet such rulings with intransigence, denial and perversity. The courts are reluctant to become involved in the mechanics of implementing their judgments. For example, much is made of the monumental decision of the U.S. Supreme Court to abolish racial segregation in schools in the fifties, but it took thirty more years of activism, court rulings, racist acts and political brinkmanship for integration to happen and it is not fully realized yet. Legal decisions are simply one move to effect change in a much larger political game. Unless politicians are prepared to force the moral weight of a legal decision, little of a substantive nature is likely to be done.

There is ongoing debate about who should be calling the shots over the making of public policy—the courts or the politicians? The fact is that the Canadian Charter of Rights and Freedoms, the law of our land, has placed the courts near the centre of public policy–making. Debate your head off—the judges are involved already. And don't forget that I went to court as a last resort. Other routes that I engaged to change police policies had proved useless.

The Jane Doe social audit ordered by Toronto City Council was the missing piece, the tool that could, conceivably, implement change in the policing of sexual assault. The city council controlled the police budget; it had the power to determine how much money police would receive and how it would be allocated.* An audit, ordered and enforced by council, could do what other interventions (legal decisions, inquests, community activism) could not.

This is how I best understand the concept of a social audit. Think of a financial audit. We all know what that looks like. An auditor examines your accumulated income and expenditures. If they do not balance, you must rectify the situation. Similarly, in the Jane Doe social audit, the city auditor, Jeffrey Griffiths, was charged with examining all of the recommendations that had come to the police over the years concerning the investigation of sexual assault (the income) and assessing how

---

* The police annual budget, currently at $600 million, is the largest single item financed by the taxpayers of Toronto.

(or if) they had been acted upon by the force (the expenditures). The idea of an audit is both brilliant and dangerous. It ties police behaviour to economic reward, kind of a financial behaviour-modification program, like the one that capitalism and the entire workforce is built on.

A NUMBER of reactions to my legal victory were playing out, and they had to play out quickly. If the police were going to ignore their masters and launch an appeal, they had to do it within thirty days of MacFarland's ruling. If they were going to obey their city hall bosses and apologize, well, apologies are best delivered warm, and the media was hot on the whole story.

First to the appeal. As I said, the council's decision that the police and their lawyers could not appeal is the stuff headlines are made of, and the police department, still represented by Weir & Foulds, could read the writing in the paper. They took a series of meetings—secret ones—with the council members responsible for the city budget in order to plead their case for appeal. The documentation was leaked to me by one of my friends in the media to whom it had likewise been leaked. It contained hundreds of pages of fault-finding with MacFarland's decision, which ultimately boiled down to a legal declaration of "Help me! I've fallen and I can't get up."

It was the city's right-wing budget chief who delivered the final blow. In the company of other councillors, he declared to the police defence team that they had "fucked up" in 1986 (during the investigation of my rape), "fucked up" in 1991 (when I was granted the legal right to proceed to trial), "fucked up" in 1997 (with the civil trial) and they should now bloody well "fuck off." There was also a story, repeated on national radio, that the city's mayor, prone to waffling, was mid-flip-flop on the question of an appeal when his wife declared in no uncertain terms that he should give that girl her money and leave her the hell alone for God's sake.

Then the police lawyers offered to give me my settlement money and proceed with an appeal anyway.* Next the Ontario Association of Chiefs of Police (led by Julian Fantino, who became Toronto's chief of police

---

* Given the opportunity, I would have considered accepting this offer. A Supreme Court decision that upheld MacFarland's judgment would have further-reaching legal consequence than her lower-court ruling. But I never got to consider it because the concept, put forward by Weir & Foulds, was deemed preposterous by city lawyers.

in 2000) considered launching a third-party appeal (but did not). Toronto Police Chief David Boothby enraged city council when he announced that they couldn't make him apologize—so there! And the police union boss, a formidably pushy cop named Craig Bromell, added my case to his list of police grievances against the city.

People watched the spectacle of judgments, audits, countersuits and apologies unfold around my court decision. Everyone saw how patently absurd the police defence had been, and they finally wondered how it had all come to this. When it came to pursuing the *Jane Doe* lawsuit, who was running the police shop and why had they let it go on for so long?

It appeared to be a *Wizard of Oz*–type situation. Everyone was suddenly asking, "Who's in charge? Who was the man (men?) behind the police curtain? Who made the decisions about their defence?" Three different police chiefs had succeeded each other as my case worked its way through the courts, but they were not directing legal strategy. The provincial Solicitor General was supposed to be in charge of all policing matters, but the trail didn't lead there. The Police Services Board, presumably, could have made those decisions, but its members had no real power. A past member who for a moment was able to steer the board progressively revealed that the board was forbidden by their insurers to even discuss my case. The hunt seemed to end with the Ontario Municipal Insurance Exchange (OMEX), which carries policies on the force and the entire city government. A little more digging (by Heather Bird and Phinjo Gombu) revealed that OMEX is not a private company but a collective of municipal governments that banded together to set up a self-insurance scheme after a series of large claims against them made them uninsurable. Apparently the big decisions about the police defence were being made by a committee of lawyers, claims adjusters and city treasurers, accountable to no one and questioned by none. Norm Gardner, chair of the Police Services Board, declined to name the bureaucrats who were calling the shots, but Weir & Foulds was the legal firm that provided them all with legal advice. George Rust-D'Eye, who came to the city's legal department from Weir & Foulds after the firm had taken on the police case, sat on that committee for a while. He returned to the law firm in time to work on the arguments for the possible appeal. Albert Cohen, a lawyer with the City of Toronto's legal department, finally pronounced that "the circumstances [concerning who was running the defence] were murky but there was no intention to mislead." The quest to find the wizard ended there. To this day, I do not know the name or nature of my invisible foes or if they are still directing police policy. And when Chief Boothby suddenly agreed to apologize to me at an upcoming Police Services Board meeting, the matter of who was in charge was dropped.

True to my nature, by this time I was questioning the motives of everyone (newly) involved. I was proud of the actions taken by Toronto City Council. The forced amalgamation of the City of Toronto and the five boroughs surrounding it had produced a large council deeply divided by regional and political differences and unable to agree on the time of day. But here it was, crossing those lines and the gender ones that separated them, standing up for me to do the right thing for the women of Toronto.

Magnificent as it was, though, they had left out a critical component in their motions—the same component that had been ignored by the courts, police and government for decades when addressing crimes of violence against women. Council didn't consult or take direction from the people most involved with the issue before drafting and presenting its motion for a social audit. Politicians did not speak with me or women working in the anti-violence sector about the issues they were advancing on our behalf. If they had, we would have advised them to at least highlight race and poverty factors in the research phase of the audit. We would have challenged their use of the term "family violence," which melds crimes against women and children in a way that can infantilize women. But we did not have that opportunity and instead had to insert ourselves after the fact, as we always did, even though this time we had a winner.

AND everyone loves a winner, if only for a moment, if only in place of other losses. The women's community embraced my victory as its own,

Who was Jane's invisible foe?

It was quite a sight the other night as Jane Doe's bandwagon rolled through city council, picking up politicians left, right and centre.

The rush to post-judgment by these jenny-and-johnny-come-latelys should be no surprise because, after all, the whole world loves a winner. No word on where most of these good folks were during Doe's lonely odyssey over the past dozen years.

While there is no quibbling with their decision not to appeal Doe's victory, there are plenty of questions which need to be asked about the process they used to arrive at that conclusion. And why council suddenly found itself with the power to make sweeping decisions in this case.

For years, Metro politicians and appointees [...] insisted [...] direct the [...] suit again[...] case was [...] company [...] were pre[...] budgets, [...] a politica[...] by any nu[...] Thursda[...]

pened to the settlement offers I sent over there?"

Both of those proposals were for amounts "substantially less" than the $220,000 which Madam Justice Jean MacFarland ultimately awarded his client.

Lawyers for the police did make one settlement offer of their own. Six days before the case was to go to trial they told Doe's lawyers that if she dropped the suit, they wouldn't go after her for legal fees.

"It was completely meaningless," says Dewart.

In the wake of Doe's resounding victory, it is becoming increasingly clear there may have been a serious abuse of the democratic process in how her legal challenge was handled.

Its ramifications are profound. In monetary terms, this could have been settled for $50,000 and political change. Instead, the case could cost taypayers up to $2.5 million. That includes Doe's $220,000 award, pre-judgment interest and the legal fees, which are expected to be in the range of $2 million.

Then there is the incalculable price paid by Jane Doe, who, in addition to the stress of a 12-year legal struggle, had to endure having her private life publicly dragged through

Heather
BIRD
CITY STREETS

NORM GARDNER
City responsible for costs

Insurers 'called shots' in lawsuit

By BRAD HONYWILL
Toronto Sun

Senior city bureaucrats are ultimately responsible for the $1.4 million taxpayers have spent on the Jane Doe case, the head of the Toronto police services board said yester[...]

Police chief kept in dark over insurer in Doe case

Taxpayers' money
to pay woman
who sued police

BY PHINJO GOMBU
STAFF REPORTER

The decision for Toronto police to fight the Jane Doe case for the past 12 years wasn't made by a private insurance company — as suggested by police services board chair Norm Gardner — but by a group of treasurers representing the former municipalities of Metropolitan Toronto.

And neither police board members, the chief of police nor city politicians were aware of that fact until yesterday.

'I'm amazed at the way things have fallen down the funnel'

It is, in fact, taxpayers money from a $45 million reserve fund that will have

ALBERT COHEN: "There was no intention to mislead," says lawyer for City of Toronto.

which it was. With the judge's decision, everything clarified for a moment. Every woman who had ever engaged in or understood activist work got it and didn't need to hear the details. Although a decade of cruel and killing government cuts and controls had replaced feminist politics in women's services with clinical models of health care and social work, we were galvanized again, revolutionaries again. Women who had been too busy patching up the poverty, trauma and murder of other women (and documenting it in triplicate) to actively support me and the issues my case represented were now returning my calls, attending meetings, agreeing to attend more. With a song in their hearts. My own dark heart mended to see them come.

A legal victory, an apology and an audit! What more could a girl want?

July 10, 1998

The police brass, lawyers and media assemble, take the best seats and use up most of the oxygen in the auditorium at police headquarters. The room is electric and I am nervous but in a positive way. A winning way.

The meeting begins and there are motions, medals are awarded, and the purchase of crime-fighting helicopters is discussed. Then Chief Boothby slowly reads a long and carefully worded letter of apology directed at me.

I hear: "On behalf of the Toronto Police Services Board and myself, please accept our sincere apologies for the pain and suffering caused by the attack and sexual assault committed on you. . . . I also regret the further stress that the twelve years of litigation must have caused you . . . ."

And then I sort of blank out, that thing I do. I hear cameras thrumming as their operators jockey for better position, completely blocking my view of my apology, and I think, "Now what? They will be all over me next, asking, 'What do you think?' 'How do you feel?' 'Can we shoot (you in) the back of your head?'"

Boothby delivers one of those conditional apologies that absolves the aggressor because they didn't really mean it, they intended no harm, so really it's your problem if you took any offence.

But you know what? This is My Apology, the one I fought for, waited for, bled for, and it's the best I'm going to get. The best they can do. We could carry on, me in one corner saying, "Screw you," and them in the other corner saying, "No, screw you," and who wins then? Maybe, just maybe, we can move this whole thing forward just a bit, just a step—what's to lose?

I get up from my seat, cross the marble floor and wedge myself between the members of the media who are thronging the chief, and they move because they know who I am. I extend my arm, handshake position, and Boothby looks at me, quite startled for a moment. "What now?" I can see him thinking. "What fresh hell is this?" Then I smile and he takes my hand, disappears it in his as he realizes who I am, and I say, "Thank you, Chief. That means a lot." He leans his head toward me, shakes my hand some more and tells me to come and see him and we'll talk. I can tell he really means it and I say, "Okay, I'd like that," and I go back to my seat.

A FEW days later, responding to the order to undergo the social audit, Boothby issued a statement promising that the force would use the *Jane Doe* decision as an "opportunity to re-examine its approach to sexual assault."

Margo Boyd negotiated the meeting between the chief and myself without media or fanfare. It took place in his office on a sad day on which the city learned of the murder of a police officer killed on duty. We began with condolences and appreciation, and Boothby was courteous and professional. He agreed that increased and better police training regarding sexual assault was critical and that he was empowered to make those changes. I reminded him that I was not representative of

Handshake seals apology to Jane Doe

By PHINJO GOMBU
STAFF REPORTER

It was the one unscripted moment of an otherwise carefully staged apology by Toronto police Chief David Boothby and the police services board to the rape victim known only as Jane Doe.

Moments after the chief read the apology letter yesterday and was talking to reporters, Doe made her way through the media throng and extended a hand to a startled Boothby.

"Chief Boothby, thank you very much," Doe said as she reached across the table where the police services board was meeting at police headquarters.

"I appreciated it. It meant a lot," she said.

The chief, clearly taken aback by the gesture, later said: "It was very spontaneous. I didn't know who she was but I made an assumption. I thought it was very nice."

The handshake was a dramatic moment, a symbolic end to Jane Doe's long quest for an apology from the police for her 1986 rape.

The woman had sued police for violating her Charter rights by not notifying her that she was the possible target of a serial rapist. A judge earlier this month agreed police had used her as "human bait" to catch a

What Boothby told Jane Doe

'On behalf of the Toronto Police Service and myself, please accept our sincere apologies for the pain and suffering caused by the attack and sexual assault committed on you by ▬▬▬▬▬▬

I also regret the further stress that the 12 years of litigation must have caused you.'

tion must have caused you," he said, adding the force was committed to reviewing its approach to crimes against women.

The litigation has already cost taxpayers more than $500,000, police board members were told yesterday privately. That doesn't include the $220,000 awarded to Doe. There's also the issue of legal costs for Doe, yet to be decided.

Doe sat quietly with her law-

REACHING OUT: Toronto police Chief David Boothby shakes hand offered by rape victim Jane Doe after yesterday's police apology.

JEFF GOODE/TORONTO STAR

Rape victim finally gets apology

Doe: I appreciate it

By ROBERT BENZIE
City Hall Bureau

Rape victim Jane Doe, once used as "bait" by Toronto Police to nab a serial rapist, burst through a crowd yesterday to thank Chief David Boothby for apologizing to her.

The dramatic scene came after Boothby read a carefully worded statement to the Po-

"It was very nice that she came up to me and shook my hand and said that she would like to talk to me at some point and, hopefully, that we could work together," he said.

"I would welcome that."

For her part, Doe said she wanted to shake his hand. "An apology always deserves you and I believe his apology was s

"I'm not sure if I'd use the word mealy-mouthed, but it (the apology) was less than one would have hoped for."

Patti McGillicuddy, a sexual assault counsellor at the University of Toronto, read a prepared response to the board on behalf of

'Sorry for pain and suffering'

Text of Chief David Boothby's apology:

• • •

Dear Jane Doe:
On behalf of the Toronto Police Service and myself, please accept our sincere apologies for the pain and suffering caused by the attack and sexual assault committed on

the larger community and could not speak for them, and that the social audit was the mechanism the community would support to effect change. He agreed and suggested we meet again.

Now I don't want to say that David Boothby was insincere. He is a farm boy from rural Ontario, who rose steadily in the force to become chief in 1995, blowing the horn of community policing. He was not welcomed by the rank and file, who were comfortable with the police-under-siege mentality polished by his predecessor, Bill McCormack. Neither was Boothby welcomed by the more enlightened members of the Police Services Board (all two of them), who had championed a different candidate as their choice for change. Within moments of his coronation as chief, Boothby failed to face down an illegal and dangerous work-to-rule action led by Craig Bromell at the notorious downtown 52 Division. Boothby never recovered and Bromell went on to lead the powerful police union.* I believe Boothby really meant what he said the day we met at his office. But within a year, he had abandoned his word and the cause of reform. And in the end, whether he was insincere or not, he foiled change. Stopped it in its tracks. As police chiefs will do.

Before Boothby betrayed himself and us, however, there was more winning to be had. While I can look back today and understand how it failed, the Jane Doe social audit was a breathtaking process. Shimmering at times.

It's clear that when it comes to crimes of male violence against women, all of the good intentions of all of the king's horses and men cannot make change. I believe they can't because these officials keep doing it on women's *behalf*, without consulting us or listening to what we define as the problems and the solutions. Without taking our direction. And without paying us for our work.

* Craig Bromell identifies himself as a bully and crows about the intelligence-gathering and intimidation tactics he uses against his political masters and opponents, reaped from workshops and strategy sessions delivered by police departments in the United States. He has provoked the outrage of citizens, politicians and media left and right in his mostly thwarted attempts to establish policing as the law as opposed to an agent of law enforcement. He and Boothby were arch-enemies on the same side.

30:

ADVISORY Most people do not find the social audit a riveting topic. Which I find puzzling, because it was the closest we came to truly winning. The closest we came to change. The audit should have worked for everyone, including the police. I don't know if it's the term "audit," which implies business and number-crunching, that invokes fear and boredom, or if it's because the subject is rape, and business and rape surely cannot go together. But the social audit is one of the most important parts of the story and the least told or understood. I've tried to keep it short.

IF YOU want to control a meeting, arrive early with copies of a formal agenda that includes "other business" at the end of the list. Once the meeting has convened, speak first and make absolutely sure that if you are interrupted, an ally will return control of the floor to you or take up the relevant issue herself. Understand and be prepared to deal with barriers. Speak with authority. Use humour when appropriate. Be as generous as possible. This is an old ploy, but the politicos and bureaucrats who saw themselves as the bosses of the social audit didn't see it coming, which was a sign of how much control they assumed they would have. They included two city councillors and their numerous staff, five members of the city's Equity Office, two members of the Police Services Board and two of that board's administrative staff. All of them appeared to be thinking, "Let's help the poor rape victims and the children and get back to the real stuff of politics."

When I asked for community support to ensure that the social audit would have some feminist teeth in it, women came running. Initially four of us convened to map out a strategy.* The city council motion recommended that police personnel be included in the community group brought together to work with the auditor and his team. The wording of the council motion also suggested that the rape of Jane Doe and the issues it addressed should be piggybacked by the litany of criminal activity that takes place within the family, as if there were no difference between crimes committed against children and those committed against adult women.

So in the first meeting with the auditor, we were determined to clarify the intent and content of the audit. The four of us had been on the phone, faxing and e-mailing about the audit and its implications. As a result, women from twenty-one agencies attended the first meeting. They represented the ethnic and racial diversity of Toronto and included women with disabilities and women from the sex trades, the majority of whom were, or had been, anti-violence workers in rape crisis centres and shelters. Other attendees included health care workers from a sexual assault care centre (SACC), hospital-based researchers and a representative from the National Action Committee on the Status of Women (NAC). In the centre of the room were the city auditor and the three staff he had assigned to the project. I spoke first and suggested, as per our agenda, that we begin with introductions. We quickly moved to introduce the following:

> Anti-violence workers would function as a community reference group to the audit team, to be called the Audit Reference Group (ARG—I know, I know . . .). Police members appointed

---

* Along with me there was Beverly Bain, a feminist educator and organizer; Beth Jordan, the director of the Assaulted Women's Helpline; and Patti McGillicuddy, a social worker and anti-violence activist. We were all teachers and counsellors with vast experience in anti-violence work, including program design, delivery of services and adult education. We all had histories of attempting to address police training and protocol and had witnessed the legal system's disregard for women at the receiving end of sexual violence.

to the audit would serve only as consultants, there to listen to what women were saying and to supply factual information rather than to give direction, hijack discussion and tell us at every opportunity how fabulous but misunderstood the police are, as this was a process designed to critique police practices. We were anxious that the audit only address violence against women, not family violence. My lawsuit was about adult women, not children—to lump the two together would compromise the importance of both.

We asked for an honorarium to cover our expenses ($50). I've already talked about how offensive it is not to be paid for work. We demanded that ARG make formal presentations about sexual assault to the auditor and his team, who would then craft the final recommendations. To ensure a balanced understanding of the issues, we asked that three women who were acknowledged community experts be hired by the auditor for his official team. Since we had seen a whole lot of reports and consultations where a whole lot of stuff got done and then left on the table, we requested that there be an implementation process built into the recommendations. Although Pam McConnell had been instrumental in arguing the motion—and she was city council's liaison and chair of the group—we believed it wouldn't do to have a politician alone in that seat and we wanted a community member to co-chair. We called for McConnell to return to council to present these conditions for its approval and amendment.

It took a few meetings, behind the scenes and in front, and the collective will of the women at the table, but we got all the changes we'd designed. We got them because we were organized and they made sense. We got them because we had nothing to lose and because we told the auditor that we would not endorse any recommendations that did not arise from a process that actively and fairly included us. We got them because the police agreed to abide by these rules and endorsed them in their management meetings and publicly, and because the media were still interested in Jane Doe. We got them because the city auditor, Jeff Griffiths, responded to community needs.

We were thrilled and exuberant, even as we reminded ourselves that we were not really in control. But at the time, in those moments, we were victorious. We cherished the opportunity to rally together to do the work we knew how to do and did so well. We were not alone. I was not alone. It was luxurious in its way.

DURING the audit, a serial rapist operating in the east end of the city propelled the police to warn women to lock their doors, stay home, leave their lights on, and so on. The investigation was being led by Inspector Tony Warr, who had been seconded from homicide to the Sexual Assault Squad to set up a stalking protocol. He and I engaged in a media war of words about the phrasing and effectiveness of the warning he had issued.

Sandy Adelson, a Police Services Board member assigned to take part in the ARG, intervened to suggest that instead of slugging it out in the press, Warr and I get together to discuss our differences in person.*

Tony Warr is a cop's cop, a man's man. He is a snappy dresser with old-school manners and a worn face. On the day we met, he sat across from me in his office and agreed that changes in sexual-assault investigation and a warning protocol, drafted with the full input of women working in the area, were necessary. He also agreed that the social audit would be an effective method to deliver change. It was as easy as that. A few weeks later, he was transferred to Internal Affairs, and Roy Pilkington was appointed commander of the Sexual Assault Squad. Warr arranged a meeting with the three of us, and at the direction of ARG, we discussed the following:

> ✧ An implementation team of an equal number of police officers and women should be appointed to oversee the inevitable recommendations for change that the auditor's report would contain.

*Sandy Adelson was a law student and the youngest person ever to sit on the board. She and I became friends.

❖ Women should be paid for their work as professional consultants to the police.

❖ To avoid the historical breakdown of communication
between police and women's groups, an outside mediator
mutually agreed upon should be hired to work with us to
develop a process and guidelines with which to proceed.

❖ The project should be time-specific and goal-oriented to
avoid make-work meetings that go nowhere.

Both Warr and Pilkington agreed. One conversation was all it took.
These senior-ranking officers had no trouble getting it. Or were they
just saying they got it as a diversion tactic to appease Jane Doe? A week
later, they both attended a city council session. Roy Pilkington, in full
dress uniform, spoke out in support of all four recommendations and
they were passed by a unanimous vote, which included the mayor.
Although present, the media did not report.

IT would be correct to say that the women who worked on the social
audit terrorized Jeff Griffiths. Especially me. Especially at the beginning. I suppose it was a gamble, but we had an advantage: If the audit
was not going to be accountable to us, the stakeholders, the women
doing the work, we didn't care if it went ahead or not. We were prepared
to walk out, and we challenged his ability and motives. Griffiths didn't
retreat. He was always clear about the audit and its carriage being his
and his alone, but he allowed the process to be as accountable as possible. Which was as good as it was going to get.
  We faced opposition from the Equity Office at city hall and from the
local sexual assault care centre, but we persevered. We made presentations and designed a confidential questionnaire for women who had or
had not reported their rapes and distributed it through the rape crisis
centre and shelters. A similar questionnaire was crafted for police officers in an effort to try to unveil their attitudes toward the investigation
of rape.

Nine months after we began, the auditor produced a document that listed fifty-seven recommendations for change in the investigation of sexual assault. The good ones focused on the need to improve and increase officer training in sexual-assault investigation on all levels of policing. Such training was to be designed and delivered by women who were experts in the field. He wrote that women hired for these jobs or as consultants should be paid for their work. The audit also directed the police to produce a written protocol regarding the issuing of warnings about stranger and serial rape in consultation with community experts.

The police shouldn't have needed anyone to recommend that they extend the Sexual Assault Squad's office hours from eight to four Monday to Friday. Whoever thought rapists observed office hours. Neither should the force have needed nudging to expand the squad's mandate to investigate all sexual assaults. Shockingly, the force's own statistics revealed that the squad only investigated 4 per cent of all reported rapes.

Some of Griffiths's other recommendations are potentially dangerous for women. For instance, he supported the increased purchase, use and development of computer profiling and forensic technology (VICLAS and VICAP systems) to investigate sexual assault. We would never have endorsed that. Nor was it discussed with us. We were also blindsided by Griffiths's recommendation that the police should work with SACCs and the Victim Services program as opposed to women's anti-violence services.* For reasons known only to himself, Griffiths recommended a rape hotline to be staffed by police. (Luckily the police also found that one unrealistic.)

For the entire nine months during which we worked with the auditor, and in every presentation, ARG stressed the absolute need for him to address the incidence and specificity of the sexual assaults of Native women, Black women and women of colour. Native women were not mentioned once in the 130-page document. Black women and women of colour rated a few paragraphs near the end, separate from the rest.

---

* Victim Services or Victim Witness programs are available to women who have been raped or beaten who enter the system. They are financed and administered by the Crown Attorney's Office and staffers work closely with police. Neither agency was mentioned once during the time we worked with the auditor.

Sex trade workers were also neglected.*

Even before the police chief made his official response to the audit recommendations, the police implemented the ones that benefited them directly (within a week they hired eleven new staff, none of whom received any of the advanced training that the audit recommended). Again we were back to the police, and the police alone, deciding how they would act. And again they decided to act their way, the old way, the my way or the highway.

The auditor did not include an implementation mechanism in his report. Apparently auditors can only make recommendations, not suggest ways to carry out those recommendations; if they talk about implementation, they breach the Worldwide Audit Rules and risk death or something.

Implementation is where city politicians are/were supposed to come in. They ordered the audit and paid for it. They were the ones who made all the speeches, expressed all the outrage and publicly apologized to me and the women of Toronto for the sorry state of the policing of sexual assault. But unless they are invested in seeing their motion through to implementation, the social audit—so lovely to look at—is doomed to join other reports, decisions and inquest verdicts on the shelves of police bureaucrats and politicians. Where it will collect dust. And we will be left with the *impression* of change.

---

* The complete text of the Jane Doe social audit, officially known as *Review of the Investigation of Sexual Assaults Toronto Police Services*, can be accessed at www.city.toronto.on.ca/audit/reports1999.htm.

31:

I PAID a high price to fight my civil suit. I chose to pay it and it paid off with a courtroom victory. I did my work and I am proud of it. But I can't recommend the course that I chose to other women. Civil justice is perhaps preferable to criminal justice, which gives women no voice at all and can never act in their interest, but not by much. Civil or criminal, the law and the manner in which it judges raped women is not nearly good enough. Women have been saying so for generations.

In the late nineteenth century, the first wave of (documented) anti-rape activism, led by the Women's Christian Temperance Union (WCTU), saw the legal age of sexual consent raised from ten to sixteen years of age. At that time, the WCTU was the largest women's organization in North America and the first mass or grassroots political organization for women in American history. (The WCTU originated in Britain, where similar organizing took place, as it did in parts of Europe.) Members recognized the double standard that required Victorian-era women to live chaste lives before marriage yet legally sanctioned consensual sex at the unripe age of ten. Their campaign initiatives addressed male sexual behaviour as detrimental to the well-being of girls and women and described sexuality as an instrument of power that worked to subjugate women. They insisted that the issue belonged at the centre of public and political debate and that the law needed to be reformed. They were successful. After that wave of reform, rape laws did not substantially change for another seventy years.

I could go on here and fill a chapter or two with the accomplishments of successive waves of feminist activism regarding rape that would bring us up to this new millennium. The pattern of reform is roughly the same in all Western democracies.* I have referred to some of this work on other pages of this book and credit it with preparing the ground for my case to proceed and be successful.

But the hard truth is that despite all this activism and legal reform, the occurrence of the crime of sexual assault is rising, rises every year. Fewer women choose to report and enter the legal system, and those who do rarely see a conviction. A history of feminist activism does not tell us that the Gayme of *Seaboyer and Gayme* was a boy of eighteen who knew the fifteen-year-old girl he raped. The list of reforms does not reflect lost or ruined lives, terror, bloodshed or injuries that never heal, economic loss or gain, social decay, health or productivity. Nor does it give us a true sense of the courage, faith and intelligence of the generations of women who got us this far and who are never far away.

To cast our eyes down the list, we might even believe that this recent work has improved the status of women. Or even helped to protect us, which is usually how women's equality demands are interpreted. To be fair, legislative changes have affected both our status and our security, but only to a degree and not nearly enough.

Try this progressive-change litmus test: Would you still caution your daughter to beware of strange men, to monitor the movements of men she does not know, to watch those she does, to not leave her glass unattended while out dancing or to not be out alone after dark? To never carry too many parcels, which might impede a quick escape, or to not trust that the man who offers her assistance has no other motive in mind than human kindness?

I'll bet that you would.

So what's a girl, a woman, a good man to do? Recognizing the problem areas that women have already identified is a start. Like this for instance: In building its response to raped women, the legal system has relied on and legalized medical definitions of how women respond to the crime. This medical pathologizing of the minds and bodies of raped women was the greatest obstacle I faced. It caused me to question

---

* A trajectory of Canada's feminist legal reforms of the sexual assault laws can be found at www.quicklaw.com.

myself, to be afraid. This alliance of the medical and legal institutions—the gathering of the materials for the sexual-assault kit, the use of medical records and expert psychiatric testimony to discredit women who file sexual assault charges—has actually worked to reduce the number of women who report the crimes and to increase the number who decide to drop charges after they have entered the system. But it's very hard to bring this reality home to the workers who staff the hospital sexual-assault centres, to the police, to the lawyers and judges of the criminal justice system, to the politicians calling the shots, all of whom seem to deeply believe they are doing the right thing.

IN 2000, I was invited to be the keynote speaker at the annual general meeting of the Ontario Network of Sexual Assault Care and Treatment Centres. "Don't they know my position on them?" I wondered. It wasn't as if I hadn't been vocal about it. When I lecture, I always include a critique of the sexual-assault evidence kit. But the organizer assured me that the association welcomed my input. All of it. In fact the conference was going to be called "Controversies in Sexual Assault Care." Another organizer had heard me speak. "All right then," I thought. Here is what I think about SACCs. This is a good summary of what I told them.

All SACCs, located in hospitals, offer counselling and health care to raped women, but their main function is to perform the testing required to compile the sexual-assault evidence kit. SACCs do not require raped women who do not report to the police to undergo forensic testing. There is, however, an institutional bias for them to do so. I described my experience earlier, but just to recap: A doctor, usually male, gives you an internal to verify penetration and to capture any rape sperm. There is usually a good chance of this as no one has allowed you to pee. You stand on a sheet in the middle of a room. Hairs are removed from your scalp and plucked from your pubic area. Skin cells are scraped from your shin. Blood is taken from your arm. Saliva from your mouth. They give you massive doses of antibiotics and morning-after pills that make you ill. Everything is put into a little box and put away, and you never see it again.

To be effective, the tests must be conducted within seventy-two hours of your rape. If you do not live in a city with an SACC you are required to drive, or in some cases be airlifted, to another place to have the tests done. You are accompanied by the investigating officer (usually male). The clock is ticking, so if it's too far and will take too long, the tests won't be carried out.

I believe that the overriding purpose of forensic testing is not to collect evidence to catch the rapist but to validate a woman's claim that she has been raped. Her story is not believed by investigating officers until a medical professional confirms it verbally and in writing. The case is then opened. Without that medical verification, the already slim chances of founding the case become minute. The prevailing myth that women lie about their rapes motivates this response. If cuts, bruises, emotional trauma or, most important of all, rape sperm are not collected in the kit, the police are predisposed to believe that the woman is lying, that no crime has occurred. Anyone would agree that the tests are invasive and intrusive. I can testify that they are experienced by the woman involved as a second assault.

Although the police tell women that the kits must be compiled in order to proceed with an investigation, they are in fact not necessary. In other words, the police are not telling women the truth. This untruth and the beliefs that motivate it coerce women into a process that is rarely in their best interest. In some provinces of Canada, forensic testing in sexual-assault cases is not required at all. In the province of Ontario, the collected kits are not used in over 90 per cent of the rape cases that come to trial.* Out on the streets, in the women's communities, there is escalating conflict between women who work in crisis centres and shelters and the medical and social workers in the hospital environment. Existing government agendas encourage a one-stop shopping program that will see the amalgamation of community-based rape crisis centres and hospital-based sexual-assault care centres under one hospital roof.

SACCs originated around 1984 to dovetail with the legislation that saw the crime of rape renamed and categorized as assault. Until then

---

* Recent advances in the area of DNA testing and DNA evidence *can* be critical in stranger-rape cases, and it has released men who have been wrongfully accused of the crime (in which shoddy police investigations usually led to the original guilty verdicts).

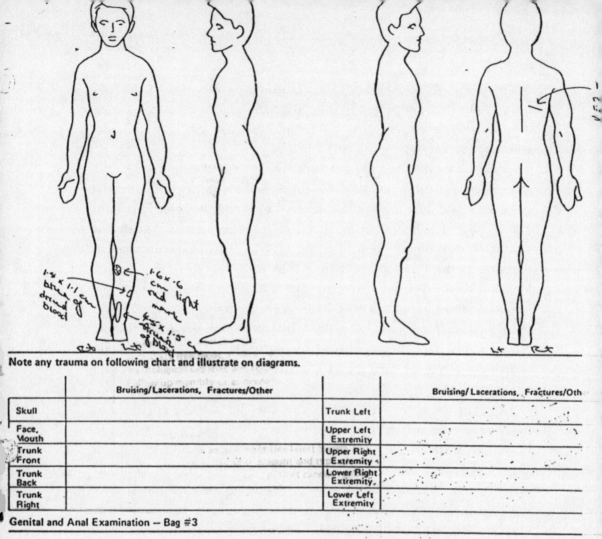

1·4 × 1·1 cm
area of
dried
blood

1·6 × ·6
cm light
red
mark

·5 × 1·5 c
area
of blood

Rt   Lt Rt   Lt Rt

Note any trauma on following chart and illustrate on diagrams.

	Bruising/Lacerations, Fractures/Other		Bruising/Lacerations, Fractures/Oth
Skull		Trunk Left	
Face, Mouth		Upper Left Extremity	
Trunk Front		Upper Right Extremity	
Trunk Back		Lower Right Extremity	
Trunk Right		Lower Left Extremity	

Genital and Anal Examination — Bag #3

For Female Patient

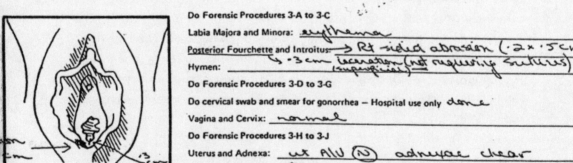

Do Forensic Procedures 3-A to 3-C

Labia Majora and Minora: _erythema_

Posterior Fourchette and Introitus: → Rt sided abrasion (·2 × ·5 cm

Hymen: ↳ ·3 cm laceration (not requiring sutures) (superficial)

Do Forensic Procedures 3-D to 3-G

Do cervical swab and smear for gonorrhea — Hospital use only _done_

Vagina and Cervix: _normal_

Do Forensic Procedures 3-H to 3-J

Uterus and Adnexa: _ut A/V (N)   adnexae clear_

Anus and Rectum: _(N)_

For Male Patient

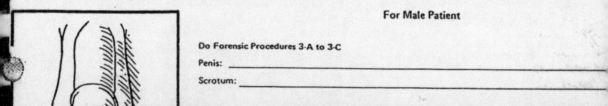

Do Forensic Procedures 3-A to 3-C

Penis: _____

Scrotum: _____

there was no standardized hospital care plan; doctors were not properly trained and emergency rooms were not equipped to deal with raped women, who were seen as a low priority compared with victims of car accidents, for example. The birth of SACCs was a combination of good intentions and government agendas; as a result, the medical profession now dictates the care of women who have been sexually assaulted. The women who were the original staffers of the SACCs were drawn from community workers already involved in feminist politics. While some of these staffers remain committed to feminism, SACCs themselves are creations of government and hospital policy, and the women who work for them find themselves having to fill out the proper forms, which include questions about whether the raped women have had children, abortions or mental health problems, which have little to do with helping women heal and a lot to do with establishing the woman's credibility. Nurses and nurse practitioners, justifiably frustrated with their low status in the hospital setting, have moved into the administration of SACCs, further undermining the community-based counselling infrastructure. For most women who are sexually assaulted, psychiatry and pharmaceuticals—used to treat diagnoses of post-traumatic stress disorder and rape-trauma syndrome—have replaced feminist counselling and advocacy. We refer to this as the woman's health care. As if her rape is an illness. We have once again turned rape into a personal tragedy rather than a social evil and a crime.

Many free-standing rape-crisis centres in smaller cities and towns have already been moved into their local hospitals. Funding originally designated and protected for such services has become part of the larger hospital operating budget. Trained rape-crisis counsellors who are not hospital staffers have gone the way of the dodo bird. Record keeping is mandatory and documentation is stored in the hospital, where it can be readily subpoenaed. SACC services are bound to operate within hospital administration hours, rules and labour contracts. They do not have the autonomy nor the analysis to advocate or represent the interests of their women clients. For a staffer to speak out could result in reprimand or job loss. To work more than eight hours a day or on weekends could violate union agreements. This is the government

<form used in rape kit

version of community health care.

The government has also begun expanding the role of SACCs to include handling wife assault, again without any consultation with existing services. Anti-violence workers are concerned that such changes will result in the further medicalizing of women who are beaten or harassed by their male partners. The team that responds to these women has been trained in a clinical model of service delivery that places the police investigation and its needs over, or on a par with, the needs of the women involved. The two are not complementary.

The SACC annual general meeting I attended was a two-day affair that included other presentations, some by police officers, and a whole floor of displays. My speech opened the conference and did not compete with other scheduled workshops. I told my stories, addressed my concerns and made my critiques respectfully. I received polite applause. When the floor was opened to questions, a woman who identified herself as a nurse in a SACC wept into the microphone as she told me that she worked long hours, sometimes getting up at four in the morning to help victims, and she didn't appreciate my coming here to say negative things about her. She got more applause than I did. I suggested that my remarks were not to be taken personally but rather addressed some real issues and problems that women were identifying. There were no more questions and no one spoke to me for the rest of the conference.

My plane didn't leave for a few hours so I went exploring in the Ottawa hotel where the conference was headquartered. There was the standard arrangement of feminist academic and legal books, a South American crafts booth, some tear-jerking anti-violence art, and displays of medical equipment and research. Then there was the Kodak booth. Yes, Kodak, the Kodak Moment people. They were there with multiple representatives in suits and good haircuts. It seems that even as I spoke, the Solicitor General's Office of the federal government (which oversees the justice system) was in the process of *adding* to the tests used to compile the sexual-assault evidence kit. The thing they were adding was a video camera, and Kodak was there to sell a sleek new model that fit perfectly into the palm of your hand. Or into a kit.

I wandered from the Kodak booth to a presentation entitled "Working with Lesbian Survivors." This basic introduction to homophobic attitudes and practices did not address the many reasons why lesbians rarely report their rapes. Other workshops dealt with "Pornography on the Internet" (the presenters were against it), "Preparing for the Enhancement of the SACC Mandate," "Male Survivors of Sexual Abuse," "Eye Movement Desensitization and Reprocessing" and "The Sexual Assault Nurse Examiner Programme." I got out of town.

I agonize still about that keynote speech—not the content but the context. Why did they invite me? Was I wrong to attend? Did my presence allow them to say they had consulted with community? Dealt with controversy? Was I simply indulging in a need to have the last word and forgetting that I am finally, always, a raped woman, a victim with the question mark of credibility punctuating everything I say? Forensic evidence to the left of me, post-traumatic stress disorder to the right. Here I am. Stuck in the middle—with myself.

I don't deny the need for someone to prescribe antibiotics and other medicines to treat women who have been raped or the severe and life-altering trauma that rape induces. I live with those things. I understand that there is a need to collect evidence in order to solve the crime, but I don't confuse what is good for me with evidentiary requirements mandated by police protocol and the legal system. Don't syndrome and disorder me half to death and then call it health care. And then use it against me in a court of law.

Besides, I am quite capable of choosing my own health care. And who said I was sick? Rape is a social crime against women that ranks right up there with murder. It is not the flu. Don't confuse the necessity for evidence to establish the identity of the minority of rapists who are strangers with those whose identity is known.

Instead of pitting women in SACCs and community-based women against each other, the government agenda should be to consult with experts in the field of sexual and wife assault.* Here's a thought: Hire those women full-time to teach doctors and nurses in medical school.

---

* Instead of consulting with community workers on its SACC initiatives, the Ontario Ministry of Health consulted with another provincial ministry, the Ontario Women's Directorate, which supported the hospital-based policy.

Or increase community-based services for women who experience these crimes so that we can better heal ourselves. Redefine the crime of rape itself as a disorder or syndrome and the reactions of the woman who has been raped as normal reactions or even coping mechanisms to the violence that has changed her life. Revisit the intrinsic harm of rape and the nature of that harm, and provide women with options and services to take care of ourselves. And do no harm. Focus instead on the socializing and pathology of male perpetrators and the codes and systems that perpetuate their behaviour.

This is not new thought. These are not new concepts. Historically, though, whenever women name barriers or craft solutions regarding rape or wife assault, our solutions are diluted through the law, academia, economics and medicine into a whole new set of problems, which then require more government legislation and interference until the original problem and the original solution are once again lost and buried. It's as relentless as a hamster wheel . . .

⁘

Still and always a feminist

32:

When I lecture, I stand in front of a group of people who are as curious to get a look at me as they are to know how I did it. What in the world caused me to pursue such a long and lonely battle? I have incorporated the answer to this last question into the talks I deliver. I tell my audiences that I am a feminist and that *Jane Doe* was a feminist political action. Brows furrow and someone usually rejoins with "Yeah, but how did you do it? What made you take on the police?" And I say it was part of a body of work, part of the women's movement, a feminist anti-oppression movement. Faces cloud, visibly shut down, and the person says, "Yeah, yeah . . . whatever . . . but what motivated you? How did *you* do it?" The few women who nod knowingly as they listen to these interchanges do not compensate for the reality that most of the audience does not know what I'm talking about or the fact that they hear the terms "feminist" and "political" as reactionary and threatening. Hardly anyone knows what anti-oppression means anymore (I'm not sure if we ever did), and I have effectively lost some of my audience.

Oh, they keep listening. I have rarely spoken without receiving an ovation. I challenge, inform, make people laugh and think. I know this is true because whenever I speak publicly, the response revitalizes and recharges me too. There is a hunger, a need for knowledge about rape, that is not sated by the current cultural response, which requires what amounts to a suspension of intellect. I hunger for that knowledge too. But this feminist stuff appears to be a pill too big, too bitter for most to swallow.

By the year 2000, anti-violence work in shelters and rape crisis centres (grassroots or frontline feminism) had all but disappeared into social work. Victims' rights groups, victims' services, psychiatric diagnosis and the courts had replaced feminist political analysis (although they appropriated heavily from it first). No one said "feminist" much anymore. We are told and tell ourselves that racism is no longer the problem it once was because we have hired more Black woman and women of colour. We do not speak of our society as a class system of haves and have-nots with an increasingly smaller percentage struggling to maintain the middle. The victory of *Jane Doe* in 1998 rewarded two decades of feminism that had actually ended around 1988, and the judgment held little practical relevance for SACCs or the twenty-first century rape crisis centre or women's shelter. *Jane Doe* was a victory out of time. Which made me a woman out of time.

Since 1986 I have been teaching in social services, studying in adult education, organizing, lecturing and demonstrating. I have seen the erosion of gender, race and class as equality issues, under the guise that we have achieved them and it is therefore no longer necessary to address them. People in power don't even pay lip service to them anymore. These mythical gains have become the mythical truths we cling to and are barely shaken by ever-increasing statistics of women who are raped, beaten and murdered by men who arc or were their lovers. Instead of creating feminist strategies to stop rape, we are caught in the disconnect that tells us that if the cops catch the rapist, the problem is solved. Let the police do their job, catch the bad guys, and for heaven's sake don't get sidelined by some rape victim screaming about feminism and a social audit, whatever that is.

A word to those who roll their eyes, bless themselves, deconstruct, tut-tut or naysay the feminist political movement without conscious knowledge or understanding of it: What's wrong with you? There isn't one of us, man, woman or child, who hasn't benefited from feminism in some way. But the nostalgia of the nineties and the new century has not limited itself to fashion and music. We have also been returned to the right-wing interpretation of feminism as man-hating and of feminists as strident and bitter, and we have many women once again rallying around patriarchy. They include successful women in positions of power. "If I can do it, you can too!" they exhort, taking absolutely no time or effort to ensure that claim. "Feministas! Feminazis!" they shout. "Gender is no longer relevant."

Which is not to say that the feminist movement hasn't made any mistakes, didn't fuck up, forget, forgo. Racism, homophobia and privilege have marked us. How could they not? Are we not caught in and dependent on the same systems we identify as oppressive?

In an early draft of this book I wrote at great length about the women's movement. I wanted to honour and examine it, and to critique it without falling into the backlashy, neo-con thinking that surrounds us. I tried to define and differentiate between socialist and liberal, radical and grassroots feminisms—but then I took it all out. The definitions have shifted and changed since I first understood them. Who am I to say that "my" kind of feminism (which hardly exists anymore and could be viewed as romantic) is preferable or better than the feminisms of women in law, in academia or working in SACCs? That is not even the nature of the exercise. I'm not critiquing feminisms but the way that feminist agendas have been co-opted. I am asserting that we must identify with the woman who has been raped and not the system that pretends to serve her, whether that's a hospital, a court of law or a rape crisis centre. We must understand that the first thing that happens to that woman, the nature of rape itself, is that she becomes diminished, reduced. The job of feminist workers is to refute that diminishment with empathy and imagination.

But how can I write that women cannot change things from inside the system, when that is exactly what I did or tried to do? How can I tell front-line workers in shelters, crisis centres or SACCs to refuse to collect or hand over personal information about raped women when they could lose their jobs or face criminal sanctions if they don't? How does my generation learn from and share information with young women who understand gender and sexuality differently from us? This is the new matrix of feminism and these are the new challenges. Or maybe they are not so new, just more complicated in difficult times.

Although significantly curbed in number and funding, feminist

313

models of women's services that are anti-oppressive still exist. Anti-oppression feminism is a package (and a mouthful). It translates as an analysis of how race, poverty, age, sexual identity, physical and mental health can affect how people respond to what is happening in their lives. In this case it works as a filter to better understand how a women responds to her rape—and how the police respond to her. These workers would be the first to tell you it is not easy to keep going. But they do. We need to listen and learn from them about the process and the strategies they have crafted to continue functioning as feminists despite the encroachment of clinical and medical models of social work.

Feminism has not gone away or become less relevant. Patriarchy has not gone away. Women are not equal. We suffer under the delusion that patriarchy no longer exists, forgetting that it rules us. The word is hard to spell and everyone looks at you funny when you use it. Patriarchy is so acceptable, so ingrained, that saying we have to get rid of it is like saying we have to get rid of bread. The male oppression of women and other similarly marginalized groups through systems has not gone away. Our work is to identify it. Feminism, with its hope and joy and commitment to equality, has not gone away. We have only just begun to sort it out.

RANT: to rave, rage, bluster, storm, spout, bellow, yell, scold, fume. So what if I'm ranting? There is truth there. Waiting, losing, winning. Why are we so frightened when women rant? It's not like we're killing anyone.

❖

Why men rape

33:

Do you remember Maya's story? The young woman who was raped by two men and lost her case on consent issues? Went on to work with the big rock star? There is another component of her story that is critical to examine if we are ever to answer the question Why Do Men Rape? An obvious answer is They Rape Because They Can. A time-honoured biological response is They Rape Because They Must. But that is too simple. Here is another thought: Men Rape Because They Think They Are Entitled to It and Therefore It Can't Be Rape.

Few men who commit the crime, whether they are charged and convicted or not, believe they did anything wrong. During their trial, I watched the two young men who had raped Maya. They were frightened, obviously ashamed of the accusation they faced, their cockiness diminished, barely visible under their distress. But they clearly had convinced themselves that Maya had really wanted it. From both of them. Fast and dirty, clothes on, no desire or fun, sort of a nightcap, might as well drink it, it's free, it's there, it's mine. The fact that she said no and pleaded with them to stop was not relevant. Women always say no. She didn't scream, fight, kick. Never mind that her child was sleeping in the next room, a particleboard wall away. Besides, they didn't hurt her. They weren't violent. They wanted it and they thought she wanted it even though she said she didn't. Therefore it wasn't rape. And that was good enough for the judge. Good enough for most of us.

What we seem to have, then, is a set of mistaken beliefs.

Under law, a rapist is not guilty if he can raise a doubt that he honestly believed there was consent, even though he was mistaken. Under law, that's not hard. But let's look at that again. *Mistaken belief in consent*. What is that? Buddy believes you want it even if you said no and, even if he was wrong, he says he honestly believed it at the time. Therefore he's not guilty. According to studies and statistics, this happens all the time.* In Ontario only 4 per cent of all reported rapes that reach trial result in guilty convictions. Does that stat sound too low for your comfort level? Okay, let's increase it just for the sake of argument. Make it 20 per cent, 30 per cent. Hell, make it 50 per cent. If only half of all charges reported result in convictions, something is very wrong. At 4 per cent we have disaster, farce, permission to rape.

Try applying the idea of mistaken belief in consent to another crime. Go ahead. Someone steals your car. You left it unlocked and the thief claims you wanted him to take it and that is what he honestly believed at the time.

Here's another example: You cross the street in traffic, and a driver assumes you are prepared to be struck down or you wouldn't be on the road. The idea is laughable, right? But if a woman finds herself in a situation where a man believes she wants sex, he can rape her and walk away on the grounds of mistaken belief in consent.

Detractors will be fuming by now, ready to point out that the feminist machine is so powerful, so odious that it has produced a rape shield law that allows women to file false charges that result in the imprisonment of innocent men. First of all, women do not file rape charges. Charges have to be investigated by the police and filed by a Crown attorney. You don't get to just charge a man with rape because you have a hate-on against him or you want attention.

Please listen: The number of false rape charges is so minute as to barely register on a statistics scale. Most of them are not "false" but rather result from a woman's mental illness or from women recanting when they realize that the process they have set in motion by reporting will backfire on them when prison sentences remove their spouses' income, separate their children from their fathers or endanger their own physical safety. (The women who back down for these reasons are utterly and completely vulnerable to the unchecked violence of the males in

* U.S., British and European legal systems have similar legislation and statistics.

their lives forever after.) Most wrongful convictions are the result of incompetent police investigations, not false reports.

Still, every few years or so false-allegation conspiracy theorists raise their voices in the halls of justice to demand that the so-called rape shield law be struck down and out. Their protests resonate with the majority of us who have not been raped, who would not dream of rape, or dream they did not rape.

In a recent feature article in the *National Post*, Wendy Leaver, a detective in the Toronto Police Sexual Assault Squad and the police chief's appointed community liaison, waxed expert about the threat of false sexual-assault allegations. She was quoted as saying that they are "a very significant problem" and that "some women enjoy the process [of filing rape charges] . . . . you wouldn't believe the attention we [police] pay to you." She rooted the problem in past attitudes: "Women will be believed. That was rammed down police officers' throats." Leaver said that when she first began lecturing about false allegations, "People said, but aren't you concerned about the harm you're doing to valid victims?" But her mission was more important, she responded. "Let's not send an innocent man to prison."

I have no argument with that. But the implication that wrongful convictions are the result of women who lie or any eagerness on the part of police to believe women is a shameful indictment of modern policing and its inability to evolve in its understanding of the crime. For an officer who claims to be trained and who lectures on the subject of rape to make those statements is proof positive of the mess we are in. It is validation for women who choose not to report and absolution for men who do not believe they have raped.*

Imagine this: In order to address so-called false sexual-assault allegations, the police engage in alternative methods of investigation, especially when they have concrete reasons to believe that mental health issues or malice are motivating the charge that they (the police) have filed. The rub is that to address these rare occurrences effectively, investigators

---

* Although the *National Post* article did not mention it, Wendy Leaver operates a private consulting firm through which she lectures on police and criminal matters such as false sexual-assault charges.

must first understand the big picture of sexual assault. To do this they must work with and take direction from (gasp) women who are the experts in the area. You can forget that. They prefer to rely on anti-quated stereotypes and training that allow them to perpetuate the myths they cling to. (Remember the potato-chip test used to investigate the crimes of the man who raped me.)

Where does this false sexual-assault myth originate? There is no doubt that men and women hold conflicting views of sex and sexuality. Current and historical sex-ed curriculum limits the understanding of sexual acts to intercourse, a biological function designed to reproduce the human species. Pleasure, communication, mutual appreciation and technique are rarely discussed or acknowledged in sex, even as we mature.

The sexual identity of boys and young men is influenced by male bonding, peer culture and the media, which separates it from any female experience or understanding. As if the male story of sex and sexuality is the only one that is known or matters.

As a result, the early experiences of many boys and young men often goes like this: They are encouraged to understand a hard-on as a defin-ing symbol of manliness. If it is not obeyed and released, manliness is denied, thwarted. Manliness denied is painful, shameful. An ambulance must attend, sirens roaring, and deliver it to the hospital. Affirmed, a hard-on is hot bliss, ecstasy released. What's to choose? And there is a woman here. She is nice, smiling, drinking my wine, smoking my pot. She has a hole that is exactly the right size. I kissed her and she liked it. Why go to the hospital, sirens screaming, when she is right here? And she did it with Joe/Michael/Bob. Uh-oh! She just stopped smiling, her body is stiff. She's saying no, stop. I'll kiss her harder, there that's bet-ter, no wait, she's pulling away again. Shit. Don't want to have to call the ambulance and deal with the incredible pain of a hard-on not obeyed. Okay baby, it's okay . . . and then it's so easy to put my weight on her, tell her she's beautiful and she's only struggling a little, not yelling, head moving back and forth. Can't stop now! Manliness is roaring, rearing, plunging, firing . . . Arrggaahhfuck! Done.

She's not looking at me. Guess I should go, tired anyway. Would have been nicer if she'd been a bit more involved . . . great without a condom though . . . thanks, baby. See ya around.

He believes this was normal consensual sex. But she has been raped. Who is right? Who wins in a court of law?

For young women, the sexual learning curve can dead-end just as suddenly. A young woman who engages in premarital sex is fallen, or at least loose. Yes, still. She alone is responsible for the unwanted pregnancies or disease that might result, although information on how to prevent them is limited, confusing and often requires parental consent. But he likes me! And it's exciting! Well at least until it gets scary, feels out of control, can't breathe, going to be sick, burning, sweaty, what's wrong with him? Why won't he stop, I said no, it hurts, can't move, he's so heavy, stop and he's kissing me, saying how pretty I am. He loves me! Happiness! What's he doing? I want to go home. Why can't we just kiss, fool around? I liked that. This fucking hurts. Don't cry. How long does it take? Oh God, if I scream, cry, he's going to think I'm so uncool. If only he'd stop. It's my fault, he says. You don't need a condom the first time and he kisses me again. It's my fault.

She believes there was normal consensual sex. It's all she knows. But under the law, she is raped. Who is right?

Sex and sexuality should be a tender experience for our young people, something special and joyful. Instead we mess it up horribly for them. Any truth in the scenarios I have just drawn exists largely because of what we teach them. Because we do not teach them well.

Women struggled to define and explain rape throughout the sixties, seventies and eighties. We worked hard to prove all of the ways in which it is a violent act of power. In the new millennium we've been rolled back to the definition of "real" rape as stranger rape. Even better, serial stranger rape with a weapon.

Stranger rape comprises about a third of all reported rapes, which is too many. But what are we to make of this "new" delineation of type and severity of rape on a descending scale from serial, stranger, date to known assailant?* Are we to believe that a man would rape once for the experience or just because he could, and then after careful consideration

---

* I have heard women refer to rape that occurs on a date or within a previously non-sexual relationship as "friendly rape."

decide that rape really isn't his thing and he won't do it again? Or should we understand that all rapists are more than likely to be repeat offenders? Date rapes are assumed to be committed by men known to the women involved (and are therefore considered not that serious). A more realistic reading is that the majority of them qualify as stranger rapes, as the crime often takes place on a first or second date with a man barely known to the woman who makes the claim. Each occurrence of rape on the scale is investigated, judged and punished differently. For the woman who has been raped, however, the act and the harm can be identical.

Take another leap of imagining. Pretend we know how to stop rape. Begin by understanding the nature of the harm it does and who benefits. Concede that the legal system is not designed to judge this particular crime, might not even be the best place for judgment. Be persuaded that lengthy prison sentences are not deterrents. Allow that women working in the anti-violence sector have critical knowledge to contribute toward a solution. And stay there for a moment. Don't bolt. This is just an exercise in rethinking. Based on true stories.

SO what is a good man to do?

In November 1997, I was deep into the drama of my civil trial. An accurate theatrical review might have read, "Harrowing! Fantastic! Four-star performances!" When my lawyer Sean told me that he had received a call from a Sexual Assault Squad detective asking if he (Sean) would help him (the detective) sue the police for discrimination, the story registered as extreme even considering the plot line I was living. It broke in the *Toronto Star* the following May, two months before a decision was released in my civil trial.

David Girdlestone was the police officer's name. In 1996, three female detectives working with him on the Sexual Assault Squad claimed to have been sexually harrassed and sexually assaulted by the squad commander at the time, Staff Inspector Brian Duff. As is common in many business institutions, no criminal charges were laid. Instead management shipped the offender out to another office and life went on. Which would have been the end of the story except that Detective

Girdlestone became aware of additional allegations by female officers against yet another male officer. He broke the silence. He could not abide such criminal conduct going unreported. After all, the squad's mantra was "Report!" Women who do not report are seen as part of the problem in the investigation of sexual assault.

The blue machine kicked in and Girdlestone found himself under attack from within for daring to speak out. He was transferred and demoted. Further protestations on his part resulted in official statements regarding his mental health. Kim Derry was assigned as the lead investigator (yes, my Kim Derry). It came out that the decision not to file criminal charges against Duff but to move him to the suburbs was made after consultation with the female detectives (the victims) involved. The women all agreed that it was a far, far better thing not to file criminal charges, and they stood by that decision throughout the investigation.

Few thinking people could have argued with them. Who is better placed to understand the perils of proceeding with an investigation than a sexual-assault investigator? Also, cops rarely take other cops to court. The police officers involved were adult women who, faced with a problem, made informed decisions about how to proceed. However, if those same officers then turned around and insisted that other women should report, they would be part of a larger moral and systemic problem.

Girdlestone resigned from the force, but persevered to see the matter tried in an internal police tribunal. At that hearing, Derry testified that while he was questioning him, foam appeared at the corners of Girdlestone's mouth. Testimony also revealed that Derry's notes of that meeting with Girdlestone had gone missing.

Yet they tell us to report.

PEOPLE believe that, as a direct result of my case, police warn more, receive better training or have developed what is referred to as increased sensitivity to sexual assault. They have not. Do not. Oh sure, we might hear more warnings, but they are still filled with don'ts. Despite their promises, Toronto police have not developed a consistent warning protocol. The fine print of the current warning protocol allows the police to determine how, when and if a warning should be issued. As always, warnings are issued at their discretion, they are fear-based and hysterical—the don'ts—or are so vague as to be completely useless. And they ultimately place the responsibility for preventing rape on the group that experiences the crime. The offending group is required to assume no responsibility at all.

I think we can all agree that crimes of violence by men against women are a mark of a society in decay. We know that most women do not tell, citing fear of the police, racism, poverty, shame and community or family ostracism as reasons not to file charges. We know that increased and additional services for these women are answers. We lobby, march, educate, protest, write and dialogue, and nothing changes. We are in agreement that the courts are rarely the solution and that often the violence escalates once the law intervenes. We agree that the result is often further victimization, racism, poverty and oppression. And yet we carry on in the same old ways.

The question we must ask—the question we must answer in order to reach meaningful solutions—is who benefits from this present and escalating state of affairs? Who benefits from keeping things the way they are? Who benefits from violence against women?

The current popular legal and political trend in addressing violence is to ram a law and order agenda down our throats. Whether we need it or not. It's a given that women's space has been effectively limited through mainstream sexism and misogyny, which prevent us from being on the streets, in clubs, out shopping or walking or living wherever and whenever we choose. In many cases, even our homes have become unsafe. Similarly, people of colour, Native and Black people think twice or three times about being in places where society's guardians—the police—are likely to roust them, suspect them, arrest them. The wheel has rolled back on young people too. Youth culture has lost its brief cachet and is also suspect to the degree that normal activity has become criminalized. In many jurisdictions, legislation has been enacted to remove squeegee persons and the homeless from city streets, from the sightlines of those more fortunate in their economic circumstances. In Toronto recently, armed undercover police officers illegally invaded an event organized by lesbians. Psychiatric survivors and activists against police and state oppression are also targets of a police department that has clearly established itself as a governing political force in our city. The list goes on.

The strategy used by police to control public space, whether directed at women, youth or people of colour, is uniform. It goes like this: Make us afraid. Once you've instilled fear, it's easier to control or limit the space in which each group, each community can function. If the authorities make us fear enough and then bill themselves as our protectors, their budget will never be at risk. In a traditional patriarchal society such as ours, the first articulated response to fear is to protect the women and children. The good ones anyway. The only way to do that, they say, is to increase police presence, to build more prisons and to enact harsher sentencing. The state response is to segregate the good people from the bad, both in community and on the streets.

So they warn us about the stranger rapist and then hold us responsible if we do not censor our movements, if we do not barricade our doors, our windows, our lives. If we do not live passively, poorly and without expressing our sexuality or politics.

Even if we obey their injunctions, the real violence in our homes—wife or partner assault—continues to escalate. I don't for a moment wish to dismiss or disrespect fear. In my home province, three women are murdered by men they know every month.* In Canada a woman is raped every seventeen minutes.** I think that we can say that fear is a healthy and even wise response to the threat of danger in our lives, especially for women who live with racism and poverty. Especially for women who work in the sex trades or have been in conflict with the law.

We must honour our fear.

The problem is that we do not get to define it or strategize around it or implement solutions to address it.

So the next time you hear the warning don'ts or read them in the paper (and you will see them again soon) think of this more effective warning:

---

* Imagine the outcry if three Canadian soldiers were killed every month (by friendly fire or otherwise), or three police officers or three judges.
** In the United States, six women are murdered every day and a woman is raped every three minutes (cited by the National Organization for Women).

MEN: Stay in the house, don't open your windows or doors. Never mind that it's thirty degrees Celsius in the shade. There is a rapist in this area, so lock yourselves up.

or:

MEN: Stay off the buses. One of you is raping women, and we don't know, can't tell which one, so until we find out, stay at home, do not use underground parking or take shortcuts through the park. Okay, okay, if you are accompanied by a woman who can vouch for your good male status, then you can come out. Otherwise, you are in danger.

The warning above and the one we are accustomed to hearing are both stupid and outrageous and call on a large group of people to censor their lives. Our response is to laugh at one and obey the other, when it is the "funny" one that would more effectively address the crime because it puts the onus on the offending group.

An effective warning regarding a stranger rapist requires adequate information that does not interfere with a police investigation and allows adult women to make informed decisions about how we live our lives. It's not difficult. A useful warning might include a description (if available), the time, method and place of attack. But please stop telling me to lock my doors and windows. I already do that. It is infantilizing. Stranger danger gets in anyway.

And where is the community response? Shouldn't we all be coming out of our homes and onto the streets and into the parks to help each other? Where is the response from all the good men who do not rape and who are the majority? Without their involvement nothing will change. What does it say about us as people if we co-operate in censoring the movements of our women through threats and hysteria? What does it say about us when our articulated response to crimes of male violence is to enact draconian measures that pretend to protect women as opposed to serving them as equal members of society?

⁘

Another turn of the wheel

34:

I WAS caught up in the fascinating politics and agendas of the social audit when the public backlash against my court victory started a few heady, giddy months after I had won. I suppose I should have seen it coming.

The YMCA in a small city near Toronto invited me to be the keynote speaker during its annual "Week Without Violence" fundraiser. I was pleased to accept. It was quite a grand affair. I stood in front of a packed house and lectured about the things I have learned, expressing the opinion that women should not enter the legal system when they have been sexually assaulted without full knowledge of the realities of that system and the treatment they are likely to receive. I was given a standing ovation. Within twenty-four hours, a wire service picked up a local newspaper article that quoted me as saying that women should not report their rapes. Period. At all. Ever.

Before the ink was dry, David Boothby had convened a media conference at which his spokesperson, Wendy Leaver, labelled me and my misquoted, out-of-context statements, as "one of the causes of rape." Leaver linked me and my supposed attitudes to the crimes of Paul Bernardo. The mayor of Toronto, the provincial minister responsible for Women's Issues and several police officers publicly labelled me as "disgusting," "dangerous" and "very bad." Television talk shows, radio phone-ins, newspaper editorials and columnists across the land condemned me roundly without so much as a phone call to check the facts. Pundits fired themselves into states of hysterical indignation and denial. Some were clearer than others in their bombast: "Jane Doe should shut up and go away," said Michael Coren, talk radio host. "Jane Doe is in the spotlight without paying the price . . . such (media) bans are noxious and paternalistic . . . her remarks are outrageous and irresponsible" wrote Christie Blatchford in the *National Post*. Even the *Toronto Star* took a piece out of me in an editorial.* And this was just the Toronto media.

I was frightened by the attack. I stayed close to home for a few days. I considered whether my phone lines were tapped, my movements monitored. I had previously believed that the media really liked me, that my work, my victory as Jane Doe had resonated at a political level, that it was acceptable for me, the rape poster girl, to define my experience publicly and that they would carry the message. It took a few days, but I recovered. Because of the media ban, my photo and real name did not accompany the public whipping. I realized that by letting my guard down, by assuming it was safe for an adult woman with some intelligence to provide a political context for sexual assault, I had precipitated my tumble into bad rape-victim status. I had crossed the line, stepped outside of the boundaries of the only role defined for raped women, which is passive, silent, suffering, and now I needed to be slapped back into place.

I was about to meet the person who would do it.

JUST as the recommendations of the social audit were released to great media fanfare, David Boothby suddenly and rather mysteriously decided that he would return to farming. The man chosen to replace him as chief of police was a former Toronto officer named Julian Fantino, who returned from exile where he had headed the police forces in the smaller cities of York and before that London, Ontario. Like Prince Charles, Fantino had been circling the Toronto throne for decades. His take-no-prisoners approach to law enforcement garnered him the leadership of the Ontario Association of Chiefs of Police. As a former homicide blueblood, he had brought public scrutiny and shame to the family of policing when he collected and publicly supported race-based crime statistics, which can be used to bolster racist assumptions

---

* The *Star* invited me to respond in an op-ed piece, which they published.

that the disproportionate number of arrests and incarcerations of Black men in Toronto is wed to that community's propensity for crime. Then he left for London, where he led a million-dollar investigation into a supposed ring of pedophiles, which resulted in the criminalizing of homosexuality and the eventual dismissal of wrongful charges. These episodes have since been erased from his resumé by a team of spin doctors he employs as media consultants.

At first the media seemed concerned about the inevitable collision between Fantino's 1950s vision and the new millennium's diversity of people and urban issues. Community activists and a few politicians also sounded alarms against him. But it was a done deal. Provincial and city governments backed Fantino. Toronto mayor Mel Lastman had just taken a seat on the police board and he supported Fantino. Few members would vote against the mayor. Rumours swirled that the provincial Tory government was pressuring its members on the board to vote for their man Julian.

Once hired, Fantino announced that his first order of business would be to meet with various cultural and political communities in Toronto, especially those historically or currently in opposition to policing. He said he wanted to mend fences, build alliances, take our great city forward in the true spirit of community policing. He would also spend the time necessary to review all matters currently before the service. A logical assumption was that women's groups in opposition to police practices for twenty-five years would be high on his list of meeting partners.*

Just days before his departure, David Boothby recommended in writing that the police not join the steering committee that was supposed to implement the auditor's recommendations but continue to consult with women on an ad hoc basis as had been done in the past. Recognizing that our only hope now lay with the new chief, the women of ARG requested a meeting with him. Pam McConnell made the first overture. Her written and telephoned requests on our behalf were ignored. I alerted members of the media, who placed calls to Fantino's office. We got our meeting.

---

*Some members of the gay community, traditionally opposed to police conduct and policies that were considered homophobic, met with and endorsed Julian Fantino, as did individual Black leaders. Other members and leaders of both communities asked for meetings with the new chief but were turned down.

Eight women, including the city councillor, sat across a massive table from Fantino, two lawyers, a media consultant and four police officers (who did not identify their rank or purpose for being there). We quickly tabled our agenda and began the meeting with introductions. I stated that our purpose was to determine the new chief's commitment to implementing the audit as recommended by city council. Another ARG member gave background information about our membership and history. Julian Fantino's face flooded purple with blood and rage as he rose to his feet and thundered his outrage and indignation. Spittle flew from his mouth, and his fists clenched as he accused us—women who had come to speak with him about sexual assault—of putting a loaded gun to his head and holding him hostage through the media. He forbade us to do it again. Then he hollered about how great the police were and how they always exercised due diligence and good faith.

It was scary stuff and, in hindsight, I wish we had walked out at that point and into the media cameras and horde of scribblers who were waiting for news of the meeting. But we had not anticipated that Fantino would allow his anger with us to surface so plainly, and we really had come to the meeting in good faith. So we talked him down a bit (the way women learn to do with violent men) and got him to give us his word that he would get back to us in thirty days.

We never heard from him again.

FANTINO submitted his draft response to the social audit recommendations at a Police Services Board meeting in November 2000. It was full of errors and focused on children and youth at risk and the investigation of pedophiles. During his presentation, which included a slide show, the term "woman" was never used. We were referred to rather as "victims," "those people" or a "special interest group."

Instead of consulting with women who worked in the area of rape and sexual assault, as directed by the auditor, Fantino originated an alternative process that excluded us. He met instead with workers from youth services and agencies affiliated with law enforcement, the medical profession, government and religious institutions. Beverly Bain and I delivered a deputation that called upon the Police Services Board to not

Women ask police for joint committee on sexual assault

May 30

BY AMIRA ELGHAWABY
STAFF REPORTER

Jane Doe and her supporters will have to wait a month before police Chief Julian Fantino responds to their demand for action on recommendations made in an audit of the way police handle sex assault cases.

"He will contact us," Jane Doe said after a closed-door meeting with Fantino yesterday at police headquarters.

About a dozen sexual-assault fieldworkers asked Fantino to support creation of a steering committee made up of their colleagues and police to oversee changes in the way police handle such cases.

we're committed to stay in. We're really not asking for much," Doe said.

The women "really had to push" to get their demands across, said Beverly Bain, who was involved in the city auditor's report.

The audit, endorsed by city council and the police services board, made 57 recommendations to reform the sexual assault squad. Two have been implemented so far.

Eleven new staff were added to the sexual assault unit, and operating hours were extended to midnight seven days a week.

But other recommendations

Jane Doe to push Fantino on overhaul of sex squad

To Star May 29, 200

Victim tired of waiting for 1999 audit to bear fruit

BY MOIRA WELSH
GTA BUREAU CHIEF

It's been seven months and four days since a city audit recommended an overhaul of the Toronto police sexual assault squad and today, the woman behind it plans to ask Chief Julian Fantino if he's ever going to create change.

Jane Doe, the pseudonym of the woman who was raped in 1986 and was victorious in a 1998 civil lawsuit against the police service for failing to warn her of the serial rapist, will meet this afternoon with the new chief after months of trying.

Why, Doe will ask, have police acted on only two of the 57 recommenda-

for change including:

■ The Oct. 25, 1999, city audit was stinging in its indictment of police sexual assault squad.

■ Doe's successful July, $220,000 civil lawsuit against for failing to warn her about the rapist stalking her neighbour and the subsequent decision of the ronto Police Services Board not peal the judge's decision.

■ The recommendations from 1998 inquest into the murder of lene May by her ex-boyfriend I lles.

■ Judge Archie Campbell's 19 port concluding the Toronto s assault squad bungled the inve tion of Paul Bernardo, the Sc ough Rapist.

Doe said she has tried for mon get an appointment with Fantino was officially sworn in as chi March 6. She was finally able to an audience after asking police

Have the police learned nothing from Jane Doe?

ROSIE DiMANNO

IT WAS SEVEN months ago that a groundbreaking and sharply critical audit made 57 recommendations for changes to the Toronto police sexual assault

29.

None of this augurs well, though, given that the main thrust of the sexual audit — which was ordered by the city and the police services board, both of which back its recommenda-

vestigations services.

Jane Doe, who fought for years for the right to sue police, and then beat them in court, says this meandering, listless response by the police force feels all too familiar. Jane Doe was a

Jane Doe does not herself support all the recommendations in the audit, nor is she foolish enough to believe that the majority of them will be absorbed by the police furce.

But there are a couple of absolute

accept the chief's response and to direct him to restart the process. We were supported by women's agencies from across the country. Norm Gardner would not allow us to deliver our deputation in full, citing time limitations. The chief, however, was granted the time to accuse us of victimizing him, to express his deep offence at our criticisms and to suggest that our motives were purely mercenary. His draft response to the audit indicated that gosh and golly, the police were *already* doing the majority of the fifty-seven recommendations, that there were only two or three that didn't work for them and that they had some additional things they wanted to add themselves. And that was pretty much the end of that story.

April 21, 2001

Fantino is presenting his final and official response to the auditor's recommendations to the Police Service Board for its approval at today's Police Services Board Meeting, and I am here to make a deputation. I was thinking this morning that Fiona's tree is in bloom. My anxiety uncoils in my chest and I struggle for breath, but there is no question that I'm going to do this. Again. I thought about passing, about giving myself permission not to go, not to stick my head into the lion's mouth again. But I am a stubborn thing and I hate to leave work unfinished and I know that the chief's final response does not vary from his draft in any manner. And Beverly Bain is here too. But still, it's nerve-racking to enter so hostile an environment, to enter the territory of armed and powerful men who see you as an enemy.

The chief and what seems to be a board entirely in sympathy with him are enthroned in the middle of the rather grand auditorium at police headquarters. One side is filled with red overstuffed chairs reserved for police officers; the other is for members of the media and the public. Our chairs are fewer, metal and fold up for easy storage.

I'm here again asking this new board what? To listen? I know they do not. To hear me? Perhaps, although I doubt if they can. I am pacing their floors watching them watch me. Roy Pilkington sees me and crosses to chat. I extend my hand and he crushes it a little in his. We smile and I tell him I am well when he asks. He says that things are good for the Sexual Assault Squad too. They have expanded and set up new units to investigate pedophiles and kiddie porn. My heart dips even as I realize that he believes this is what the women who worked on the audit would like. I understand that he will stand his watch, push a conflicted police agenda forward, even though he might prefer it were otherwise. I think he knows I will also stand mine. I

regret that I cannot be more appreciative of his kindness
and show of respect. I will receive no more today.

A volunteer from the Toronto Rape Crisis Centre has come
to witness and support. None of the staff could make it.
She has brought her infant son who coos and gurgles
throughout the meeting. My friend Fatima spends her lunch
hour here and of course there is the brilliant and relentless Beverly. The rest of the gallery is full of media
types, three of whom ask me for interviews, none of them
familiar with the details and history of the audit and my
case, even though it fronted their papers and newscasts for
over a decade.

The first item is a call by a city councillor for more
cops on the streets, and then the mayor chimes in with
an addled memory of the good old days when cops could
go right into your house when there was a problem and how
they successfully fielded calls from distressed wives who
suspected their husbands were drinking their paycheques in

Chief accused of ignoring sex assault issues

**But Fantino says
force is acting
on audit suggestions**

BY BRUCE DEMARA
AND MOIRA WELSH
CITY HALL BUREAU

ble. City council must act now to move
their audit forward," Doe said at a
news conference yesterday.
"We do not need another death, another inquest, another audit, another
commission or summit. We have a
wealth of recommendations to assist
us in the implementation of policy and
training programs," Doe said.
Fantino dismissed the criticism as

the force has boosted the number of
officers doing sexual assault investigations by 11 and has increased normal working hours beyond "9 to 5,"
other initiatives have been ignored.
The audit, produced last October,
was endorsed by council and the police board. There was a requirement
that within six months the chief provide a report detailing a "specific

spond.
"The question is, are the lives of
women a priority?" Chow asked.
"These are good recommendations."
Doe hinted that city council should
consider removing Fantino for his inaction.

'It is obvious that the police

the chief on May 29 to ask when he'd
present his report.
Fantino, she said, promised a written report within 30 days. They have
yet to receive it, she said.
"It is obvious that the police have
disengaged," Doe said.
Patti McGillicuddy, a long-time sexual assault counsellor at the University of Toronto, said she has seen little

local speakeasies. The boys in the media gallery erupt in
laughter, and the mayor's aides, young and in good suits,
circle the room, making mental note of those who dare make
game of their boss.

The police chief's lips barely move as he evokes the war
on drugs, which he swears is not lost and certainly not in
his town and to which he will never surrender. I think,
"Haven't you seen Traffic? It won Academy Awards!" And then
a new board member, a councillor from the suburbs, says,
"Yes, it's just like in the film Traffic. We have to keep
on fighting for our children." Did we see the same film?

I'm up next.

I take my seat on their altar beside Chief Fantino, who swivels to face me. Sweat trickles down my arm. The feel of it cools me, calms me. I disengage emotionally. I inform the board that I am here to resubmit the objections we placed before them when the draft document was presented five months ago. I read the names of the women's agencies, local, provincial and national, that have signed on, and the parts of our deputation that we were prevented from reading at our last appearance. I close with a caution about accepting the word or the handshake of the chiefs and other officers who say one thing about sexual assault when they mean something else entirely.

Chief Fantino levels his gaze on me and opens fire. He is once more, but even more so, deeply offended by my comments. The cop gallery and other board members rumble assent. He has proof—indisputable—that I have acted to prevent community

---

Globe & Mail FRIDAY, JULY 28, 2000 • A15

Police chief accused of not coming to grips with women's issues

Fantino denies he's insensitive as coalition demands he do more to combat violence

COLIN FREEZE
NATALIE SOUTHWORTH
The Globe and Mail, Toronto

lice Chief Julian Fantino en-
aged in a war of words yester-
with women's groups who
sed him of being "complicit"
he issue of violence against
en.

ief Fantino responded that it's
large he "categorically dis-
ts." "I've heard this refrain
for a while and it seems to be
condescending and it certainly
ks the very fibre of any integ-
t to these issues," he said as he
red a Toronto Police Services
'd meeting.

does an employer do when an em-
ployee doesn't do his job?" asked
Beverley Bain, who acted as chair-
woman for the news conference.

"Fire him!" replied a chorus of
voices from the back of the committee room.

The news conference was called
to push for action on recommendations from five major coroner's inquests and a city-council-led audit.

Speakers called for police to
implement the recommendations
to improve training and policies
specific to violence against women.

Many of those recommendations
come from the Jane Doe Social
Audit into the police investigation
of sexual assault.

A meeting he missed

Fantino puzzles women by sidestepping crucial sex assault discussion

POLICE

By ENZO Di MATTEO

Julian Fantino has been eager
to pass himself off as a man
of the people. But the
revved-up top cop has been
reluctant, or too busy, to
meet with women's groups
over their concerns about the
operations of the sexual assault
squad.

A steering committee representing women's groups had been meeting with higher-ups in the squad to
discuss how the force should implement the 57 recommendations —
particularly those around training
— in a highly critical city auditor's
report tabled last fall.

The group had the
blessing of both council
and the police services
board.

But former police
chief David Boothby
unexpectedly pulled the
plug on the working
group before he rode
into the sunset in Febru-

gence.

The working group, of which Doe
is a co-chair, has since asked Fantino for a meeting.

Despite a letter and follow-up
phone calls, there's been no response from the chief who's made it
his mission to meet with anyone
and everyone since he took over.
That is, until NOW began to ask
questions. There may be a meeting
after all.

Seeks meeting

"There's been a little communication problem here or something,"
says inspector Jane Dick, the
chief's media liaison.

Suddenly, I get a call from Doe
that the chief, mysteriously, is seeking a meeting with her group.

But Fantino's recent moves where
the sexual assault squad is concerned signal that women's advo-

Exhibit B: Fantino has passed the
task of dealing with the women's
concerns to deputy chief Joe Hunter, who, for legal — and optical —
reasons may not be the best choice.

Hunter is one of several senior officers named in a civil suit brought
by David Girdlestone, a former detective with the sexual assault
squad.

The suit has been dropped with
the proviso that the particulars of
Girdlestone's complaint, including
the seeking of damages, will be
dealt with in a labour arbitration.

Girdlestone, who was eventually
transferred out of the unit, claimed
in his suit that he became the target
of reprisals, threats and
slanderous statements
— among them, that he
was mentally unfit —
after he reported the al-
leged harassment.

Hunter did not respond
to requests for comment.

Will the recommenda-
tions in the city auditor's
report also be swept un-

AUDITOR'S RECOMMENDATIONS

■ Sexual assault squad staff be restricted to cops trained in sexual assault investigations.
■ Training provided to recruits and front-line officers be re-evaluated.
■ All training courses and conferences attended by sexual assault squad officers be evaluated.
■ Skills and qualifications required to become a trainer at police college be formalized.
■ Community groups be asked for input on training.

groups from coming to the table. Despite that, he and his
troops have soldiered on to save Gotham and its fairer sex.
I blank out a little, not because I don't care but because
it is the only way I can stay in my seat, not be enraged,
cut by his hostility and scorn. Staff Sergeant Wendy Leaver
trots up to provide proof once again of my wayward, if not
criminal, behaviour. According to her files, which are
numerous, time-coded and dated, I or my agents contacted
the entire women's community and persuaded them not to meet
or work with the police. She is relieved to announce that
at least one woman who worked with homeless youth managed
to thwart my manipulation and trickery and agreed to assume
the position of co-chair.*

When I ask if I might respond, the chair of the board
says no. The mayor hems and haws and then sputters, "Isn't
this just . . . what's this I hear—aren't you in this for
the money?" Shocked but not surprised, I ask him if he is
accusing me of extortion. "Extortion!" he screams. "Whaddaya
mean extortion! Who said anything about extortion? I asked
ya if you were in this for the money." Several months
prior, the mayor was part of the unanimous vote that supported our request that women be paid for their work as
professional consultants to implement the audit. When I
remind him of this, his eyes glaze over and he turns his
chair away from me.

I leave their podium, my high heels tattooing the marble
floor, the assembled officers copping a good look. They
carry on discussing what I have said.

There is a new guy on the board, a lawyer and clearly a
"sensitive man." He observes that my deputation was delivered calmly and eloquently and that it was signed by some
big names in the women's community. He suggests that it

---

* In conversation with another ARG member about her decision to work with the police, this
woman stated that she had signed on because she had no experience in sexual assault and therefore was not biased.

Sex-assault victim still faults police

Jane Doe sees little meaningful change in training, policy 14 years after rape

BY COLIN FREEZE
POLICE REPORTER, TORONTO

The woman whose 1986 rape prompted a review of the way in which Toronto Police investigate sexual assaults remains critical of the force, despite a promise by the police chief to implement nearly all of the review's recommendations.

Chief Julian Fantino is to formally present his response to the Jane Doe social audit to the Toronto Police Services Board tomorrow. A document written in advance of the meeting indicates the police service agrees wholly, or in part, with 54 of the audit's 57 recommendations.

But in an interview yesterday, audit fully in 2002. But last night, the auditor said that he's "reassured" by some responses, such as increased staffing for the sexual-assault squad that has also taken on more investigations and expanded its hours, which once were 8:30 a.m. to 4:30 p.m.

Ms. Doe, however, is not so reassured. Though there were elements of Mr. Griffiths's audit of which Ms. Doe did not approve — too much focus on computer technology for investigations, for example.

Ms. Doe's biggest specific quarrel is with the consultation process. A steering committee that would have involved equal numbers of police and women who work with sexual-assault victims was never set

might behoove the board to pay a little attention, and motions for a vote that would see letters sent to each signee asking for her input. "But fellah," I think, "you have their input! They've signed the letter I just gave you."

The chair shouts down my request to respond. The new woman from the suburbs inserts herself then and illuminates the room with her insider information that contrary to statistics, sexual assault crimes are not really on the rise, it's just that more women are reporting now due to the excellent work of the police department. The chair bellows that I know dang well I can't respond and that this isn't a debating society. I tell him that there is no confusion there and ask for his direction to access a forum in which I might respond. He suggests I write a letter and sneers that I certainly know how to access the media. The mayor rouses himself at that and tries to rise from his chair but abandons the effort when one of his aides leans in and whispers something.

At the elevator, I bump into Wendy Leaver and her boss Roy Pilkington. Wendy and I have never met face to face. Our interactions have always been on the phone or in the media. I remind her that she has not contacted me to be part of her consultation group. She responds that I'm not on any of her lists but that if I want to be involved I should give her a call. I start to laugh and she reaches for her holster, I mean business card, as Roy bustles her into the elevator and the doors close.

I walk around for a while, wondering if any of the reporters who had spoken with me earlier still think there is a story to pursue, but they do not. Beverly is shaking her head, I am a little stunned, the TRCC volunteer has taken her baby home and Fatima is back at work.

The next day the Toronto Star carries a piece that is not bad but is confused about the history of the audit and police-community relations. The article doesn't mention the dismissive, vicious attacks of the police chief or the Police Services Board and their fawning, single-minded support of Toronto's finest.

It's like travelling full circle.

A note from the parole board

35:

IN August 2002 the National Parole Board called to inform me that the man who raped me would have his annual detention review the following month. They would follow up in writing. In keeping with their initiatives to better represent the interests of victims, the parole board regularly invites me to take part in the process of deciding my rapist's future by attending in person to give a statement or by submitting a written response. The worker who called this time referred to me as "victim" at least five times, and I was five times reduced to that place although her intent was clearly to elevate me to an active, participatory role.

I have received these calls and letters before.

At first they unnerved me greatly. The telephoned voices begin benignly, identify themselves, their geographic location, the name of the institution and *bam*, a knife is at my throat and the man whose name I never say is named, is real, is in my life again and I am expected to play the role his crime designed for me. Again.

The letterhead of the parole board is stark. Dark. In script that demands your full attention, it pushes the stamp, even your address, off the envelope. Sometimes I leave their letters in the mailbox for days, weeks. Sometimes I put them away unopened. I know what they say.

I will receive the calls and letters every year until he is released in 2007, after serving his full sentence of twenty years' imprisonment. The National Parole Board weakens me, frightens me. I hate it. One telephone call came at nine in the morning. My first conversation of the day. A woman identified herself and asked how I wished to be notified in the event that the man who raped me escaped from prison. Would I prefer direct contact, or a message left on my machine or with a relative or friend?

Sometimes I play a bit with the "regional communications officers" who telephone. They are always courteous as I try to trick them, get them to say something outrageous, which I write down, save for later, get to feel superior about—"You fools, don't you know who I am," I think, "which one I am, don't you know? Can't you leave me alone? Don't you dare leave me alone!"

But they are only workers, doing a job they probably hate, and I never get much out of them because they do not know. I go on anyway, set them up with loaded questions. "If I attend, will the parole board pay for my airfare and accommodation? Pay me a fee for my work?" And they are always astounded, never see it coming, never write a note in the margins of my file: *She's the nutty one, hang up if she answers.* They never register the pain, or the point I am making. They do not know.

This call is a little different. They have a new option, she tells me. I can hear the excitement in her voice. I can send a videotape of my statement! This is the result of a recommendation from the Standing Committee on Justice. Apparently they consulted with victims' rights groups nationally and regionally, and everyone agreed that videotaped statements would result in greater victim representation and participation in the criminal sentencing process. The victims incur the cost of production and are given guidelines within which to speak. Buddy doesn't get to view the tape but he receives a full transcript. If you elect to submit a letter, he also gets a copy. Even though it's creepy, I have no problem with this. It is his right under the law, as it would be mine, to see the evidence gathered against him. My problem is more layered, personal, political.

Why am I being asked to take responsibility to keep this man in prison? Surely that is not my job. Surely I have done enough. If only by surviving. The pretense that my participation in his parole and detention hearings could or should affect his sentencing is just that. The National Parole Board is pretending that I, the person against whom a crime was committed, has informed or meaningful input into the legal process. If I did, they would at a minimum engage with me and others in a dialogue about what is in the best interests of women who experience crimes of male violence.

The national lobby of victims' rights groups has commanded a significant portion of media attention, which conflates and confuses victims' claims for justice in the form of criminal sanctions and women's claims for equality as guaranteed under the Charter. Victims' rights groups and movements, championed by parents who have lost children to murderous psychopaths, are the experts to whom police and politicians point when challenged about their embrace of increased sentencing and the construction of U.S.-style super-jails to house more prisoners. These groups, with their legitimate anger and grief, do not speak for me. They won't even speak to me. I am one of many women across the country who has attempted to bring the needs and the political realities of women who experience rape and assault to so-called victims' rights groups. We have been dismissed and ignored, even though we are legion, the marjority of the victims of crime.

The man who raped me is a bad man. He raped before and there is no reason to believe he will not do so again. During his first incarceration for a series of sexual assaults on the West Coast in the seventies, he sexually assaulted a female corrections worker. After his 1987 sentencing for the Balcony Rapes (at his request), he was returned to that same prison, where he made "sexually inappropriate actions" toward two more female corrections workers. In 2000, after serving two-thirds of his term, he became eligible for parole. At that first hearing, it was decided that he was a serious risk to reoffend and that he should serve his full twenty-year sentence. The decision will be reviewed every year until he is released in 2007, middle-aged and institutionalized with no probationary requirements and no support services, into a society where two decades of industrial, technological, economic and cultural growth and change have passed him by.

Yeah, yeah, I know, boo-hoo and all that—but listen, what is served? Who benefits? Me? I don't think so. Am I suddenly unraped? Was I involved in any of the decision-making? Consulted? Responsible? Could what happened to me that night in 1986 happen again? Has it

happened to other women? Has anything been put in place to prevent it or to prevent the negligence and discrimination that were the hallmarks of the police investigation into his crimes? Would a dangerous-offender application in 1986 have better served us all? Made it worse? The answer is, spare me the nonsense about prison as a deterrent and law and order, until you understand my questions.

IN 1990, Johnny was released on probation from a penitentiary. He had served sixteen months in the same prison as the man who raped me. Before he went in, I made him promise that he would not engage in any cowboy prison-vengeance on my behalf; if he did, it would come back on me. I figured Johnny would be okay because he wasn't like that anyway. (He was just a thief.) He wrote me once to say he'd seen my rapist and described him as a loner who did not engage in prison programs or pastimes. When Johnny got out, I let him use my phone number as a contact for jobs and appointments for a little while. One day I got a call from a friend of his who was still in prison and looking for him. I took the message and chatted a bit, asked him how he was, where he was from. Normal stuff. I could tell that he appreciated the contact. After a few false starts he told me that he and others were aware of my situation and my alter ego, Jane Doe, and that if I were so inclined, and now that John was out, he could set things in motion that would deal with the author of my troubles. I thanked him for his offer and stated clearly that that was not what I wanted. He said he heard me and we both hung up.

I don't really believe, and I certainly don't support, the popular belief that prison inmates should or would exact eye-for-an-eye retribution on our behalf. The notion mostly makes for popular movies and novels. Besides, why would a civilized society committed to humanitarian legislation and justice look to the people it incarcerates to punish others through criminal acts of violence? Unless of course the structure of penal institutions itself perpetuates criminal behaviour.

But lofty notions aside, I would be a liar if I didn't admit to some gratification and sense of power as a result of the offer. Johnny told me later that the guy blew hard but was simply trying to make me feel better. Men, huh? You can't live with them and you can't put them in prison.

There has been great debate and proposed legislation about the release into our communities of repeat sexual offenders who have served their sentence. I am enormously conflicted about it. There was a situation in Toronto where a man convicted of sexually abusing children was released into the custody of his aging mother. The media printed their names and location. Mother and son were scorned, spat on, threatened and shamed into moving far from the home where the woman had lived for most of her life. He reoffended. She now lives alone and isolated. The feelings and actions of her neighbours were human. They were also primitive. Frankly, I don't want a child abuser living next door to me either, but how and why and for whose benefit have we allowed the situation to evolve to the point that vigilante justice and emotional outrage have replaced services and prevention? I mean, let's be clear, it's not as if we are a society committed to child welfare. The same legislators and courts who rail against the lawful release of sex offenders support the right of parents to use physical force when disciplining the children in their care. Our courts and existing services are overloaded with cases of child sexual and physical assault. The United Nations cites high rates of child poverty in Canada and the United States as human rights abuses. Let's get a grip here. Let's stop pretending that there is no correlation. Stop pretending that we are progressively seeking solutions and methods of prevention.

The man who raped me has given us reason to believe that he will reoffend. I don't think of him much. The National Parole Board informed me that he chose not to take part in anger management and other behaviour modification programs available in prison. (I know, too, that these programs are clinical and dated, with waiting lists that last for years, and have limited success rates.) He did not embrace the brotherhood of the many other Native men in prison. He expresses no remorse or responsibility for violently altering the course of so many women's lives, including the lives of his daughter, his mother, his wife and other women who loved him.

There are bad men among us. Men who are lost to us. They cannot, will not, should not come back. But the places we put them, the manner in which we treat them, the degree to which we forget them, will determine our future well-being individually and as a society. So when the man who raped me is released, as he must be under the law, and the alarm is raised in the interest of law and order, I will not be part of it. Just as I will not engage in presentations or videos at parole board hearings that dismiss my intelligence and insights in order to maintain a knife at my throat and keep me a victim.

When the man who raped me is released, I will not live in fear of him. Certainly he has more to fear than I do. I do not wish him well or ill or anything at all. But I am clear about this: If he comes near me again it will be the last thing he ever does.

I told you I was conflicted.

The only ending so far

36:

I STOPPED writing for a while after September 11. Who cares about rape and sexual assault, I thought. There are larger issues. How do I write about anything else? Oh right! The women of Afghanistan— the most disappeared, murdered, invisible, raped women we have acknowledged in ages. Maybe since the burning times. Why, if you listened and read, you might even have believed that we were bombing their country for them. Terrorizing Afghani women to end terrorism. The white men saving the brown women from the brown men. But what do those women say? Who records their voice, their image? Easier to believe they have none. What can I possibly write?

I always knew that I would document my rape in a public manner and in a manner over which I had control. I was sure at first that it would be a documentary film and it almost was. But I gave away control to close friends whom I assumed had my best interests at heart. Silly girl. Their hearts were reserved for their own best interests. And why not? They tried to take my story from me, we quarrelled bitterly and I never spoke with or saw my friends again or the footage I had shot during the civil trial.

The tapes are out there somewhere. Pieces of me that I knew I would forget. That I am sure I miss.

ANOTHER friend, now a lawyer, who had been intimately involved in my case almost from the beginning and who contributed immensely to my work as Jane Doe, wrote an article about my case for a big-deal law journal. In it she removed me from all agency in my civil suit, situated herself as my advocate and alleged that her partner created the "women as bait" analogy, which has become the calling card of my case. I e-mailed her, challenging her claims, but she has not responded. The article circulates in legal and academic communities in this country and in others. How do I write around that?

A GIRLHOOD friend phoned to say that I didn't deserve to win any money or to have a book published and that I lived a charmed life with horseshoes up my ass. One of the women raped by the man who raped me wrote a letter to the *Toronto Sun*, which they published as an editorial and in which she roundly condemned me. The women of LEAF hold firmly to the belief that they did right by me, my protestations and experience of our relationship be damned, and they regularly workshop the many issues involved in my case in my absence. Although I have cautioned him several times, my lawyer continues to speak of the remarkable serendipity of my case. How the pieces just came together as if by magic. My parents do not know. My siblings—some of whom do know—never speak of my rape or ask about my writing.

While my pre-rape nature, the person that I was before I became Jane Doe, contributes significantly to my positions in the sketches above, I wonder sometimes if it is my rape-victim status that ultimately defines me for the other parties involved. If it allows them to think around me, remove me, act as if I am not here and cannot, or do not, wish to control my environment or direct actions. It is a view that is popular socially, legally, in families and among friends. It's hard to fight for, analyze, deconstruct or create alternative readings for rape victims when the popular one dictates that all such women must be protected, taken care of. Silent. Dumb. Unable to write.

My editor says to go where there is a pulse of energy, remember why I am writing the book, create another character who will express all of the criticism I fear will be directed my way when the book is published, who will say it first but from my mouth, my fear. This is good. I like it but still I cannot write. Don't even mind not writing that much. Do you know how glamorous this is? I am the writer in residence at Random House. My editor is a beautiful Governor General's Award–winner who dresses well and is of sterling character. The other women in the office

could be in magazines. I dress up every day and walk among handsome men in good suits. I read all the papers, drink all the coffees, make phone calls. I cannot write. But my agony becomes me. When it wakes me at night now, it is because I cannot write.

I attend the inquest into the murder of Gillian Hadley. She is—was—a woman who ran naked, baby in arms, through the streets of her lovely neighbourhood, chased by her estranged husband, who caught her, hauled her inside and shot her dead. I think the inquest will be a chance for me to revisit the scene of the legal crime where women who have experienced violence are disappeared. Spoken for. And Gillian Hadley is the most desirable of those victims. Completely silent. Too many lawyers move around her, through her, motioning, filing, casting, renouncing blame and guilt. There is even a lawyer for a fathers' rights group (who looks like Spencer Tracy) who is granted standing by the coroner. His presence and defence of the murderer reduces the entire process to its paltry, pitiful essence, enlightens the court as to its own insignificance. The coroner's jury will produce a tome of recommendations and proposals for legislation that echoes others, and nothing will change. And Gillian Hadley will run forever in the streets. I am reclaimed by smells and sorrow and legal culture, but I cannot write.

I READ the news today. George W. Bush was denied a portion of the front page in order to tell the story of a young girl. A child really, twelve years old and gang-raped by three white, twenty-something sons-of-pillars of a tiny prairie town. She is Native. They are released without bail, claiming consent, innocence. She bled for two days and became infected, ran away, has no legal representation or voice. They are sure to win. She is in grade seven. I cannot write.

And how is it that no one remarks on the male gender of the players in this "war against terrorism" in the East and in the West? The leaders, soldiers, husbands, decision-makers, killers, pundits, rapists, politicians are men. Driven by an excess of testosterone and religiosity.

Better not write about that.

Toronto Police Service

NEWS RELEASE

TPS 600 1998/04
40 College Street,
Toronto, Ontario.
M5G 2J3

Unit/Telephone:

Corporate
Communications
808-7100

Media Release*

For immediate release
May 23, 2002, Toronto

Chief of Police Julian Fantino announced today that in keeping with the recommendations of the Jane Doe Social Audit, the nationally acclaimed Sexual Assault Squad has amalgamated with Vice and Morality to become the Sex Crimes Unit.

The new unit will expand its mandate to investigate child prostitution and kiddie porn. The official launch will take place at the next Police Services Board meeting.

There will be an accompanying PowerPoint presentation.

For further information please contact:

-30-

* While accurate in content, this version of the official media release put out by Toronto police has been modified by me.

IN the eighties, the work of WAVAW, and the work of women before us, caused the police force to remove sexual assault from its archaic sex-crimes definition, as investigated by morality, vice and robbery squads. For the following fifteen years, the City of Toronto had a sexual-assault squad that was something quite different from what had previously existed. In 1987, money was poured into SACO, the first office of its kind in Canada, and it was mandated to investigate stranger rapes against adult women. In 1989, after the botched investigation into the serial rapist and murderer Paul Bernardo, the unit was recharged as the Sexual Assault Squad, complete with the latest technology and career-building cachet. (Shortly after, a provincial inquiry led by Justice Archie Campbell called for increased training and a transparent protocol in sexual-assault investigation in recommendations identical to the work of the WAWAW committees. While some changes took place, Campbell's recommendations were not officially implemented.)

Women who were professionals in the area of sexual assault were not included in the training or protocol design of the new squad. Through deputations, petitions and brief audiences, we attempted to make the Sexual Assault Squad user-friendly and demanded that all sexual assaults be investigated under its mandate. We were ignored. In 2002, and again without political or public consultation, the squad was stripped of its focus on crimes committed against adult women and was reformed as the Sex Crimes Unit. It was re-amalgamated with vice and morality to include the crimes of child pornography and child prostitution. The new unit has not been scrutinized with regard to the training, protocol and education of officers who investigate crimes against youth; the same officers have yet to receive the improved and increased training in sexual-assault investigation recommended in the social audit. The new mandate is not entirely clear. If you question it in any way, you risk being judged as indifferent to crimes of sexual violence against children.

The term "woman" is not used anywhere in police documents and presentations about the newly re-formed squad. Chief Julian Fantino has taken to raising his hands in the universal expression for quotation marks when he uses the phrase "sexual assault."

Tiny steps forward, military charges back.

I DON'T know how to end this book. It is the most difficult part. I've lived with the beginning and the middle for a long time—I memorized everything that happened to me, to everyone, and I've written it all down. That is my real victory, and gift. That could have been my ending.

But there is not enough joy here, it is not uplifting enough, does not transcend or transform. In fact it feels kind of depressing, and I do not want to leave you like that. There is not enough hope, and I am a creature of hope.

I used to imagine myself as an old woman picketing, rallying, ever the activist within a community of women, teaching, learning, challenging. What was I thinking? How do I reconcile this with the present-day void where there seems to be no place to make that ruckus? Today's activists are punished for their work and beliefs. They are relegated in popular culture to a hair above nutcase status, a step behind criminal. It has become commonplace to attend a demonstration against poverty, against racism, and to be outnumbered by armed and threatening police officers. To see mounted police or special forces charge on unarmed protestors, clubs swinging, shields raised. Unless there is violence at a demo, the media doesn't report.

At women's demos, hardly anyone shows up anymore. Social activists and union leaders no longer include "women's issues" in their platforms. As if globalization, free trade, unemployment, poverty and war are not felt most by women and their children. As if violence against women is not cause or effect of those scourges. As if we are not the first line of assault, as if it is not political.

For a moment I thought I could have an ending about the labour movement as a possible beacon, but it is not. It says it is, but name a woman labour leader. Name a labour leader who is not white. When was the last time labour activists said the word "feminism" or included it in their literature and positions? And really meant it.

AT the time I was trying to write an ending, I responded to a call for submissions from a group of university students called Activists Against Sexual Assault. They were compiling a magazine of "writing and political analysis to clearly link the roots of sexual assault to patriarchy, power and domination." They appealed to activists involved in work of a leftist, grassroots and feminist nature.

I was really excited about the magazine and sent them a piece I wrote about the social audit and the policing of rape. A few months later I received a polite note saying that their editorial collective had decided against printing my submission because *it was not radical enough*. Yes, it's true! And it made me so happy. There it is. There is my hope—our hope. Young women and men resisting, thinking, building, carrying on, declaring that rape "is an issue we must work on as regularly as, for instance, capitalism, globalization and poverty. We should be thinking, talking and writing about systems of oppression constantly, how they interlock with each other, how they are enhanced by capitalism and how they are replicated in our own work—even our anti-oppression work." Declaring that they will not work within systems that cannot work for women, and will look to their own community for answers, organizing, consciousness-raising and insisting that "leftist" or "left wing" is not the same as "feminist," using art, the Internet, rage, pride and glee to tell us.

I love those women. And I must go find them. Join them.

But maybe I can rest a while first.

November 11, 2002. Sleeping in an early winter storm. Wet snow pelts the windows of my third-floor apartment. (No balcony.) I stir, almost wake up, but then keep on dreaming.

Where Are They Now?

An alphabetical index of the main characters and their current status in one or two lines.

Beverly Bain is pursuing her doctorate in women's studies, with a focus on anti-racism, feminism and sexual assault.

Rosemary Barnes continues to practise psychology and has frequently worked as an expert witness with Sack Goldblatt Mitchell.

Heather Bird is on a maternity leave from the *Toronto Sun*.

Bill Blair is a staff superintendent of police and is favoured by some to be the next chief of police in Toronto.

Margo (Pulford) Boyd retired from policing in 2002 as the second woman to achieve the rank of superintendent. She is now the director of the Ontario Civilian Commission on Police Services, which investigates police wrongdoing.

Shary Boyle currently lives in Winnipeg, where she continues to create, educate and sing country and western ballads.

Bill Cameron retired from policing and works in the insurance industry. Jane has not seen him since the civil trial.

Vince DeMarco left psychiatry in the late nineties to become the director of the Clinic for Optimal Health and Rejuvenation in Toronto.

Kim Derry was promoted to superintendent of police in 2003.

Sean Dewart joined the law firm of Sack Goldblatt Mitchell shortly after the trial ended. He is now a partner and uses his fine mind and remarkable legal skills to successfully defend other political women and causes. He is becoming quite famous for it. He and Jane remain friends.

Jane Doe is learning to draw and looking for a job. A movie of the week about her aired in 2003. Although it twisted and revised her story—apparently for dramatic purposes—Jane did not hate it. Especially the first thirty minutes and the extraordinary performance of Wendy Crewson, who played Jane against the impediment of a truly awful wardrobe.

Richard Element became a lawyer.

Julian Fantino remains the chief of the Toronto Police Service as of this writing. In the fall of 2002, he travelled to Lithuania to instruct its military police force in community policing. On his return, he denounced as "trash" a *Toronto Star* investigation of six years of police records that demonstrates racial profiling by the force. Fantino plans to head an inquiry into the matter. He has yet to meet with women working in the area of sexual assault.

Graham Glancy continues in his psychiatric practice and as an expert witness. Although he used to frequently work on cases represented by Sack Goldblatt Mitchell, he now refuses to.

Eric Golden is a partner in the law firm Blaney McMurtry.

Jim Hodgson left his position at Longwood College in 2002 and is currently the manager of juvenile programs at the Virginia Department of Criminal Justice Services in the United States.

LEAF acts as an intervener in legal cases and issues that affect women's equality rights under the Canadian Charter. They do not sponsor individual cases.

Lori Martin feels grateful that she has been given the gifts of health and self-expression through music, dance and acting. She works with Usana Health Sciences.

Gregg McCrary continues to appear on U.S. talk and news shows as an expert on serial murderers and rapists. He was one of several profilers who jumped on (but then fell off) the Beltway Sniper investigation bandwagon.

Patti McGillicuddy continues to advocate for women and works in health care.

Cynthia Petersen is a partner with Sack Goldblatt Mitchell.

Elizabeth Pickett writes poetry, does readings and is at work on a manuscript.

Kim Rossmo, geographic profiler, was booted from the Vancouver Police Department and then lost the wrongful dimissal suit he filed against them. He now works in the U.S. In 2002 he was part of the profiling posse flown to Virginia to consult in the investigation of the Beltway Sniper.

WAVAW grew in membership and continued to organize and demonstrate until it disbanded around 1989.

To date, police training and protocol have not undergone the changes recommended by the social audit. Similar recommendations from the inquests into the murders of Gillian Hadley and Aileen Mays, another Ontario woman killed by her husband, have yet to be implemented. November is designated as Partner Abuse Awareness Month on the force's calendar. To promote it in 2002, they offered workshops on animal abuse (they are against it), and sexual harassment in the workplace. The term "woman" was not used.

Some relevant statistics

✣ Around the world, as many as one woman in every four is physically or sexually abused during pregnancy, usually by her partner. In Canada, 21% of women abused by a partner were assaulted during pregnancy, and 40% reported that the abuse began during pregnancy. Abuse often begins or worsens during pregnancy, when a woman is most vulnerable, and most dependent on her partner's support.

✣ Research repeatedly shows that a vast majority of Native women have been assaulted. Violence may have begun while at residential school or been inflicted by parents who were damaged by the residential school experience of rape, physical abuse, and cultural genocide. Violence continues into adulthood, with 48% to 90% of Native women being assaulted at the hands of their partners, depending on the community in which they live. Native women also experience racially motivated attacks and are harassed on the streets by the public and police more often than non-Native women.

✣ In addition to racist violence, women who are of minority racial, ethnocultural or linguistic groups also suffer violence at the hands of their intimate partners. However, their access to the justice system and to services are not the same. Only 57% of Canadian shelters offers services that are sensitive to cultural differences. Women who have difficulty speaking the official language where they live face enor- mous barriers in accessing services and dealing with the justice system.

✣ Violence against women crosses socio-economic lines. However, low-income women may be more often trapped in abusive relationships because of a lack of financial resources for housing and income support. For Inuit women and others, "The virtual absence of alternative housing arrangements often forces women and children to stay in dangerous and potentially deadly situations."

✣ A DisAbled Women's Network (DAWN) survey found that 40% of women with disabilities have been raped, abused or assaulted. More than half (53%) of women who had been disabled from birth or early childhood had been abused. Women with disabilities may also be physically, sexually or financially abused by people who aid in their care. Less than two-thirds of shelters for abused women report being accessible to women with disabilities. However, women with disabilities report that only one in ten who sought help from women's shelters were accommodated.

✣ Women working in certain occupations are also more vulnerable to violence. For example, foreign domestic workers work for low wages isolated in private homes and are vulnerable to threats of deportation if they complain of physical or sexual abuse. They are often unaware of their legal rights or of services. Other occupations in which women are very vulnerable to workplace violence are health care workers, and women in the military. All women in subordinate positions are vulnerable to sexual harassment in the workplace, and women in male-dominated occupations may be subject to workplaces that are hostile toward women. Women working in the sex trade are at enormous risk of sexual and physical assault, on-going abuse, and murder. They receive the least amount of support due to the stigma surrounding prostitution, and the belief that prostitution is a "lifestyle" decision. This ignores the fact that [many] young women who end up in the sex trade are flee-ing abusive homes, and that economic options for young women on their own are minimal.

✣ Young women and female children are highly vulnerable to sexual assault. In 1997, persons under 18 were 24% of the population but represented 60% of all sexual-assault victims and one-fifth (19%) of physical-assault victims. Of sexual offences against kids under twelve, the ages at which boys are most likely to be sexually assaulted, girl victims outnumber boys by two to one. Women under twenty-five are also at greatest risk of being killed by their male partners.

Reprinted from the Canadian Research Institute for the Advancement of Women Website, www.criaw-icref.ca. Log on for endnotes and sources, and for links to other related sites.

Acknowledgements

I wish to thank my friends and family who supported me in my personal life and in the lawsuit; the women of WAWAW and the social audit; the people who read my manuscript for fact and for a safety net; those who helped me in the writing or who came up with alternative titles; the staff at Random House Canada for their support, generosity and good company, especially my editor, Anne Collins, copy editor Stacey Cameron and production manager Sharon Bailey. I thank Carmen Dunjko for her artist's eye, and the incomparable Shary Boyle.

I also want to acknowledge people who show up at demonstrations and engage in political actions; producers of art, zines and stuff on the Internet; voters; squatters; little kids; people who grow things; community workers; *The Sopranos*; seniors; teachers; the Canadian women's hockey team; writers; mothers; the labour movement; everyone who recycles, bicycles; and the city of Toronto, which I love.